THE WILD PLACES

Also by Robert Macfarlane

Mountains of the Mind: A History of a Fascination
The Old Ways: A Journey on Foot
Holloway (with Dan Richards and Stanley Donwood)
Landmarks
The Lost Words (with Jackie Morris)

THE WILD PLACES

ROBERT MACFARLANE

GRANTA

Granta Publications, 12 Addison Avenue, London W11 4QR

First published in Great Britain by Granta Books, 2007
This paperback edition published by Granta Books, 2017

A CIP catalogue record for this book
is available from the British Library.

5 7 9 10 8 6

ISBN 978-1-78378-449-3

Typeset by M Rules

Printed and bound by CPI Group (UK) Ltd, Croydon, CR0 4YY

Topping & Company Booksellers
2 Blenheim Place
Edinburgh
EH7 5JH

Telephone: (0131) 546 4202
edinburgh@toppingbooks.co.uk
www.toppingbooks.co.uk

23-12-20 10:51 SALE 2 23315
You were served by: User1

PRODUCT	QTY	VAT
MOUNTAINS OF THE MIND		
9781783784509	1	9.99 Z
WILD PLACES		
9781783784493	1	9.99 Z
Zero Rate	19.98	19.98
TOTAL	2	19.98
VAT		0.00
Card - Pin Pad		19.98
TOTAL TENDERED		19.98
CHANGE		0.00

Opening Hours
Monday - Sunday: 9am - 9pm

VAT number: 794805691

For my parents,
and in memory of Roger Deakin (1943–2006)

I only went out for a walk, and finally concluded to stay out till sundown, for going out, I found, was really going in.

JOHN MUIR

Blakeney Spit

The Northumbrian
Tree Ring

Red Pike

The Black Wood   Rannoch
Moor

The Lost Valley
of Bidean nam Bian

Orwell's house

The Strathnaver broch

Ben Hope

Sandwood Bay   Isle of Raasay   The
Coruisk Basin

N

Orford
Ness
Dengie Peninsula
Walnut Tree Farm
The Beechwood
The Holloway
The Tor of
the Snow Hares
Sharpnose Point
Ynys Enlli
The Burren
Bin Chuanna

CONTENTS

1

Beechwood

The wind was rising, so I went to the wood. It lies south of the city, a mile from my home: a narrow, nameless fragment of beech-wood, topping a shallow hill. I walked there, following streets to the city's fringe, and then field-edge paths through hedgerows of hawthorn and hazel.

Rooks haggled in the air above the trees. The sky was a bright cold blue, fading to milk at its edges. From a quarter of a mile away, I could hear the noise of the wood in the wind; a soft marine roar. It was the immense compound noise of friction – of leaf fretting on leaf, and branch rubbing on branch.

I entered the wood by its southern corner. Debris was beginning to drop from the moving canopy: twigs and beech nuts, pattering down on to the coppery layer of leaves. Sunlight fell in bright sprees on the floor. I walked up through the wood, and midway along its northern edge I came to my tree – a tall grey-barked beech, whose branches flare out in such a way that it is easy to climb.

I had climbed the tree many times before, and its marks were all familiar to me. Around the base of its trunk, its bark has sagged and wrinkled, so that it resembles the skin on an elephant's leg. At about ten feet, a branch crooks sharply back on itself; above that, the letter 'H', scored with a knife into the trunk years before, has ballooned with the growth of the tree; higher still is the healed stump of a missing bough.

Thirty feet up, near the summit of the beech, where the bark is smoother and silver, I reached what I had come to call the observatory: a forked lateral branch set just below a curve in the trunk. I had found that if I set my back against the trunk and put my feet on either tine of the fork, I could stay comfortable there. If I remained still for a few minutes, people out walking would sometimes pass underneath without noticing me. People don't generally expect to see men in trees. If I remained still for longer, the birds would return. Birds don't generally expect to see men in trees, either. Blackbirds fussing in the leaf litter; wrens which whirred from twig to twig so quickly they seem to teleport; once a grey partridge, venturing anxiously from cover.

I steadied myself in the observatory. My weight and movement had made the tree rock, and the wind exaggerated the rock, so that soon the summit of the beech was creaking back and forth, describing arcs of five or ten degrees. Not an observatory that day; more of a mast-top crow's-nest in a sea swell.

From that height, the land was laid out beneath me like a map. Dispersed across it were more fragments of woodland, some of whose names I knew: Mag's Hill Wood, Nine Wells Wood, Wormwood. To the west over corduroy fields was a main road, busy with cars. Directly north was the hospital, its three-piped incinerator tower rising far higher than my hilltop tree. A deep-chested Hercules aeroplane was descending towards the airfield on the city's outskirts. Above a road verge to the east, I could see a kestrel riding the wind, its wings shivering with the strain, its tail feathers spread out like a hand of cards.

I had started climbing trees about three years earlier. Or rather, re-started; for I had been at a school that had a wood for its playground. We had climbed and christened the different trees (Scorpio, The Major

Oak, Pegasus), and fought for their control in territorial conflicts with elaborate rules and fealties. My father had built my brother and me a tree house in our garden, which we had defended successfully against years of pirate attack. In my late twenties, I had begun to climb trees again. Just for the fun of it: no ropes, and no danger either.

In the course of my climbing, I had learned to discriminate between tree species. I liked the lithe springiness of the silver birch, the alder and the young cherry. I avoided pines – brittle branches, callous bark – and planes. And I found that the horse chestnut, with its limbless lower trunk and prickly fruit, but also its tremendous canopy, offered the tree-climber both a difficulty and an incentive.

I explored the literature of tree-climbing: not extensive, but so exciting. John Muir had swarmed up a hundred-foot Douglas Spruce during a Californian windstorm, and looked out over a forest, 'the whole mass of which was kindled into one continuous blaze of white sun-fire!' Italo Calvino had written his magical novel, *The Baron in the Trees*, whose young hero, Cosimo, in an adolescent huff, climbs a tree on his father's forested estate and vows never to set foot on the ground again. He keeps to his impetuous word, and ends up living and even marrying in the canopy, moving for miles between olive, cherry, elm and holm oak. There were the boys in B. B.'s *Brendon Chase*, who go feral in an English forest rather than return to boarding-school, and climb a 'Scotch pine' in order to reach a honey buzzard's nest scrimmed with beech leaves. And of course there was the team of Winnie the Pooh and Christopher Robin: Pooh floating on his sky-blue balloon up to the oak-top bee's nest, in order to poach some honey; Christopher ready with his pop-gun to shoot Pooh's balloon down once the honey had been poached.

I also came to admire some of tree-climbing's serious contemporary exponents, in particular the scientists who study the redwoods of California and Oregon. *Sequoia sempervirens*, the giant redwood, can grow to over three hundred feet high. Most of the height of an adult redwood is near-branchless trunk; then comes a vast and complex crown. The redwood researchers have developed exceptional techniques of ascent. They use a bow and arrow to fire a pulling line up over a firm branch in the crown. By means of this line they then raise and secure a climbing rope. Once in the crown, their rope-skills are so refined that they can move about safely and almost freely, like latter-day spidermen. Up there, in that aerial world, they have discovered a lost kingdom: a remarkable and previously uninvestigated ecosystem.

There was nothing unique about my beech tree, nothing difficult in its ascent, no biological revelation at its summit, nor any honey. But it had become a place to think. A roost. I was fond of it, and it – well, it had no notion of me. I had climbed it many times; at first light, dusk and glaring noon. I had climbed it in winter, brushing snow from the branches with my hand, with the wood cold as stone to the touch, and real crows' nests black in the branches of nearby trees. I had climbed it in early summer, and looked out over the simmering countryside, with heat jellying the air and the drowsy buzz of a tractor audible from somewhere nearby. And I had climbed it in monsoon rain, with water falling in rods thick enough for the eye to see. Climbing the tree was a way to get perspective, however slight; to look down on a city that I usually looked across. The relief of relief. Above all, it was a way of defraying the city's claims on me.

Anyone who lives in a city will know the feeling of having been there too long. The gorge-vision that streets imprint on us, the sense of blockage, the longing for surfaces other than glass, brick, concrete and tarmac. I live in Cambridge, a city set in one of the most intensively farmed and densely populated regions of the world. It is an odd place for someone who loves mountains and wildness to have settled. Cambridge is probably, hour for hour, about as far from what might conventionally be called 'wild land' as anywhere in Europe. I feel that distance keenly. But good things hold me here: my family, my work, my affection for the city itself, the way the stone of its old buildings condenses the light. I have lived in Cambridge on and off for a decade, and I imagine I will continue to do so for years to come. And for as long as I stay here, I know I will also have to get to the wild places.

I could not now say when I first grew to love the wild, only that I did, and that a need for it will always remain strong in me. As a child, whenever I read the word, it conjured images of wide spaces, remote and figureless. Isolated islands off Atlantic coasts. Unbounded forests, and blue snow-light falling on to drifts marked with the paw-prints of wolves. Frost-shattered summits and corries holding lochs of great depth. And this was the vision of a wild place that had stayed with me: somewhere boreal, wintry, vast, isolated, elemental, demanding of the traveller in its asperities. To reach a wild place was, for me, to step outside human history.

The beechwood could not answer my need for wildness. The roar of the nearby roads was audible, as were the crash and honk of the trains that passed to the west. The surrounding fields were treated with fertiliser and herbicide to maximise productivity. And the hedgerows were favourite locations for fly-tippers. Junk heaps would appear overnight: brick rubble, water-swollen plywood, rags of newspaper. I had once found a bra and a pair of lacy pants hanging from the thorns, like oversized shrike kills. Fly-tipping, I guessed, rather than a fit of roadside passion – for who could make love in a hawthorn hedge?

For weeks before the windstorm, I had felt the familiar desire to move, to get beyond the fall-line of the incinerator's shadow, beyond the event-horizon of the city's ring-road. And up there in the crow's-nest that day, looking down at the roads, the hospital and the fields, and the woods cramped between them, I felt a sharp need to leave Cambridge, to reach somewhere remote, where starlight fell clearly, where the wind could blow upon me from its thirty-six directions, and where the evidence of human presence was minimal or absent. Far north or far west; for to my mind this was where wildness survived, if it survived anywhere at all.

Time and again, wildness has been declared dead in Britain and Ireland. 'Two great wars demanded and bequeathed regimentation,' wrote E. M. Forster in 1964, 'science lent her aid, and the wildness of these islands, never extensive, was stamped upon and built over and patrolled in no time. There is no forest or fell to escape to today, no cave in which to curl up, and no deserted valley.' For Jonathan Raban the extinction of the wild happened far earlier: by the 1860s Britain was 'so thickly peopled, so intensively farmed, so industrialised, so citified, that there was nowhere to go to be truly alone, or to have . . . adventures, except to sea'. John Fowles, writing in 1985, was grimly adamant: 'We are now, in hard fact, on the bleak threshold of losing much of the old landscape. We have done unimaginably terrible things to our countrysides. It is only here and there along our coasts and on the really high hills and mountains that the ancient richness of natural life is not yet in danger.'

Five years later, the American author William Least-Heat Moon described Britain as 'a tidy garden of a toy realm where there's almost no real wilderness left and absolutely no memory of it. Where the woods are denatured plantings. The English, the Europeans, are too far from the wild. That's the difference between them and us.' Repeatedly, the same lament, or the same contempt.

An abundance of hard evidence exists to support these obituaries for the wild. Over the last century in particular, disaster has fallen upon the land and the seas of Britain and Ireland. The statistics of damage are familiar and often repeated, more as elegy now than as protest. In England, between 1930 and 1990, over half of the ancient woodland was cleared, or replaced with conifer plantation. Half of the hedgerow mileage was grubbed up. Nearly all lowland pasture was ploughed out, built on or tarmacked over. Three-quarters of heathland was converted into farmland, or developed. Across Britain and Ireland, rare limestone pavements were cracked up and sold as rockery stones, peatbogs millennia in the making were drained or excavated. Dozens of species vanished, with hundreds more being brought to the point of crisis.

In Britain, over sixty-one million people now live in 93,000 square miles of land. Remoteness has been almost abolished, and the main agents of that abolition have been the car and the road. Only a small and diminishing proportion of terrain is now more than five miles from a motorable surface. There are nearly thirty million cars in use in Britain, and 210,000 miles of road on the mainland alone. If those roads were to be stretched out and joined into a single continuous carriageway, you could drive on it almost to the moon. The roads have become new mobile civilisations in themselves: during rush-hours, the

car-borne population across Britain and Ireland is estimated to exceed
the resident population of central London.

The commonest map of Britain is the road atlas. Pick one up, and
you see the meshwork of motorways and roads which covers the surface
of the country. From such a map, it can appear that the landscape has
become so thickly webbed by roads that asphalt and petrol are its new
primary elements.

Considering the road atlas, an absence also becomes visible. The
wild places are no longer marked. The fells, the caves, the tors, the
woods, the moors, the river valleys and the marshes have all but disappeared. If they are shown at all, it is as background shadings or generic
symbols. More usually, they have faded out altogether like old ink,
become the suppressed memories of a more ancient archipelago.

The land itself, of course, has no desires as to how it should be represented. It is indifferent to its pictures and to its picturers. But maps
organise information about a landscape in a profoundly influential way.
They carry out a triage of its aspects, selecting and ranking those aspects
in an order of importance, and so they create forceful biases in the
ways a landscape is perceived and treated.

It can take time and effort to forget the prejudice induced by a
powerful map. And few maps exercise a more distortive pressure upon
the imagination than the road atlas. The first road atlas of Britain was
produced in 1675 by John Ogilby. It was a six-volume work, which
claimed to be the only 'Ichnographical and Historical Description of all
the Principal Road-ways in England and Wales'. Ogilby's maps showed
a scrupulous attention to landscape detail: they depicted not only roads,
but also the hills, rivers and forests that the roads ran round, along,
through and over.

In the centuries since Ogilby's innovation, the road atlas has grown in ubiquity and influence. Over a million are sold in Britain and Ireland each year; twenty million are thought to be in circulation at any one time. The priorities of the modern road atlas are clear. Drawn by computers from satellite photos, it is a map that speaks of transit and displacement. It encourages us to imagine the land itself only as a context for motorised travel. It warps its readers away from the natural world.

When I think of this map – when I think *in* this map – I see the landscape in grainy CCTV splices, in images of direction, destination, purpose: vehicle brake-lights at dusk, the hot breath of exhausts. The road atlas makes it easy to forget the physical presence of terrain, that the countries we call England, Ireland, Scotland and Wales comprise more than 5,000 islands, 500 mountains and 300 rivers. It refuses the idea that long before they were political, cultural and economic entities, these lands were places of stone, wood and water.

It was at some point soon after the windstorm that the idea first occurred to me. Would it be possible to make a series of journeys in search of some of the wild places that remained in Britain and Ireland? I did not believe, or did not want to believe, the obituaries for the wild. They seemed premature, even dangerous. Like mourning for someone who was not yet dead, they suggested an unseemly longing for the end, or an acknowledgement of helplessness. The losses to the wild places of Britain and Ireland were unignorable, and the threats that they faced – pollution, climate change – appeared greater in number and vigour than ever before. But I knew that the wildness had not wholly vanished.

I began to plan my journeys. I wrote to friends, asking them where and when they would go to find wildness. 'Birmingham city centre on a Friday night, just after closing time,' one replied. Another told me about the Grind of Navir in Shetland, where during the spring tides, waves a hundred feet high hurl boulders a quarter of a mile inland, to form a storm-beach out of sight of the sea. Then my friend Roger Deakin rang, to recommend Breachan's Cave on the lonely north-west coast of Jura, and a peninsula on Loch Awe in the Southern Highlands, whose ruined castle was enticingly rook-haunted, and on which, he said, he had enjoyed an invigoratingly bad-tempered encounter with an estate manager. But – why didn't I come over, he suggested, and we could sit and talk properly about it all.

There could have been no one better with whom to discuss wildness than Roger. A founder member of Friends of the Earth, he had been fascinated by nature and landscape all his life; a fascination that had culminated in the late 1990s, when he set out on a journey to swim through Britain. Over the course of several months, Roger swam in dozens of the rivers, lakes, llyns, lochs, streams and seas of England, Wales and Scotland. His aim was to acquire what he called 'a frog's-eye view' of the country, to immerse himself in an unfamiliar element, and see the land from an untried perspective. The book he wrote describing his journey, *Waterlog*, is a classic: a funny, lyrical travelogue that was at once a defence of the wild water that was left, and an elegy for that which had gone. It also rang with his personality: vigorous, digressive, passionate. 'He's over sixty years old,' a mutual friend of ours once said to me, 'and he's still got the energy of a fox cub!'

Roger and I had met a few years before, brought together by a shared love of the wild. I had written a book about mountains, he one about rivers and lakes. Although he was over twice my age, we quickly became close friends. When my daughter Lily was born, he assumed the role of a *de facto* great-uncle. On her first birthday, he gave her a wooden steam engine, wrapped up in sycamore leaves and tied with grass. Before her first visit to his rambling house, he told me that he had made her another present: it turned out to be a leaf maze – thousands of bright yellow mulberry leaves that he had raked and shaped into a Lily-sized labyrinth.

So on a bright day, a week or so after our conversation on the phone, I drove across to Mellis Common in Suffolk to see Roger, turning in past the wide self-coppiced willow stump that marked the start of the lane leading to his farm.

Roger lived in the most unusual home I had ever known. In 1969, when he was twenty-six, he had bought the ruined remains of an Elizabethan steading and twelve acres of surrounding meadow. Little survived of the original sixteenth-century structure except its spring-fed moat and its vast inglenook fireplace. So he put a sleeping-bag down in the fireplace, and lived there while he built a house around himself.

Walnut Tree Farm, as Roger christened it, was made largely of wood. Its frame was of oak, chestnut and ash, and more than three hundred beams kept its roof and its floors from falling. When big easterlies blew, its timbers creaked and groaned, making a sound 'like a ship in a storm', as he once put it, 'or a whale on the move'. It was as close to a living thing as a building could be. He kept the doors and the windows open, in order to let air and animals circulate. Leaves gusted in through one door and out of another, and bats flitted in and out of windows, so that the house seemed almost to breathe. Spiders slung swags and trusses of silk in every corner. Swallows nested in the main chimney, and starlings in the thatch. Ivy and roses clambered up the outer walls, and sent prying tendrils inside through knot-holes and cracks. At the front grew the eponymous walnut tree, which in early autumn clattered green hard fruit down on to the roof of his barn and the heads of visitors. At the back was the moat in which he bathed most days during the summer months, and which was kept clean by a colony of thousands of ramshorn snails – the hygienists of the pond world.

I had visited Roger often, and had come to know his home and his land well. His fields, tended but unfarmed, were busy with life. Sparrowhawks cruised the sky overhead, hedgehogs slept under corrugated iron, and tawny owls hooted from the wood of hornbeam and oak that he had planted. Over the decades, he had established in his meadows a variety of outlying structures, including a shepherd's hut into which he had fitted a bed and a stove with a stove-pipe, an old wooden caravan with a cracked window and a railway wagon he had painted Pullman-purple. He liked to sleep in the railway wagon on stormy nights: 'An amazing thunderstorm last night as I lay listening,' he had once written to me after a summer tempest. 'Like being inside a kettledrum with a whole symphony going on out there and with thunder in wraparound quadraphonic!' One morning, he woke in the shepherd's hut to find that the whole structure was shaking. An earthquake? No, a roe deer scratching itself against a corner of the hut, unaware of its occupant.

The day I went to see him, we sat and talked for hours about the wild, drinking tea from big fired-clay cups, occasionally pulling books or maps down from his shelves, comparing our different understandings and experiences of the idea. Roger told me about some of the places in England he found strangest and most wild: the Brecklands of East

Anglia, the Undercliff at Lyme Regis, Canvey Island in Essex. I told him about a waterfall pool far up Glen Feshie, which was overflown by peregrines and whose water was horseback brown; and about the Shelter Stone, a huge balanced boulder in the heart of the Cairngorms, beneath which it was possible to spend the night, even in winter.

I asked if he would accompany me on some of my journeys, and he said he would, especially those in England and Ireland – and that he was particularly keen we do some trespassing together. He declared his specific desire that we mount an expedition into the grounds of Madonna's Wiltshire estate, in order to assert a right to roam in that beautiful wooded land. I demurred, muttering something cowardly about man-traps and gamekeepers – but already looking forward to our adventures together. I did not at that point know how vital a presence Roger would become in my journeys, or how powerful his influence would be in helping to change my understanding of wildness.

For weeks after my visit to Roger, I carried on planning. I bought and borrowed specialist maps – geological, meteorological, natural-historical – and let my mind wander out over them, dowsing for possible sites, trying to imagine in full what the maps only suggested might be there. I traced rivers as they dropped from escarpments, and guessed at the shapes of the rocks they carved. I ringed unnamed wooded islands in Scottish lochs and Irish loughs, and imagined swimming out to them, climbing their trees, and then sleeping out on them. I marked up areas of roadlessness and openness: the altiplanos of Rannoch Moor and the Fisherfield

Wilderness. I tracked different rock types – gabbro, hornblende, serpentine, oolite, boulder clay – watching them submerge and then resurface
across the landscape. To my desk I pinned a paragraph written by the
mountaineer-explorer W. H. Murray as he researched an expedition to
the Highland mountain of Ben Alder, using the old one-inch maps:
'Even on coloured paper, all that country bore the unmistakable stamp of
the wild, recessed by corries great enough to have at their backs still
wilder fastnesses, where secret things awaited inquiry. What kind of
things? you might ask. But, of course, I did not know.'

I listed hill-forts, barrows and tumuli in the Welsh marches and the
south-western counties, and plotted routes between them. I spotted
cliffs: the legendary rock prow of Sron Ulladale on North Harris, the
escarpments off the south-west arm of Mull that plunge nearly 1,000
feet to boulder-beaches; the sheers of Clo Mor near Cape Wrath; and
the north-facing corrie walls of Braeriach in the Cairngorms, where
snow lies all year round, sintering slowly into ice. And I noted where
certain animals and birds had their refuges: golden eagles, dotterel,
greenshank, otters, snow hares, ptarmigan and even the ghostly snowy
owl, making its rare forays south over the Arctic Circle.

Almost all of these places were in the far north or far west: the high
hills and remote coasts of Scotland and Wales. But that cardinal bias
seemed to supply a rough natural shape for the journeys. I would begin
with what I knew and loved, casting outwards and upwards to the
peaks and littorals that Fowles had declared as the last enclaves of 'old
nature', and that conformed most purely to my private vision of wildness. Then at some northerly point I would turn south, back down
through Ireland and eventually into urban England, where the wild
seemed most at risk, most elusive and most foreign to me.

I also decided that, as I travelled, I would draw up a map to set against the road atlas. A prose map that would seek to make some of the remaining wild places of the archipelago visible again, or that would record them before they vanished for good. This would be a map, I hoped, that would not connect up cities, towns, hotels and airports. Instead, it would link headlands, cliffs, beaches, mountain-tops, tors, forests, river-mouths and waterfalls.

This book is that map. And I began its making by heading west, out along the pointing arm of the Lleyn Peninsula of North Wales, to a remote island where the first glimmerings of a wild consciousness could be found.

2

Island

Low evening light glowed in the bow wave. The wind was strong, and the boat was heeled over at twenty degrees to the horizontal. The sails were tight, the sea grey, agitated. All three of us on board were braced against wires and wood in order to keep our footing on the sloped deck. I was at the helm, trying to hold a steady course towards the island. I could feel the current pushing us sideways, forcing a sly lateral slide north, towards the distant rocks of the mainland, upon which broke a line of fine pale surf. Above the mainland hung two thin layers of cloud, black over white: a sign of disturbed air.

Early evening, early summer, off the westernmost tip of the Lleyn Peninsula. We had left harbour late, knowing that the wind was high, and darkness three hours away at most.

The boat was moving at nearly eight knots, and had settled into a steady battering bounce over the waves, when there was a crack, and a fierce white flapping, like a swan taking off. The boat slewed round to leeward and slowed, as though the water had suddenly thickened, and we were all jolted forwards. Cold spray broke up and over the starboard side, and slapped my face. I could hear a noise like an irregular drumbeat.

The staysail had torn out from the deck, near the bow. The thick pin that clasped it in place had sheared through under the wind's pressure, and the sail was lashing almost free, secured only at the masthead.

The heavy metal spool fixed to the sail's loose lower end was flinging about and pounding at the fibreglass deck.

John, the skipper, issued brief and exact orders. He took the helm, brought the boat round into the wind, and then left me to keep it there. Wave water soaked the deck. Jan, John's wife, edged out along the boat's bucking side, caught the spool and lashed it to a railing. The sail was lowered, and we wrestled it back from the wind and rolled it, so that it could be laid flat along the deck and taped down.

The final hour passed in the quiet that follows a crisis. With less sail up, we moved slowly. Four knots, rarely more.

The island, to the south-west of us, was silhouetted against the setting sun: a big back of cliff and crag, rising five hundred feet out of the water, then tapering off to a long shallow arm of land. On the arm stood a tall lighthouse, its opal mirrors glinting every few seconds.

We sailed at last into the wind-shadow of the island's cliffs, and the single sail slumped, airless, from the mainmast. Then, by way of welcome or miracle, though of course it was neither, the low sun broke fully through the clouds and turned the sea silver, and we motored into the small sheltered harbour on the surface of that bright water.

As we drew close to the shore, the air filled with a high keening noise, which grew in volume the nearer we came to land. I thought that it must be an acoustic effect of the wind – quick air singing in the boat's tight wires – and I looked around at my companions, unsure if I were the only one hearing it. As it became louder, I realised that it was not a single note, but a braid of dozens of notes, each of a slightly different pitch. And then I understood. Seals! Seals were making the sound, the hundreds of seals that were hauled out on every rock and kelp-hung skerry in the bay, and on its curved shoreline. They were giving off noise without seeming to, as bees do, or water. They were of many different colours: grey, black, white, fawn, fox-red and leather-brown. As we passed close by three smaller females, I saw that their fur was elegantly marked in swirls and contours.

John rowed me ashore in the dinghy, running it up on to the pebbled beach in the dusk light. I moved off alone inland, down the island's thin south-western arm, passing through the plainsong of the seals, prospecting for a place to sleep.

The island's name is Ynys Enlli, which means Island of the Currents. The name is well given, for several fierce tide races meet around Enlli. A tide race occurs when a rising or falling tide drives the sea rapidly through a channel. The water in tide races, especially at points where two or more races converge, behaves erratically. At the turn of tides, it can achieve a sleek calmness, but when the tides run, the water seethes and there is a submarine twining of currents. Where the races meet, waves stand up like shark-fins, and bubbles rise in gouts, as though the seabed itself were being stirred.

Tide races can also reach into apparently open water. When a race meets a headland, as it does at the tip of the Lleyn Peninsula, it is deflected outwards. The distance of the deflection depends upon the speed of the race: a quick race can reach out a menacing arm for miles. It is easy to see how early navigators, caught in the pull of such a current, ascribed supernatural malevolence to certain headlands and peninsulas.

Ynys Enlli was among the many remote places of the west and

north-west coasts of Britain and Ireland to be settled between around
AD 500 and 1000. During those centuries, an extraordinary migration
occurred. Monks, anchorites, solitaries and other devout itinerants
began to travel in their thousands to the bays, forests, promontories,
mountain-tops and islands of the Atlantic littoral. In frail craft and
with little experience of seamanship, they sailed out across dangerous
seas, in search of something we might now call wildness. Where they
stopped, they built monasteries, cells and oratories, dug cemeteries for
their dead and raised stone crosses to their God. These travellers were
known as *peregrini*: the name derives from the Latin *peregrinus* and
carries the idea of wandering over a distance, giving us our word 'pilgrim'. Before coming to Enlli, I had plotted on a map the known
routes and landfalls of these migrations, and I had ended up with a
tracery-work of what are still among the wildest parts of Britain and
Ireland.

This Celtic Christian culture of retreat originated in the Ireland of
the fifth and sixth centuries. Begun by St Patrick in the 430s, and
inspired by the desert saints of the preceding centuries, the practice of
retreat spread to what are now western Scotland and coastal Wales: a
centrifugal motion, carrying men to the brinks of Europe and beyond.

It is clear that these edgelands reciprocated the serenity and the
asceticism of the *peregrini*. Their travels to these wild places reflected
their longing to achieve correspondence between belief and place,
between inner and outer landscapes. We can surmise that the monks
moved outwards because they wished to leave behind inhabited land:
land in which every feature was named. Almost all Celtic place-
names are commemorative: the bardic schools, as late as the
seventeenth century, taught the history of places through their

names, so that the landscape became a theatre of memory, continually reminding its inhabitants of attachment and belonging. To migrate away from the named places (territories whose topography was continuous with memory and community) to the coasts (the unmapped islands, the anonymous forests) was to reach land that did not bear the marks of occupation. It was to act out a movement from history to eternity.

From the early years of Celtic Christianity, Ynys Enlli was renowned as a destination for the *peregrini*, and it is thought that the first monastery was built there in the sixth century. For all its difficulty of access, however, it is among the least remote of the monks' habitations. You wonder at how the monks reached and settled landscapes such as the Garvellochs – the islands off the Argyll mainland where, over 1,000 years ago, people lived in clustered mortarless huts shaped like beehives – or Skellig Michael – the rock fang that juts 700 feet out of the Atlantic, nine miles west of the Kerry coast. The uppermost slopes of Skellig Michael are pocked with cells, built on the rock by the monks who landed there in the sixth century. The cells, which were used for penance and meditation, face out on to the Atlantic. Below them, the rock swoops away so abruptly and steeply that it is hard even to believe you are on land, and not hovering above only air and sea. There, with the ocean extending away from them, and nothing on the horizon to abbreviate or delay the eye, the monks were free to consider infinitude.

George Bernard Shaw travelled to the Skelligs in September 1910 in a clinker-built rowboat. The journey out took two and a half hours in calm weather; the way back was longer and more unnerving. Rowing in thick mist and darkness, compassless and moonless, over tide races and currents, Shaw's guides steered by instinct and know-ledge alone. The following evening, sitting by the fire in the Parknasilla Hotel in Sneem, Shaw wrote a letter to his friend Barry Jackson about his experience on Skellig Michael. 'I tell you the thing does not belong to any world that you and I have lived and worked in: it is part of our dream world . . . I hardly feel real again yet!' For Shaw, as for the monks who once lived there, on the Skellig you were brought to think in ways that would be possible nowhere else. It was a place for deep dreaming.

The sea journeys that the *peregrini* made are extraordinary to con-template. We had difficulties reaching Ynys Enlli in a thirty-three-foot ocean-going yacht. Shaw had feared for his life returning from the Skelligs in a well-manned rowboat. Yet the monks had got to the Skelligs, and had made longer, riskier voyages – to Iceland and to Greenland, over the rough seas of the North Atlantic – in far more exposed and unstable craft.

The boats in which they travelled went by different names in differ-ent traditions: the coracle or curricle in Wales, the carraugh in Gaelic, the knarr in Norse. Their shapes differed, too: the curragh was generally long and thin, with a snub nose and squared-off bows, while the cor-acle was lenticular. What they shared was a method of construction. Their hulls were of oxhide, which was oak-tanned, then wetted and stretched over a framework of bent wood and wicker. As it dried, the hide shrank around the framework, setting it rigid. Once it had set, it was caulked with tallow. What these craft had in common, too, was a logic of motion. They were designed, in their lightness and their shal-low draft, to slide over the currents and the tide-rips, to slip up and over waves. This was their talent as vessels: they possessed a kind of maritime guile, barely displacing water, moving over the sea with the delicate touch of a pond-skater.

At last light, near the tip of Enlli's southern arm, I walked through a field of dead sea pink, the compact plant that grows so well in the saline conditions of coastal margins. The crisp heads of the flowers, on their stiff stalks, vibrated in the breeze, so that in the twilight it seemed as though the ground were shivering. On water to the south, I heard the clatter of a cormorant taking off. I could see the glimmer of the cabin lights of the boat, swaying in the bay, and briefly wished I were there with John and Jan: hot food, a glass of whisky, the company of friends.

I glanced back towards the mainland. It was visible only as a line in the dusk, wire thin. The monks would have launched their boats from the coves of the peninsula. Even now in summer, if the weather is poor, it can be two to three days before it becomes possible to reach the island. When the winter storms set in, Enlli can be isolated for weeks at a time.

The monks would have gauged their timing carefully. The long wait for flat weather. The watching of tides. Then the launch, feet crunching in the pebbles, splashing in the water. The boats lurching even in the swell of the coves, and then tacking out into the open waters of the Sound, the currents stacked in descending storeys beneath them.

How exposed they must have felt, I thought. Yet perhaps they did not, perhaps their faith was so absolute that it resembled fatalism, which is a type of fearlessness. Certainly, many of them – unnamed, unchronicled – died there in the Sound, drowned by wave and current. 'There is an island there is no going to / but in a small boat,' wrote the priest-poet R. S. Thomas, whose parish of Aberdaron looked out on to Enlli:

> *The way*
> *the saints went, travelling the gallery*
> *of the frightened faces of*
> *the long-drowned, munching the gravel*
> *of its beaches . . .*

We can know little for certain about the *peregrini*. We know few of their names. Yet, reading the accounts of their journeys and of their experiences on places like Enlli, I had encountered a dignity of motive and attitude that I found salutary. These men were in search not of material gain, but of a hallowed landscape: one that would sharpen their faith to its utmost point. They were, in the phrasing of their own theology, exiles looking for the *Terra Repromissionis Sanctorum* – the Promised Land of Saints.

A long Christian tradition exists that considers all individuals as *peregrini*, in that all human life is seen as an exile. This idea was perpetuated in the Salve Regina, the chant often recited as a last night prayer. *Post hoc exilium*, the prayer declares: all will be resolved after this exile. The chant, when sung, sounds ancient and disquieting. It is unmistakably music about wildness, an ancient vision of wildness, and it still has the capacity to move us.

Much of what we know of the life of the monks of Enlli and places like it, is inferred from the rich literature which they left behind. Their poems speak eloquently of a passionate and precise relationship with nature, and of the blend of receptivity and detachment which characterised their interactions with it. Some of the poems read like jotted lists, or field-notes: 'Swarms of bees, beetles, soft music of the world, a gentle humming; brent geese, barnacle geese, shortly before All Hallows, music of the dark wild torrent.' Others record single charmed instants: a blackbird calling from a gorse branch near Belfast Loch, foxes at play in a glade. Marban, a ninth-century hermit who lived in a hut in a fir-grove near Druim Rolach, wrote of the 'wind's voice against a branchy wood on a day of grey cloud'. A nameless monk, responsible for drystone walling on the island of North Rona in the ninth century, stopped his work to write a poem that spoke of the delight he felt at standing on a 'clear headland', looking over the 'smooth strand' to the 'calm sea', and hearing the calls of 'the wondrous birds'. A tenth-century copyist, working in an island monastery, paused long enough to scribble a note in Gaelic beside his Latin text. 'Pleasant to me is the glittering of the sun today upon these margins.'

Gleanings such as these give us glimpses of the nature of faith of the *peregrini*. They are recorded instants which carry purely over the long distances of history, as certain sounds carry with unusual clarity within water or across frozen land. For these writers, attention was a form of devotion and noticing continuous with worship. The art they left behind is among the earliest testimonies to a human love for the wild.

Ideas, like waves, have fetches. They arrive with us having travelled vast distances, and their pasts are often invisible, or barely imaginable.

'Wildness' is such an idea: it has moved immensely through time. And in that time, two great and conflicting stories have been told about it. According to the first of these, wildness is a quality to be vanquished; according to the second, it is a quality to be cherished.

The etymology of the word 'wild' is vexed and subtle, but the most persuasive past proposed for it involves the Old High German *wildi* and the Old Norse *villr*, as well as the pre-Teutonic *ghweltijos*. All three of these terms carry implications of disorder and irregularity, and as Roderick Nash has written, they bequeathed to the English root-word 'will' 'a descriptive meaning of . . . wilful, or uncontrollable'. Wildness, according to this etymology, is an expression of independence from human direction, and wild land can be said to be *self-willed* land. Land that proceeds according to its own laws and principles, land whose habits – the growth of its trees, the movements of its creatures, the free descent of its streams through its rocks – are of its own devising and own execution. Land that, as the contemporary definition of wild continues, 'acts or moves freely without restraint; is unconfined, unrestricted'.

This basic definition of wildness has remained constant since those first appearances, but the values ascribed to this quality have diverged dramatically.

On the one hand, wildness has been perceived as a dangerous force that confounds the order-bringing pursuits of human culture and agriculture. Wildness, according to this story, is cognate with wastefulness. Wild places resist conversion to human use, and they must therefore be destroyed or overcome. Examples of hostility to the wild are ubiquitous in cultures ancient and modern, Eastern and Western. 'Except for the true civilisation builders,' hallelujahed the American preacher and writer James Stalker in 1881, 'the very land in which we live would still be an

undiscovered wilderness! These men see teeming cities, and thriving fac-
tories upon the desert, where others see only sage brush and alkali
plains . . . these men have tunnelled our mountains, have spanned our
great rivers, and opened our mines of wealth!' The Old English epic
poem *Beowulf* is filled with what the poet calls *wildéor*, or 'savage
creatures'. In the poem, these monstrous dragon-like beings inhabit a
landscape of wolf-haunted forests, deep lakes, windswept cliffs and
treacherous marshes. It is against these wild places and *wildéor* that the
civilisation of Beowulf's tribe, the Geats – with their warm and well-lit
mead halls, their hierarchical warrior culture – sets itself.

Parallel to this hatred of the wild, however, has run an alternative history: one that tells of wildness as an energy both exemplary and
exquisite, and of wild places as realms of miracle, diversity and abundance. At the same time that the *Beowulf*-poet was writing his parable
of the conquest of the wild, the monks of Enlli, Rona, the Skelligs and
elsewhere were praising its beauty and its riotous fecundity.

Even earlier than the *peregrini*, indeed, evidence can be found of a
love for the wild. It is there in the Chinese artistic tradition known as
shan-shui or 'rivers-and-mountains'. *Shan-shui* originated in the early
fifth century BC, and endured for two thousand years. Its practitioners –
T'ao Chi'en, Li Po, Du Fu, Lu Yu – were usually wanderers or self-exiles
who lived in the mountain lands of China, and wrote about the wild
world around them. Their art, like that of the early Christian monks,
sought to articulate the wondrous processes of the world, its continuous
coming-into-being. To this quality of aliveness, the *shan-shui* artists
gave the name *zi-ran*, which might be translated as 'self-ablazeness',
'self-thusness' or 'wildness'.

Pilgrims and walkers, they explored their mountains in what they called the 'dragon-suns' of summer, in the long winds of winter and the blossom storms of late spring. They wrote of the cool mist that settled into valleys at dawn, of bamboo groves into which green light fell, and of how thousands of snowy egrets would take off from lakes like lifting blizzards. They observed the way winter light fell upon drifted snow, and how shadows hung from cold branches, and wrote that such sights moved them to a 'bright clear joy'. Night was especially marvellous to them, because of the clean luminous presence of the moon, and its ability to silver the world into strangeness. Beauty did not always connote benignity: Li Po so loved the moon, it is said, that he drowned while trying to embrace its reflection in a river. Nevertheless, reading the poems and viewing the paintings of the *shan-shui* tradition, you encounter an art in which almost no divide exists between nature and the human. Form imposes itself on content so absolutely that these artefacts do not represent the world's marvels, but partake of them.

A hundred yards from the black-rock headland that marked the end of the island's peninsula, I searched for a sleeping place. The night air was loud with the pennywhistle piping of oystercatchers and the gulls' yowls. It felt exciting to be out there in the dark, among the birds, and with the sea surging and sloshing all around me.

The ground was uneven, and sloped down to a set of cliffs that were cleft by big wave channels. Finally I found somewhere I could sleep: a body-length patch of grass on a terraced bank, above a deep gorge-like inlet. The bank tilted slightly inwards; there was no danger of me rolling off it in my sleep. I could make out the shapes of seals moving through the water. Sweeping above me were the beams of the lighthouse, long thin spokes of light opening out into the darkness, turning in slow predictable yellow rotation. It was warm enough for me not to need the bivouac bag I had carried, so I laid out my mat and sleeping-bag on the grass.

The noise began at around midnight, or that was when I woke to it. Birds were falling through the air above me, screaming while they fell, leaving long curved trails of sound as they plunged. I could hear them landing with soft thumps on the ground around me.

Every few seconds, one of the plunging birds and one of the turning lighthouse beams would coincide, vertical through lateral. I began to see them, here and there, momentarily outlined in the light – birds, with arrow-wings swept back from their little bomb-bodies, so that even as they disappeared, my eye retained an image of their streaking forms.

Shearwaters. Of course – they were shearwaters. Migratory, long-travelling, long-lived birds, which nested in burrows, and which waited until the cover of darkness before coming into land. Their name derives from their habit of gliding low over the water, wing-tips skidding the waves and striking droplets from them. The longest recorded wave-top glide of a Manx shearwater is one and a half miles. They are remarkable, too, for the distance of their pilgrimages. In a single day, they can cover as much as 200 miles. When the breeding season is over, obeying impulses beyond our cognition, the shearwaters of Enlli will fly thousands of miles to spend the rest of the year at sea in the South Atlantic.

Ynys Enlli, like so many of the islands and marshes on the east and west coasts of Britain, is a refuge for migrating birds. Hundreds of species stop off during their search for undisturbed feeding grounds. Tides and currents of birds, sweeping seasonally north and south, dispersing and returning, linking remote place to remote place.

Around two o'clock, the shearwaters settled. I lay in the quiet dark, watching the light beams turning silently above me, until I slipped back into sleep.

I woke to a still dawn. The sea, breathing quietly to my south, was pearly, with a light low mist upon it. The sky was pale with breaks of blue. The splash made by a black-backed gull diving fifty yards away sounded like a stone lobbed into the water nearby. I sat up, and saw that dozens of tiny dun-coloured birds were littering the rocks around me, making a high playground cheeping. Pipits. They gusted off when I moved.

I clambered down the shallowest side of the gulch, to the sharp angled rocks at the sea's edge, and washed my face in the idle water. On a rock ledge, I found and kept a heart-sized stone of blue basalt, beautifully marked with white fossils: coccoliths no bigger than a fingernail, the fine fanwork of their bodies still visible. I set a thin shell afloat, carrying a cargo of dry thrift heads. As I placed it on the water, it was sucked out away from my fingers on an invisible back eddy, bobbing with the gentle swell.

Two big seals were hauled out on the rocks on the far point of the gulch. They watched me, and when I neared them they began to toil off their perches. Then they slipped into the water, rolled onto their backs, and sculled past the mouth of the gulch, gazing at me. They both dived. One disappeared. The other surfaced close to me, his thick head rising like a periscope. His big liquid eyes locked on to mine, and he watched me with a calm intransitive attention. For ten seconds or so we stared at each other. Then he ducked his head under the water with a splash, as though to rinse it, and disappeared.

Seals have long figured in the folklore of the Atlantic fringes as pos-
sessors of an uncannily double nature: in-between creatures,
half-human and half-marine. In the 1940s, the writer David Thomson
travelled between the westerly sea communities of Ireland and Scotland,
gathering stories about the seals. Everywhere he went, he found that the
tales told were the same: of the capacity of the seal's gaze to compel and
hold its subject, of seals stepping from the sea and becoming humans,
and humans slipping into the form of seals. The seal was a living
reminder, he noted, of how close we are to animals, and of our aquatic
ancestry. 'Land animals may play their roles in legend,' he concluded in
the book he wrote about his journeys, 'but none, not even the hare, has
such a dream-like effect on the human mind as the seal.'

I walked back to the shingle beach on that still morning, past the
burrows of the shearwaters, over the soft moulded grass, back through
the field of thrift. I tried to imagine the conversations the monks would
have had with one another about the places in which they dwelled: their
discussions, implicit and explicit, about what it meant to be in affinity
with the land they occupied. I admired the ways in which their spirituality found expressions and correlations in the physical world. In the
view over a low-misted sea from a headland. In the fall of light upon the
margin of a page, or a bay. In feathers rocking down through still air like
snow, or snow rocking down through still air like feathers. Of course
there were physical discomforts to their lives in these places; of course
there would have been disagreements, dislikes, currents of bad feeling
between the men themselves. But these ascetics had desired and celebrated an affluence which was beyond the economic, and which found
its forms in the clearness of the air over the sea, or the shoaling patterns
of a flock of seabirds in flight. Henry David Thoreau had written about

such ideas of value. A lake, he said, a hill, a cliff, or individual rocks, 'a forest or ancient trees standing singly', 'such things are beautiful, they have a high use which dollars and cents never represent.'

Much had changed since the time of the *peregrini*. Plastic flotsam washed up in Enlli's coves and gulleys. Power-boats thumped over the water near the mainland. There were problems with sewage, piped out into the Irish Sea from the Welsh coastal towns, and with chemical pollution which, on certain days, set the water foaming like shampoo on the rocks. And I could not have survived on the monks' island, could not have lived on it even for a month, probably – the draw of the city, my own routines, my need for libraries, luxuries, connection, variety. Yet aspects remained of what had attracted the *peregrini* there, centuries earlier, and it felt somehow right to have begun my journeys in a landscape where people had, in the past, lived companionably with the wild.

Later we sailed back across the Sound to the mainland, at the turn of the tides, passing as we did so over water that was plump and gleaming, as though it were covered in a sheeny surface membrane beneath which the upwelling current seemed to pause and tremble.

John moored the boat a hundred yards offshore, near a point jutting west towards Enlli, facing a small bay. To either side of the bay rose jagged cliffs, complicatedly recessed and cut into by caves, off which bird cries pinged. The boat rolled on the subtle green swell, snapping its anchor rope tight with each roll, so that water sprang from it. Its mast, seen from the stern, ticked from side to side like a metronome.

I dived in. Blue shock. The cold running into me like a dye. I surfaced, gasping, and began to swim towards the cliffs at the eastern side of the bay. I could feel the insistent draw of the current, sliding me out to the west, back towards Enlli. I swam at a diagonal to it, to keep my course.

Nearing the cliffs, I moved through different ribbons and bands of temperature, warm, then suddenly cold again. A large lustrous wave surged me between two big rocks, and as I put a hand out to stop myself from being barged against them, I felt barnacles tear at my fingers.

I swam to the biggest of the caves. Holding on to an edge of rock, and letting the swell lift me gently up and down, I looked inside. Though I could not see the back of the cave, it seemed to run thirty or forty feet into the cliffs: cone-shaped, tightening into the earth from its mouth. I released the rock, and drifted slowly into the opening. As I crossed the shadow cast by the cave's roof, the water grew cold. There was a big hollow sucking and slapping sound. I shouted, and heard my call come back at me from all sides.

As I got deeper in, the water shallowed. I swam breast-stroke, to keep myself as flat as possible. I was passing over dark red and purple rocks: the voodoo colours of basalt, dolerite. The lower sides of the cave were lined with frizzy green seaweed, which was slick and shiny where the water reached it, like wet hair.

Further back into the cave, the light was diffused and the air appeared powdery. The temperature had dropped, and I sensed the whole gathered coldness of the unsunned rock around and above me, pushing out into the air and water.

I glanced back over my shoulder. The big semicircular mouth of the cave had by now shrunk to a cuticle of light. I could only just see out to the horizon of the sea, and I felt a sudden involuntary lurch of fear. I swam on, moving slowly now, trying to sense the sharp rocks over which I was moving.

Then I reached the end of the cave, and there, at its very back, and in its very centre, lifted almost entirely out of the water, sat a single vast white boulder, made of smooth creamy rock, shaped roughly like a throne or seat. It must have weighed five or six tons. I climbed awkwardly out of the water, slipping on weed, and sat on the rock, while the water slopped around its base, and looked back down the cave to the curved rim of light, all that remained of the world beyond.

Remembering the white rock now, it seems like a hallucination. I cannot explain what it really looked like, certainly not what it was doing there, among the red and purple basalts. Nor could I conceive of the might of the storm waves that, over the centuries, must have brought that boulder to the cave, and then shifted it deeper and deeper in, until finally they had heaved it into that position, placed perfectly at the centre and the back of the cave.

That afternoon the sun returned, filling the air with low warm light. We climbed steep cliffs near the cove, above deep sea water which would catch us if we fell, and gathered the rock samphire that grew in vertical fields. We perched in little nooks and sentry holes, facing out to the setting sun, and talked to each other across the cliff, as we chewed on the samphire's pale green leaves, relishing its saltiness.

As dark was finally falling, we returned to the cove off which the boat was moored. It lay at the mouth of a small steep-sided valley, cut by a stream. The valley's two banks were thick with small trees – ash, elder, rowan – hung with wild honeysuckle, and bindweed, whose almond scent gathered in the air and moved with the wind in currents through the dusk, and whose white trumpet-shaped flowers shone in the fading light.

The cove's beach was formed of hundreds of thousands of stones, some as smooth as eggs. Several old rusted tractors with black plastic bucket seats were pulled up to either side, near the cliffs, ready to haul fishing boats out of the water. Where it was sandier, near the water, three wading birds moved forwards together in a line, swinging their beaks from side to side in arcs as they advanced, like a team of metal detectors. We moved boulders to make seats, and sat for a while, watching the sun complete its combustion over the western sea.

When it was fully dark, we lit a birchwood fire in a pit of stones beneath the westernmost cliff edge of the cove, and sat round it, drinking, eating, talking. The orange fire popped bright sun-flares out into the darkness. Resin hissed, and wood cracked as it tore itself along its grain. Sparks rushed in flocks into the darkness, before passing out of sight. The sea hushed on the shingle. Time became measured by the fire's failing and flaring. Later in the evening, I walked across the cove. I looked back through the dark at the fire, to see its orange sway, and the figures, visible only as shadows, moving about it.

By two in the morning the fire had dulled down to a pyre of embers, which pulsed black and orange with the light wind. The night was moonless and tepid. It was then that I saw the glimmering of the water. A line of blinking light – purple and silver – rimming the long curve of the beach. I walked down to the edge, squatted, and waved a hand in the water. It blazed purple, orange, yellow and silver. Phosphorescence!

I left my clothes on the stones, and waded into the warm shallows. Where it was undisturbed, the water was still and black. But where it was stirred, it burned with light. Every movement I made provoked a brilliant swirl, and everywhere it lapped against a floating body it was struck into colour, so that the few boats moored in the bay were outlined with luminescence, gleaming off their wet sloped sides. Glancing back, the cove, the cliffs and the caves all appeared trimmed with light. I found that I could fling long streaks of fire from my fingertips, sorcerer-style, so I stood in the shallows for a few happy minutes, pretending to be Merlin, dispensing magic to right and left.

Then I walked out into the deeper water, and slipped forward and swam in a squall of tangerine light. I rolled on to my back, and sculled along the line of the shore, looking back at the land, and kicking my legs so that complex drapes of colour were slung outwards. What was it Thoreau had written about a similar experience at Walden Pond? 'It was a lake of rainbow light, in which, for a short while, I lived like a dolphin.' I remembered Roger describing how he had stood one night on the beach at Walberswick in Suffolk and seen dozens of swimmers out in the phosphorescent water, their bodies 'striking through the neon waves like dragons'.

It was dark in the cove, and there was little loose light in the sky, and I realised that I could not see myself, only the phosphorescence that surrounded me, so that it appeared as though I were not there in the water at all: my body was unclear, defined only as a shape of darkness set against the swirling aqueous light.

It is now understood that marine phosphorescence – or, more properly, bioluminescence – is a consequence of the build-up in the water of minute organisms: dinoflagellate algae and plankton. By processes not entirely understood, these simple creatures ignite into light when jostled. They convert the energy of movement into the energy of radiance. For their phosphorescence to become visible to the human eye, the collaboration of billions of these single cells is required, from each of which light emanates.

The existence of these plankton, long remarked upon by sailors, especially warm-water sailors, has produced some extraordinary phenomena. During the Gorda Basin Earthquake, which struck California on 8 November 1980, witnesses on the coast saw vast areas of the ocean light up. In the 1970s, several sea captains navigating the Indian Ocean and the Persian Gulf reported the sight, in calm seas, of vast phosphorescent wheels with luminous rotating spokes, up to 200 yards in diameter, trembling in the wake of their ships. Sometimes these wheels appeared to be below the water and sometimes they seemed to hover just above its surface.

In 1978, while crossing the Persian Gulf, under a starry sky in which stars were falling with long green tails, the captain of the Dutch vessel *Dione* saw several such wheels. There are no pre-twentieth-century records of this phenomenon, and it is generally assumed to be a function of the turbulence caused by the ships' engines. It has also been proposed that the wheels' apparent transcendence is due to the still water acting as a kind of lens, projecting the phosphorescence on to a thin layer of mist hanging just above the water's surface.

In 2004, a father and son were sailing in the Gulf of Mexico when their yacht was capsized by a gust of wind, sixty miles offshore. They clung to the hull, as it was carried on the powerful currents of the Gulf. After night fell, the water became rich with phosphorescence, and the air was filled with a high discordant music, made of many different notes: the siren song of dolphins. The drifting pair also saw that they were at the centre of two rough circles of phosphorescence, one turning within the other. The inner circle of light, they realised, was a ring of dolphins, swimming round the upturned boat, and the outer circle was a ring of sharks, swimming round the dolphins. The dolphins were protecting the father and his son, keeping the sharks from them.

When at last I left the sea, and came out on to the beach, the light-filled water shed from me on to the stones, flashed and vanished. I walked slowly inland, fading back into darkness as the water ran from me, and then lay down and slept by the low embers of the fire.

3
Valley

The journeys of the monks, moving from wild place to wild place in search of their innominate lands, had provided one precedent for the map I was making. After returning from Enlli, I found another. It was an Irish saga, thought to have been written in the fourteenth century, and called *Buile Suibhne* – which translated variously as *Sweeney Astray*, and *Sweeney, Peregrine*. It told of an Ulster king, Sweeney, who so offended a Christian priest that a curse was put on him. The curse declared that Sweeney would be transformed into 'a creature of the air', and could live only in the wild places of Ireland and western Scotland. Like a wandering bird – a peregrine – he would have to shun human company, and to seek out remoteness wherever it could be found.

When the priest's curse fell upon Sweeney, the poem said, he became 'revolted' by the thought of 'known places', and he 'dreamed strange migrations'. Thus began his long period of wandering. He ranged far over mountains and wastes, passing through narrow valleys and dark woods, shouldering through scrub of ivy and juniper, setting pebbles rattling on scree slopes, wading estuaries and walking on unsheltered hills in starry frosts and wind-blown snow, until he was clad in black ice. He moved up and down rivers, swimming from pool to pool, and he wintered among wolf packs. He made lairs and dens for himself: on mattresses of soft bog, in root-nooks at the foot of big trees, by waterfalls.

Despite the severity of these places, Sweeney came to find their harshness beautiful, and to admire the rhythms of time and weather that they kept.

On two large-scale maps, I charted as far as possible the places to which Sweeney had gone, researching the names that occurred in the poem, trying to establish either their present-day locations or their modern counterparts. Dal'Arie, Glen Arkin, Cloonkill, Ailsa Craig, Swim-Two-Birds, Sliebh Mis, Cruachan Aighle, Islay – the names joined up to make a poem of wildness. Several of his haunts no longer existed, lost to history. Others were now far from wild: they had roads running through them, or towns built over them.

Despite the changes, the form of Sweeney's quest and the intensity of the poem's vision remained powerful. I stuck pins in the maps for each of Sweeney's stations, and joined the pins with white thread, so that soon there was a hectic cotton zigzag marking his travels. His journeying from wild place to wild place, his wintering out, his sleeping close to the ground: all this made inspiring sense to me. What also made me warm to Sweeney was his occasional wish, when out in the wild, for a 'soft pillow', a bed and a hot meal. These were longings I recognised with sheepish affection.

Of the many places to which Sweeney travelled, the one he found most magical and strange was the valley of Glen Bolcain. I could find no trace of Bolcain in any contemporary gazette or record, but its character was clear from the poem: this was a lost valley, steep sided, a 'glen of winds and wind-borne echoes', where watercress grew in clear-water streams, and moss flourished in banks firm and wide enough to sleep on. Daydreaming about Bolcain, I remembered the most extraordinary valley I had ever been to: the valley of Coruisk, on the Atlantic coast of the Isle of Skye. And so I thought that I would go there for my next journey; moving north from one igneous west-coast island, Ynys Enlli, to another, Skye.

We are accustomed to the idea that ice-caps and mountains can grip the mind or compel the imagination. But the capacity of valleys – gorges, canyons, arroyos, ravines – to shape and shock our thought is less well documented. Of the many types of valley, by far the most potent is the sanctuary: that is, the sunken space guarded on all four sides by high ground or by water. Sanctuaries possess the allure of lost worlds or secret gardens. They provoke in the traveller who enters them – cresting a ridge at a pass, finding the ground drop away beneath your feet – the excitements of the forbidden and the enclosed. Among the world's great sanctuaries are the Annapurna and the Nanda Devi sanctuaries in the Himalayas, and the Ngorongoro Crater in Tanzania. Accounts exist within the literature of Western exploration of those who entered these spaces for the first time. They are accounts of wonderment and fear.

There are sanctuaries in Britain and Ireland, too. Though they are of a different magnitude to their Asian and African counterparts, I find them almost as remarkable. Versions of the sanctuary are to be found in the combes of Exmoor, in the swales and dips of the Mendips and the Yorkshire Dales, or in the Devil's Beeftub near Moffat. My cousin once told me of a small unnamed sanctuary in a lonely area of Assynt in north-west Scotland: he spoke of sleeping out there one night, alone, beneath an overhanging boulder, and watching a herd of red deer, led by a stag, pick their way down into the valley. The deer were surprised but not disturbed by this human presence, he said.

Between the first and second guardian spurs of Bidean nam Bian, the broad and complex mountain which stands near the western mouth of Glen Coe, there is a valley known to some as the 'Lost Valley', which is enclosed on three sides by the black rock fins and battlements of Bidean, and protected on its fourth by the double barrier of a rockslide that closes off the mouth of the valley, and the River Coe, which in spate becomes uncrossable. Late in the winter of 1939, W. H. Murray escaped into the Lost Valley in order to attempt new climbs on the crags of Bidean. Its floor was covered by a foot of snow, whose spotless surface heightened the loneliness of the valley, and deepened its silence. It was a place, Murray wrote, in which 'it is easy to be still', and in which 'the natural movement' of the heart was to 'lift upward'. To enter the valley was to be 'as much out of sight and sound of civilisation as if one dwelt at the North Pole'.

The greatest of the sanctuaries, though, is Coruisk: the loch-filled valley which lies on the south-western coast of the Isle of Skye. Coruisk is an Anglicisation of the Gaelic *Coir'uisge*, which means 'the cauldron of the waters', and its isolation is legendary. On three sides of Coruisk are mountains, and on the fourth is a deep inlet of the Atlantic, Loch Scavaig. The mountains are the Black Cuillin, the most austere and gothic of all Britain's ranges. They are the roots of ancient volcanoes, fifty-five million years old, which have eroded down into a six-mile battlement of smashed basalt and gabbro.

The only way into Coruisk on foot is over one of the steep passes of the Cuillin, or the walk of many miles along the brink of Loch Scavaig, which includes a traverse of the 'Bad Step' of Sgurr na Stri, an angled plane of glacier-smoothed rock that tilts twenty feet above the green waters of Scavaig. The valley is by no means inaccessible, but its solitude is formidably guarded. And its world is exceptional. Coruisk determines its own weathers, its own skies and clouds. Light behaves unexpectedly within it. The rock of the Cauldron's sides changes colour frequently, depending upon the weather's accent. It can be grey in cloud, toffee-coloured at noon, liverish at evening, and metallic in rain and sunshine.

At the heart of the sanctuary is Loch Coruisk, fed by the cold river waters that drain from the ridge. The water of the loch alters colour, too, depending on one's angle of vision of its surface: black when you are beside it, sky-blue when you are on the peaks and ridges above it, and a caramel brown when you are in it. In Coire na Creiche on the far side of the Cuillin ridge from the Basin, there are deep river pools that contain underwater rock arches. On summer days, it is possible to dive down and swim through the arches, in the blue filtered light of the water.

There is something in Coruisk's forms and its habits that has long attracted stories of wildness. When Murray first reached what he called 'the basin of Coir-uisg' in 1936, he found that his 'wild dreams fell short of the wilder reality'. Walter Scott, the impresario of Caledonian wildness, visited Coruisk in 1814 and described it as 'dark, brooding, wild, weird and stern'. Such a summary, coming from Scott, was a spur to the romantics and melancholics of the nineteenth century. Successive parties of Victorian artists, writers and explorers made elaborate efforts to reach the Basin. They travelled there in their hundreds, on foot and by boat, braving midges, rain and storm, and living in tents and caves, or on boats anchored in Loch Scavaig: aesthetes willing to tolerate the harshness of life in the Basin in order to celebrate its

form. What a curious colony they made! Among them was the little
red-headed Victorian poet Algernon Swinburne, and J. M. W. Turner,
who in 1831 arrived to see the wildness that Scott had described, and
nearly fell to his death while executing a painting in which the Cuillin
are distorted into spindly peaks, resembling whipped egg-white more
than rock.

I came to Coruisk from the south on a hot August day, along the edge
of Loch Scavaig, with Richard, my oldest friend, with whom I had
over the years climbed several hundred mountains. For hours, we followed a narrow path that kept to the loch-shore as neatly as a hemline.
The Atlantic was always to our left, turning slowly to brass as the day
proceeded and the sun lowered. Shags were perched here and there on
boulders, staring out to sea. Some stood motionless with their wings
open, hinged at the carpals, drying themselves off in the sun and wind:
iron crosses. Foam, the creamy colour of writing paper, gathered
between shore stones.

Four miles into the approach, we passed through a miniature forest,
200 yards long, and with no tree over ten feet tall. The steady onshore
wind had warped the trees eastwards, so that they had taken the curved
shape of the land against which they were pressed. We had to bend and
sidle to fit through the narrow space between the wood and the hillside.

There are few trees left now on Skye, as there are few people. The
island lost many of its inhabitants during the Clearances of the nineteenth century, and it had lost most of its woodland only a few centuries
earlier, through burning and felling. One of the first surviving descrip-

tions of Skye, from 1549, describes it as an island with 'maney woods, maney forests, maney deire'. Now the only real trace of Skye's wooded past are the old paths through its remoter reaches, several of which were first paced out by foresters. Skye's celebrated bleakness is a relatively recent acquisition, and one which speaks sadly of its past. Like so much of Scotland's wildest land, this is not an empty landscape but an emptied one. On Skye, one recalls that 'bleak' comes from the Old Norse *bleikr*, meaning 'white' or 'shining'; that it is a word through which the bone shows.

After we had traversed the forest, the path dropped steeply into a cove, and Richard and I stopped there to comb the stony beach. Lurid debris was everywhere, far more than in the coves of Enlli: blue milk-bottle crates, pitted cubical chunks of furniture foam, cigarette butts, bottle caps, aerosol canisters and Tetrapak cartons, printed with faded lettering in dozens of languages. Even here, on this remote Atlantic-facing bay, evidence of damage was unmistakable, pollution inescapable and the autonomy of the land under threat.

Thousands of tons of debris wash up each year on the coasts of Britain and Ireland. The amount is increasing annually, and the effect of this debris, beyond its visual impact, is severe. Whales, dolphins and porpoises are dying, their digestive tracts blocked by plastic. A minke whale washed up on the Normandy coast in 2002 was found to have nearly a ton of plastic packaging and shopping bags in its stomach. Seals and seabirds are becoming entangled in the 'ghost' fishing nets which – abandoned or lost from trawlers – drift through the sea. Loose oil, chugged out by the marine traffic or by offshore drilling, coats the forests of kelp, and fouls birds and seals.

I sifted through fragments of plastic, and found a shard that had been chafed by the rocks until it was rough and light as a shell. When I rubbed it against the ball of my thumb, it rasped like a cat's tongue. I picked up a twist of rope, blue and black, its fibres plaited in interlocking rhomboids, like the pattern on an adder's back. Oystercatchers stood about on the beach, neckless, in tuxedoed groups. A trio of eiders puttered around twenty yards offshore. The wind and water had woven heather stalks and grass into a mess of harvest wreaths, which lay along the tideline for miles. On a series of sloping rock ledges, the sea had arranged big stones into different calibres and gauges; the lighter boulders carried up on to the higher ledges, the heavier ones lined nearer the water.

Caught in a little ravine was the body of a seagull, recently dead, with its wet wings flung out. There were traces of oil on its wing feathers, like fretmarks, though it did not seem to have died from this contamination. Its eyes had misted over, so that they had the scuffed consistency of sea-glass. I bent down and folded its wings across its chest, and then we walked on towards the gateway to the sanctuary, with its black guardhouses of rock.

We reached the entrance to Coruisk at dusk. Cliffs on one side, and a cut wall of rock, waterfall-seamed, on the other. The sky was black out to sea: a storm was building somewhere over the horizon's rim. As we passed between the cliffs I felt a strong sense of having crossed a portal, or stepped over a threshold. I remembered my grandfather telling me how, growing up in Switzerland, he had once managed to gain access to the mysterious Val de Susanfe, a sanctuary valley locked behind the

Dents du Midi. Entry to the valley involved climbing to a high rocky ledge above a waterfall. The ledge appeared to terminate in thin air, but in fact led to another, broader ledge, and from there to the valley itself. 'This secret way,' he said, 'was the door to a magical place,' where edelweiss and aster grew in profusion.

Near the outflow of Loch Coruisk into Loch Scavaig, just above the point where fresh meets salt, we found the hut. Richard saw it first, and called out. It was well camouflaged, hunkered in the lee of a thirty-foot basalt escarpment, facing out over the Atlantic, barely visible in the twilight. In the calm air of the escarpment's lee, midges gathered and danced in clouds, and settled maddeningly in their hundreds on our faces and hands.

A pine panel screwed into place above the fireplace recorded that the hut had been built in 1952, paid for by the parents of two young men who had died during a winter ascent of Ben Nevis's Tower Ridge. It stood in memory of the two men, the board said, and 'to assist those whose spirit of adventure, courage and good companionship finds outlet in the high hills'.

Around nine o'clock, the cold blue dusk gave way to full storm. There were volleys of rain on the windows, like handfuls of gravel being thrown at the glass. I went to the western window of the hut, cupped my hands round my eyes and stared out. I could see only the miniature landscape of the raindrops on the window pane: silver tumuli and barrows. The darkness beyond the glass was absolute and featureless. Except for the noises of the wind and rain, our hut might have been hurtling through deep space.

On a window-sill I found the hut's guest-book. It held decades of comments from people who had been drawn to Coruisk. Fishermen,

walkers, wilderness pilgrims, painters and solitaries had come here from
all over the world. The Mensa Mountaineering Club claimed that they
had failed to work out how to open the door. An entry for 21 April
2001 read: 'Major Leek in water pipe near to burn.' It was not explained
how Major Leek had got there, or what was done to remove him, but
apparently the water supply had been satisfactorily restored.

One group from Cornwall described how on a clear night they had
seen the sea water in the bay shining with green phosphorescent light.
They had all walked out to the shore, and thrown rocks into the bay,
and watched emerald fountains spring up from the dark water. I read
their description enviously, remembering the phosphorescence of Enlli
and wishing for another such swift miracle of light.

When we woke next morning the storm had passed. Pale sunshine lay
in stripes across the floor. Outside, big scarps of white cloud hung over
the ocean, with blue between them. Gulls wheeled easily, gleaming as
they passed through columns of light. Scavaig was tranquil, the storm
forgotten. The only noise was the quiet talk of the waves floating in
with the wind, and the lazy clack of lanyard on mast, from a yacht
moored in the bay. It must have fled here from the open water during
the night, seeking shelter. Seals basked on the rocks, prone and incuri-
ous.

We left the hut and walked further up into the sanctuary. Our plan
was to explore the long northern coast of Loch Coruisk, passing
through the land that lay between the base of the cliffs and the water.
Then, from the loch's end we would scale the headwall to the ridge, and

finally try to climb the 'Inaccessible Pinnacle' of Sgurr Dearg – the shark's fin of black rock that jags hundreds of feet out of the ridge above Coruisk, and which had long been, to my mind, one of the wildest points in the world.

Along the north shore, we traversed acres of soaked marsh, pocked with deep sink-holes. The steep ground to our left was a mosaic of brown rock, grouted with grass and streaked vertically with water from the previous night's storm. The angle of tilt of the mountain's face and the angle of fall of the light were such that every wet face of rock was set glinting – thousands of them at once, all on the same alignment.

The sink-holes in the marsh brimmed with water. The mild ferrosity of the rocks meant that the water in the holes was stained red around the edges: they shone like pools of drowned blood. Only faint deer paths showed us a safe way through.

The air was moist and smelt swampish, oozy. The ground was dense with plant-life: mare's tails, among the oldest plants in existence, and the dark green leaves of a plant whose name I did not know. I reached out and scooped one of the leaves up from beneath. It felt heavy and limp as an old vellum map, drooping loosely over my palm.

Weather blew rapidly in and over us as we walked: squalls of sunlight, then rain, then a sudden fusillade of hail. Near the head of the loch, after three miles in the marshlands, we emerged on to a hard rock landscape of flat gabbro floors, each up to a quarter of an acre in size and punched with holes. Glaciers had flattened and rounded these off tens of thousands of years ago. In the bottom of each hole, I noticed, was a pebble or rock that fitted the hole snugly, like the head of a counter-sunk screw.

At the head of the loch, we began to climb. Around us, exploiting the unpredictable wind laws of the Cuillin, ravens practised their flying skills – stalls, rolls, flic-flacs, Immelmann turns – and their sharp calls rang off the cliffs like ball-bearings striking tin. Here and there were rugged rowans, their knuckly roots binding the wet scree together.

Progress was hard, and we stopped to rest by a flat-topped rock over which a stream ran. Hanging from the rock's lip were three plump green hives of moss, the shape of weaver-bird nests. The water that ran over the rock was so smooth it resembled plastic, sheened and artificial. I put my hand just beneath the surface and watched the water flow over it and take its shape, like a second translucent skin. Looking up, I could see the fin of the Pinnacle. The wind up at the height of the ridge was strong, and shreds of white cloud were tearing over black rock. I felt a quick buzz of fear, remembering the description of the Pinnacle by one of its first ascensionists: 'a knife-edge ridge with an overhanging and infinite drop on one side, and a drop on the other side even steeper and longer'.

As we climbed higher, we entered the cloud and the temperature plunged. The rock was slick with settled moisture. We reached a bealach – a narrow notch in the ridge between two peaks – then scrambled up to the false lower summit of Sgurr Dearg, and from there picked our way down the steep overlapping scales of basalt to the base of the Pinnacle.

A small circular refuge of rocks, like a rough sheepfold, offered some shelter. We hunched in it for a few minutes, sharing a chocolate bar, not speaking. I kept looking up at the Pinnacle's black summit, hundreds of feet above me, angled up into the racing white cloud.

I stood, walked to the start of the Pinnacle's incline, and laid a hand against its rock. It was so cold that it sucked the warmth from my skin.

But this rock had once been fluid, I thought. Aeons ago it had run and dripped and spat. On either side of the Pinnacle, the ground dropped immediately away. I took a few steps up the fin. Suddenly I felt precarious, frightened: balanced on an edge of time as well as of space. All I wanted to do was get back off the ridge, back down into the Basin. We had talked of climbing the Pinnacle, had brought ropes to do so. But here, suddenly, there seemed neither point nor possibility to such an act. It would be dangerous, and impertinent.

So we retreated; back up the dragon-skin of the basalt, along the ridge, and then back down to the bealach again. We rested there for a while, in the wind shelter of the ridge. I sat quietly, trying to work out what had just happened. Where had that sudden fear come from? It had been more than a feeling of physical vulnerability, more than a vertiginous rush – though that had been part of it. A kind of wildness, for sure, but a fierce, chaotic, chastening kind: quite different from the wildness, close to beauty, of Enlli.

The clouds to the west of the bealach were moving quickly and complicatedly, like sliding panels, parting to give a view back out over the Atlantic, then sealing it off again. In one gap, I saw out to the island of Rum and far beyond it the long low boundary of the Outer Hebrides, running from Barra Head to Lewis in the north. Another opening gave me a glimpse back down into the Basin. It would have been, I thought, somewhere just like this bealach that the first of the Skye glaciers would have formed – the glaciers that had ground out the great valley space of the Basin itself, during the Pleistocene period: from two and a half million years ago, until the last glaciers receded from Skye around 14,700 years ago.

For as a river begins with a droplet falling on a slope, so a glacier

begins with a snowflake settling in a hollow. The snowflake becomes a
drift, and the drift sinters under its own weight into ice. The ice over-
flows the hollow, and then, following the impetus of its own gathering
mass, it runs down the ledges and scree slopes of the mountain, pursuing and widening the channels that have already been carved by water
run-off. At the height of the last glacial period, the ice would have
filled the Basin, and only the highest mountain-tops – the Inaccessible
Pinnacle among them – would have protruded, like *nunataks*, the rock
spires that jag out here and there from the snows of Greenland and
the Poles.

Fowles had been right, it seemed to me then, to locate the 'old nature'
in places such as Coruisk and the Cuillin. If the wild were to come close
to extinction, its final fastnesses would be the mountain-tops, and the
valleys they protected. These were places that, in the main, still kept
their own patterns and rhythms, made their own weathers and their
own light. But there were warnings here too against dreams of purity or
invulnerability – in the plastic debris that gaudied the beaches, in the oil
that slicked the kelp and the seabirds: evidence of incursion and change.
Subtler warnings, as well, which took the form of absences: cleared glens,
treeless hillsides.

Later that day, back down in the valley, we stopped and swam in the
wide blue river which gathers the waters of the headwall and ridge, and
fills Loch Coruisk itself. Richard found the spot: a long flume of
smooth rock, perhaps ten yards long, down which the river rushed
before pouring into a deep clear pool. The perfect swimming place!
Roger would have loved it, I thought. So too would my father, who had
always swum outside: in waterfall holes, in rapids under stone bridges,
in sea coves. During my childhood, whenever we drove from our home

in the Midlands up to the Highlands, which we did most summers, he would stop the car at the same bay on Loch Lomond's western shore, and plunge into the water for a few minutes, regardless of the weather. Then – smiling, damp, restored – he would get back in and drive on north.

Richard and I took it in turns to launch ourselves into the flume, letting the current whizz us down, arms held high, before dropping into the pool. Rain teemed on the water's surface, and midges bobbed in the air around us, settling and biting if we stayed still for even a few seconds. By the side of the river were firm podiums of green moss, and I remembered Sweeney's beloved Glen Bolcain. But you never mentioned the midges, Sweeney, I thought reproachfully . . .

As we were walking the final miles back down the side of the loch, the weak sun seething in the water drops still on our skin, and the river beside us shaking out its own light, I saw that a rainbow had formed in the sky over the valley below us, joining both sides of the sanctuary. We walked on towards the rainbow, and as we advanced, it seemed always to retreat, keeping the same patient distance from us. I recalled a quotation I had once written down in a notebook, but for which I had lost the source: 'Landscape was here long before we were even dreamed. It watched us arrive.'

The morning we left, the sky was a slurless blue. Before beginning the walk out, we took a last swim in the water of Loch Coruisk. We slipped into the loch from a warm tilted shore rock, having laid our clothes out on boulders to take up the sun's heat. The water was cool from the night, and still as stone. Its peaty colour gave my skin a goldish lustre, the colour of old coin.

A hundred yards or so out across the loch was an island. Just a shallow hump of bare black rock, smoothed by the passage of the glaciers, and no more than a foot above the water at its highest point. It looked like the back of a whale, and its form reminded me of the outline of my beechwood.

I swam across to it, clambered out and stood there, dripping, feeling the roughness of the rock beneath my feet, and the warmth it had already gathered from the sun. Then I lay down on my back, tucked my hands behind my head and looked into the sky.

After three or four minutes, I found myself struck by a sensation of inverted vertigo, of being on the point of falling upwards. The air was empty of indicators of space or time; empty, too, of markers of depth. There was no noise except the discreet lapping of the water against the island. Lying there, with no human trace except the rim of my own eyes, I could feel a silence that reached backwards to the Ice Age.

In the Basin I had come to imagine time differently, or at least to experience it differently. Time seemed to express itself in terms not of hours and minutes, but of shades and textures. After only a few days I found it hard to think out of Coruisk: to the ongoing world of shops, colleges and cars, with its briskness and urgency, or even to my family, my city home and my garden, where the branches of the apple tree would be lolling with fruit.

The Basin kept many different kinds of time, and not all of them were slow. I had seen quickness there too: the sudden drop of a raven in flight, the veer of water round a rock, the darts of the damselflies, the midges who were born, danced and died in a single day. But it was the great chronologies of its making – the ice's intentless progress seawards, down the slope of time – which had worked upon my mind most powerfully.

To be in the Basin, even briefly, is to be reminded of the narrow limits of human perception, of the provisionality of your assumptions about the world. In such a place, your conventional units of chronology (the century, the life-span, the decade, the year, the day, the heartbeat) become all but imperceptible, and your individual gestures and impulses (the lift of a hand, the swimming stroke taken within water, the flash of anger, a turn of speech or thought) acquired an eerie quickness. The larger impulses of the human world – its wars, civilisations, eras – seem remote. Time in the Basin moves both too fast and too slowly for you to comprehend, and it has no interest in conforming to any human schedules. The Basin keeps wild time.

In a valley of such age, you feel compelled to relinquish your habitual methods of timekeeping, to abandon the grudging measures and audits that enable normal life. Time finds its forms minerally and aerially, rather than on the clock-face or in the diary. Such human devices come to seem brittle and inconsequential. You want quietly to yield them up – to surrender your diary at the sanctuary's gateway, to turn your watch so that it faces inwards. There will be opportunity afterwards to recover these methods of record, you think.

Birds began to move across the empty sky above me. Nothing more than black marks at first, until my eyes started to sort them. Gulls turning on their wing-tips in the lower terraces of the air; three crows above them, crackling; and finally in the upper reach, a buzzard. Suddenly the sky's depth was fathomable, its space divided into tiers and circles. And Coruisk itself was changed: this place, so alien to me, was home to these birds, the place in which they hunted, played and lived.

I swam back to shore. Near the mouth of the loch, where the water was only eight or nine feet deep, I dived down to the floor, seized a big black fin-shaped rock and held myself there, so that my body and feet tilted up to the vertical, and then inclined downstream, nudged by the gentle current, like water-weed. As my breath ran out, I let go of the rock and bobbed to the surface, back into the bright air.

We left the sanctuary by an old forester's path, which followed a stream up and over the lowest of the passes to the south of the Basin. A hundred feet or so from the pass, which was indicated by a wide cairn, I found a little beach of stones, rinsed by the water and shiny white, as if in affinity with the ice that had shaped them. I took one for the cairn, and put one into my mouth to keep myself from getting thirsty, rolling it round, and keeping up a steady molar clatter as we followed the path upwards.

At the cairn, which marked the point of exit from this magical place, I stopped and looked around. To the north-east was the cleared valley of Sligachan, where the scattered wall-stones of ruined houses lay in the river's loops, grown over by grass and moss. Away to the west I could see the Inaccessible Pinnacle casting a sharp dark shadow. Far below it, Loch Coruisk gleamed and tilted like a mirror. We began the walk down into Sligachan, and the landscape watched us leave.

4

Moor

Years ago, on a warm autumn evening, I climbed Buachaille Etive Mor, the arrowhead-shaped mountain which stands at the eastern gateway to Glen Coe. When I reached its summit, the sun was low over the sea behind me, so that the Buachaille had become the pointer of a sundial, casting a triangle of shadow eastwards across the golden circle of Rannoch Moor. I stayed for an hour, watching the mountain's shadow narrow and lengthen over the Moor, changing its form from pyramid to chalet gable to obelisk. I decided then that, at some future point, I would return to cross the Moor on foot, and spend a night out somewhere in its distant centre.

Many people know Rannoch Moor, for they have looked down on to it from the mountains on its perimeter, or driven through it on the road that crosses its western marches. More know of it who have never seen it, for it is across the Moor that Alan Breck and Davey Balfour flee in Robert Louis Stevenson's *Kidnapped*. After travelling over 'wild, and houseless mountains' and 'among the well-heads of wild rivers', the two fugitives come across a region of 'low, broken, desert land' that lies 'as waste as the sea; only the moorfowl and the peewees crying upon it, and far over to the east, a herd of deer, moving like dots'. This is the Moor, and crossing it nearly kills Davey. And people have died there in winter, lost in its expanses, harassed to death by the cold that settles upon it, hardening its extensive waters and binding its few trees in ice.

Many know the Moor, then, but relatively few enter it, for it is vast and trackless and has a reputation for hostility at all times of year. Sea storms blow across it, funnelling down through Glen Coe. It is a high-level, hyena-coloured prairie – etched and roughened by glaciers, and still bearing the marks of those harrowings. Skeins of swans land on its two main lochs, intricate Loch Bà and antler-shaped Loch Laidon. On a clear night, from the top of one of the mountains that surround it, you can see its uncounted lochans, streams and rivers gleaming in the moonlight. It is only at such moments that you realise how much of the Moor is made of water.

Later that same warm autumn, I drove through the Moor at night. The crossing seemed to go on far longer than I had thought possible, mile after empty mile of it. It was as though I had driven into a pool of black and limitless space, and were passing through another, not altogether earthly, place. On the downslope of the Moor, I had to brake sharply and slow almost to a standstill, for deer were flowing across the road before me, making for their haunts in the Black Corries. In the brightness of the car's headlights, I could see the deer crowded closely together as they crossed the road, each laying its nervous head against the back or flank of the one in front. In the cold air their breath clouded out from their nostrils, and the whites of their eyes caught and returned the car's light, so that they glowed orbishly in the dark. As I drove down the waning slope of the Moor, towards the Bridge of Orchy, two or three more herds crossed the road before me, off to the corries of the Black Mount.

Four years after that deer-haunted crossing, I returned to Rannoch Moor to keep the promise I had made on the Buachaille's summit, and to add another panel to my map of the wild. I had also been drawn back to the Moor by W. H. Murray, whose essays I had been reading in the weeks after Coruisk, and who was, along with the monks and Sweeney, another quester for the wild, another precedent for my own journeys.

Although he was brought up in Glasgow, Murray had not thought of venturing into the Highlands until in 1933, when he was nineteen, he heard an acquaintance describe a winter traverse of An Teallach in Wester Ross: 'clouds lifting off a high and rocky mountain ridge, sun-shafts lighting a glen deep below'. Murray was entranced; a desire to experience such things struck him, he remembered, 'with all the sud-denness of a conversion in faith'. From then until the outbreak of the Second World War, he explored the islands, moors and mountains of Scotland whenever he could – in all four seasons, and by night as well as by day – journeying up into what he called the 'wildland of the skies'. He came to know the glens and the peaks superbly well: their weather habits and weather histories, the natures of their rocks, plants and animals. Wildness assumed for him a near-mystical importance: it would also, though he was not then to know it, save him from madness.

Several of those who met Murray in adulthood, noting his curved nose, his precise, observant manner and his capacities for sustained calm and sudden action, spoke of him as a raptor – 'a frugal, contem-plative eagle', as Hamish MacInnes put it. Of all his wild eyries, none was more important to Murray than Buachaille Etive Mor, with its dove-grey and pale pink rocks, and its vantage at the brink of Rannoch Moor.

On 3 September 1939, Murray was crossing the Moor en route to

Glen Coe. He stopped at the King's House, the inn on the western edge
of the Moor, and there he was told that war had been declared. He
knew that mobilisation would take him away from the Scottish landscape he loved, perhaps for ever. 'My instinctive reaction', he
remembered afterwards:

> was to turn to the mountain that had given me most – the
> Buachaille. So I walked across the moor in a smirr of rain, and
> climbed the Crowberry Ridge to the summit. I remembered many
> days and nights on this mountain – the beauty and brilliance of
> moonlight, ice glinting, the climbing hard. I remembered the still-
> ness and the music of silence when it seemed to merge with the
> mountain . . . Were those days over? Days of inner and outer
> exploration? . . . I spent a full hour on the top, and came down as
> slowly as I knew how. Every rock and stone seemed familiar to me.

Murray joined up in April 1940. After training, he was commissioned
and posted to the Highland Light Infantry. His crack battalion, the
2nd, was posted to the deserts of North-East Africa to fight Rommel's
newly formed Afrika Korps.

On 19 June 1941, Murray and his men were moved west to the
Libyan frontier, and entered an expanse of rock and sand vaster than
France and Germany combined. So empty and featureless was the terrain, wrote Murray afterwards, that maps of it resembled 'sea charts,
blank sheets apart from the coastline'. Despite the deprivations and the
dangers of the situation, he found a beauty in that hard and hostile sand
world. He grew to love the desert: its clarity of line, its fiery sunrises –
'when the huge sun-disc lifted up from the horizon, the cool stillness

then, the vastness of blue skies' – and the light, which at the brightest hours gave the impression of having bleached the sand so white that it seemed as if snow had settled upon the desert.

In 1942, on what would be his last leave before action, Murray climbed the 'arête' of the Great Pyramid of Giza, and then tried a bold new ascent of the Sphinx. Diplomacy overcame audacity, however. 'The chin,' he reported later, 'was the main obstacle, and it seemed . . . a dubious act to use pitons on the rock of a friendly state.'

The fun ended in August of that year. In the part of the Libyan desert known as the Cauldron, his battalion was thrown into the first of a series of infantry advances against Rommel's Panzer divisions. The tactic was a Great War relic, and fatal in its anachronism. Murray and his men were ordered to advance on foot, over half a mile of flat ground, in daylight, against tanks.

Murray would later recall that advance. First, the deafening silence after the supporting artillery barrage had stopped. Then the enemy guns opening upon the walking men: the whine and zip of bullets, the noises of the falling shells. A truck full of hens struck by a mortar, feathers blown skywards. Murray turning to speak to his runner, to find only a pair of legs, trunkless and smoking.

Murray survived that day; six hundred men did not. The battalion was given little respite. On 28 June, having been restored to strength by a new draft of men from Scotland, it was ordered to dig in near El Fuka, a coastal position forty miles west of El Alamein, and there to hold its line against Rommel's advancing 15th Panzer Division. Murray and his men excavated shallow slit trenches, and positioned their light two-pounder guns, the only ordnance they had with which to repel the oncoming Mark IV tanks. Dusk was falling, and the first glimmer of stars lit the smooth desert sky, when news arrived of the approach of Rommel's division. They were to be expected within half an hour. Murray's brigadier approached him in the failing light. 'By tonight,' he said, 'you'll be either dead meat or a prisoner.'

Down in the half-light of the slit trench, Murray sorted through his pockets and destroyed anything which might be of use to the enemy: his prismatic compass, his identity cards, his cartographic notes. He found his address book and glanced through it. Most of the names were of mountaineers. At that instant, Murray later recalled, he was overwhelmed by a sudden access of memory of the mountains and moors over which he had ranged, and the people with whom he had done so. The memory came to him 'whole, in an instant's flash – the mountains . . . charged with a beauty not theirs pouring through them'.

The first wave of German tanks struck an hour later. Dark bulks on the top of the escarpment, twenty of them abreast, their tracks whisking the sand into ochre clouds. The shells from the two-pounder guns glowed in the dusk, and made short red arcs through the sky. The tanks fired their .88mm guns, pouring white tracer into the backs of the Allied trucks, and down into the trenches and the gun emplacements. The slaughter was swift and almost total. Again, Murray escaped harm. He was taken prisoner, and flown 600 miles to Campo 21, in the province of Chieti in north Italy.

Conditions in the Chieti camp were onerous, but not appalling. There were books, and there was food, though never enough. Brutality was expedient rather than gratuitous: prisoners were clubbed with rifle butts for misdemeanours, but nothing worse than this. Most importantly, there was a view: away and up to the west, through the wire mesh of the camp's perimeter fence, Murray could see the Abruzzi mountains.

Those mountains became, during his months of imprisonment, the home of his hope. When winter arrived, the first snows settled on the Gran Sasso, the highest of the range, and it appeared to Murray like a blue and white ghost floating in the sky, the embodiment of 'a freedom of spirit' that could not be constrained by fence and hut and sentry.

Ten weeks after arriving at Chieti, Murray began to write: about the wild places he had known before his incarceration, about the Scottish mountains, moors and ridges he had loved and explored.

Paper was scarce. At first he wrote on toilet paper, but the diet of the camps meant that there was little to spare. Then Murray's mother sent him via the Red Cross a copy of Shakespeare's *Complete Works*, 'printed on the finest India paper'. He bartered pages of the book – pages whose firmness and texture were much appreciated by the men of the camp – for sheets of blank toilet paper on which he could write.

The writing Murray did there was a kind of dreamwork: a casting back and a summoning up of the open spaces of Scotland, its 'rock, snow and ice, as well as the high plateaux and long ridges and wide moors', from within his confinement. As his stamina waned, his imagination grew stronger. He thrived on the recollections of openness and freedom. The book that Murray began in Chieti, *Mountaineering in Scotland* – 'a book written from the heart of a holocaust', in his phrase – must stand as one of the finest expressions of the power of the wild to act, even in retrospect, even remotely, upon the mind.

In October, Murray was moved to the Moosburg camp in Bavaria. Prisoners were housed in wire-fenced compounds, in jam-packed bunkrooms, 'like rats in a slum'. Fleas and lice proliferated, and at night bedbugs swarmed from the mattresses. Still he wrote.

After a short time, he was moved again, this time to a camp in

Bohemia, the westernmost province of Czechoslovakia. The prisoners were searched on arrival. Murray's thick wad of toilet-paper manuscript was found, and he was interrogated by Gestapo officers, who believed it to be a coded account of troop movements. They took the manuscript from him, and destroyed it. Even to a man of Murray's mental resilience, it was a severe blow.

During the years of his confinement, Murray's health deteriorated. Towards the end of the war, Red Cross parcels were prevented from reaching the camps. The inmates of Murray's camp had to survive on black bread and minimum rations of potato and turnips. When possible, they would catch and kill dogs and cats, and eat strips of their flesh. Tuberculosis was rife. 'I am literally a skeleton,' Murray wrote in a sad letter to a friend. His fingernails became corrugated through vitamin deficiency. His hair had thinned. He could not walk ten yards without stopping to rest, could not walk at all without dizziness. He assumed that, even if he were to survive the war, he would never again be able to climb mountains.

But through all this, the dreaming continued. In Bohemia, in secret, Murray restarted the manuscript that had been taken from him on his arrival. Weak from lack of food, he became imaginatively uninhibited. 'I shed,' he remembered, 'any reticence about feeling for beauty.' When he closed his eyes, the mountains and glens sprang to mind, vivid in every detail. He dreamed of the violet dusk of moors, of the green water of the sea lochs in which he had once swum, and the beaten-gold sky of dusk seen from the Buachaille's top, and then he wrote of these things. During the last year of his confinement, he recalled, 'I had not once thought of myself as imprisoned. I lived on mountains, and had the freedom of them.'

On May Day 1945, Murray's prison camp was liberated by American troops. A month after his release, Murray returned to Rannoch Moor. Weak and emaciated in body, but exhilarated in spirit, he climbed the Buachaille again and on its summit he stayed, looking out over the Moor, in the space of those wide skies.

By the time I set out to cross the Moor in November, Coruisk's rich summer light had ceded to autumn's browns. The air was cooler, and in place of the long evenings of July and August were quick dusks.

I had hoped for an early onset of winter, because I wanted to make an ice-bound traverse of the Moor, following its frozen waterways from one side to the other, on skis or even ice-skates. This was something which I knew had been done once before, in the 1950s, and I greatly liked the idea of keeping to a single element for the crossing, of using only water to cross such an expanse of earth. But my father, who had agreed to accompany me on the crossing, pointed out two minor problems with my plan: neither of us could ice-skate, and the weather was damp, so we would sink. I acknowledged the force of his logic; walking it would have to be.

We caught the sleeper-train north together from London. The romance of the train, its Edwardian miracle of conjuring you to a different land while you sleep, was still perceptible. We left Euston Station – fast-food outlets, the tannoy's squash-ball *bing-bong*, crushed beer cans in corners, the shifty body-mass of the crowds – and woke to chilly air, white mist and a stag disappearing into the drizzle. Fog pooled in the low ground. At Rannoch Station, we stepped down from the train and on to the Moor.

That morning, we began to learn the habits and the obligations of the Moor, its resistance to straight lines of progress. As Murray knew, going on the Moor is slow, to be measured in hours, not miles. Much of the Moor is loch, and much is peat hag, and between the lochs and the peat hags bog streams wriggle, their water dyed black and shiny as oil.

We leapt from hag to hag, jumped peat crevasses and picked our way through the maze-work of stream and tussock. Later, crossing a name-less river, I saw a big trout arrow across its pool and set chevrons rippling out over the surface. Here and there, sunk in the peat, we came across the big swooping roots of ancient pine trees, thousands of years old. How I would love to have climbed one of those great pines, I thought. Peatbogs are so preservative of wood that, during the Second World War, the US Navy used 3,000-year-old white cedar logs, re-covered from sphagnum bog in New Jersey, to build the hulls of their motor-torpedo boats. From one of the stumps I took a loose dolphin-shaped fragment of wood, stained a deep brown by the peat. In another black bank, I found a white stone, bedded like an eyeball. I brushed it clean, and turned it in my hand as I walked.

The Moor's vastness and self-similarity affected our perception of dis-tance. Objects and movements showed more clearly in its spareness. So extensive was the space within which we were moving that when I glanced up at the mountains west of the Moor, to try to gauge the dis-tance we had come, it seemed as though we had not advanced at all: that, like explorers walking against the spin of pack ice, our feet fell exactly where we had lifted them.

Hours into the day, we stopped for shelter in a ruin named on our map as Tigh Na Cruaiche. A rusted iron brazier stood in one corner.

Otherwise, the interior was empty. It smelt green. We sat on stones, and looked out through the doorless entrance. Beyond the series of wooded islands slung across the centre of Loch Laidon we could see the Black Corries – the high holding grounds of deer, snow and fog – and the air which gathered in them had a deep cold blueness of tone. I thought enviously of Murray, who had returned after the war to cross the Moor on a hot August day, with only his dog for company. Halfway across, he had taken off all his clothes, put them in his pack, walking naked for the rest of the day, bathing here and there in pools and loch bays. Perhaps, I daydreamed, on the right winter day – bright sun, no wind – it might be possible to combine the traverses, and ice-skate naked from one side of the Moor to the other . . .

Later, on the top of a fifty-foot-high knoll, we sat and ate black rye bread with cheese, watching rain fronts gather miles away in the mouth of Glen Coe and then billow towards us over the ground. Velvety rags of lichen hung from the rocks on the drumlin and rippled as wind passed over them. My father pointed west: a kestrel, hunting fast over the ground. Then it stopped, hung, collapsed its wings and dropped hard into the heather.

That far into the Moor, the vast space we were in resolved the land around us into bacon-like bands: a stripe of sky, a stripe of white cloud, a stripe of dark land, and below everything the tawny Moor. The Moor's colours in that season were subtle and multiple. Seen from a distance it was brindled; close up, it broke into its separate colours: orange, ochre, red, a mustardy yellow and, lacing everything, the glossy black of the peat.

It took us all that day to reach what I had come to think of as the Moor's centre, the Abhainn Bà – the point where the River Bà flows into Loch Laidon. We stopped there, for dusk was spreading over the Moor, and pitched a small tent. We lay talking in the dark: about the ground we had covered, the ground still to go, about the odd mixture of apprehension and awe that the Moor provoked in us both. Our sleeping-place was cupped in a curve of the river, on a miniature flood-plain that the winter spates had carved out and flattened: a shelter in the middle of the Moor's great space.

In a land as densely populated as Britain, openness can be hard to find. It is difficult to reach places where the horizon is experienced as a long unbroken line, or where the blue of distance becomes visible. Openness is rare, but its importance is proportionately great. Living constantly among streets and houses induces a sense of enclosure, of short-range sight. The spaces of moors, seas and mountains counteract this. Whenever I return from the moors, I feel a lightness up behind my eyes, as though my vision has been opened out by twenty degrees to either side. A region of uninterrupted space is not only a convenient metaphor for freedom and openness, it can sometimes bring those feelings fiercely on.

To experience openness is to understand something of what the American novelist Willa Cather, who was brought up on the Great Plains, called 'the reaching and reaching of high plains, the immeasur-able yearning of all flat lands'. To love open places – and they have, historically, not been loved – you have to believe, as Cather did, that beauty might at times be a function of continuous space. You have to believe that such principalities might possess their own active expansiveness. Anyone who has been in an empty sea, out of sight of land, on a clear day, will know the deep astonishment of seeing the curvature of the globe: the sea's down-turned edges, its meniscal frown.

Open spaces bring to the mind something which is difficult to express, but unmistakable to experience – and Rannoch Moor is among the greatest of those spaces. If the Lake District were cut out of Cumbria and dropped into the Moor, the Moor would accommodate it. The influence of places such as the Moor cannot be measured, but should not for this reason be passed over. 'To recline on a stump of thorn, between afternoon and night,' Thomas Hardy wrote in *The Return of the Native*, 'where the eye could reach nothing of the world outside the summits and shoulders of heathland which filled the whole circumference of its glance, and to know that everything around and underneath had been from prehistoric times as unaltered as the stars overhead, gave ballast to the mind adrift on change, and harassed by the irrepressible New.'

For Murray, it was not even direct exposure to the spaces of moor and mountain that consoled him during his prison years, but the memory of that experience. He knew that these places continued to exist; this was what sustained him.

In 1977, a nineteen-year-old Glaswegian named Robert Brown was arrested for a murder he did not commit, and over the course of the following days had a confession beaten out of him by a police officer subsequently indicted for corruption. Brown served twenty-five years, and saw two appeals fail, before his conviction was finally overturned in 2002. When he was released, one of the first things he did was to go to the shore of Loch Lomond and sit on a boulder on the loch's southern shore in sunlight, to feel, as he put it, 'the wind on my face, and to see

the waves and the mountains'. Brown had been out on the loch shore
the day before he was arrested. The recollection of the space, that place,
which he had not seen for a quarter of a century, had nourished him
during his imprisonment. He had kept the memory of it, he recalled
afterwards, 'in a secret compartment' in his head.

We have tended to exercise an imaginative bias against flatlands:
moor, tundra, heath, prairie, bog and steppe. For Daniel Defoe, travelling in 1725, the moors above Chatsworth were abominable: 'a waste
and a howling wilderness'. Reactions like Defoe's occur in part because
of the difficulty of making the acquaintance of flat terrains. They seem
to return the eye's enquiries unanswered, or swallow all attempts at
interpretation. They confront us with the problem of purchase: how to
anchor perception in a context of vastness, how to make such a place
mean. We have words we use for such places, half in awe and half in dis-
missal – stark, empty, limitless. But we find it hard to make language
grip landscapes that are close-toned, but that also excel in expanse,
reach and transparency.

The consequences of this difficulty of engagement with open land
have been considerable. It has been hard to make and hold a case for its
worth, and so, over two centuries, the area of lowland heath in
England – the Dorset linglands, Cannock Chase, New Forest – fell by
three-quarters, lost to the plough, plantation or development. Of those
heaths that have survived, most have done so because they have kept
their designation as 'common ground' – that is, as areas open to all-
comers, and that are invulnerable to conversion by private interests.
Much of the now vanished heathland was brought under tillage for the
first time during the 'Dig for Victory' campaign of the Second World
War. Other areas of openness – Salisbury Plain, the Brecklands of East

Anglia – were sealed off and converted for military purposes, their unbroken expanses making them ideal for firing ranges, tank manoeuvres or airstrips. Strange Bodmin Moor, with its gorse uplands, shrank in area by nearly half between 1800 and 1946. Elsewhere, quarrying works, such as those on Titterstone Clee in south Shropshire, have taken industrial bites from the open landscapes. Nearly a sixth of the North Yorkshire Moors and the Northumbrian Moors are now planted with conifer for commercial use. Across England in particular, openness has been closed down.

The Pennine moors of northern England – to whose slopes and plateaux hundreds of millions of people from the cities of Nottingham, Derby, Sheffield, Manchester and Liverpool have, over the centuries, escaped – were for much of the nineteenth and early twentieth centuries run as a series of private grouse moors. Until the Mass Trespass on Kinder Scout of 1932, led by Benny Rothman, access to the moors was restricted to wealthy sportsmen, and the land was patrolled by gamekeepers who would treat walkers as trespassers. These gamekeepers were also responsible for the culling of predators. Raptors, mustelids and other carnivores were killed in their tens of thousands, their deaths recorded dispassionately in the columns of game books.

The contemporary appearance and nature of the moors is, then, in large part determined by their sporting history and use. Some of the marks left are subtle: on Stanage Moor, the Victorian owners – the Wilsons of Sheffield – employed masons to cut channels and holes into the rocks, so that rainwater collected there and provided drinking water for young grouse in the breeding season; their chisellings are still visible on the rocks. Other marks are more obvious: the large areas of moor that are burnt each year to stimulate the growth of young heather shoots, the staple food of grouse.

Yet despite the human influences in their making, the moors of Britain and Ireland have become wild places for numberless people, who leave behind the confines of their cities to enter another realm: of mazes made by troughs and hags, of wheatears flicking between stones, and of mica sand that causes stream-beds to flash in the sunlight with a silver fire.

Out on the Moor, some time around midnight, I was woken by a rumbling noise, the sound of stones rolled in water. It was a herd of deer sloshing across the river a few yards from us, turning rocks with their long sharp legs, as they followed their paths across the heather.

In the early hours, the sky cleared and the temperature dropped. We woke to a dawn of indigo and bronze, and we walked within that light for hours, passing in and out of the bays along the serried northern shore of Loch Bà. Thin beams of sun were probing down through gaps in the clouds. They looked like searchlights sweeping the Moor's emptiness for fugitives, or lasers measuring its extraordinary extent.

During those hours, the Moor seemed to reveal itself in odd forms, abstract shapes that recurred wherever I looked. The curve was one such shape: the little gold sand beaches that bracketed the loch's bays; the arc of a dark hillside held against the snowy backdrop of a higher mountain; a bough of a birch tree glimpsed through the window of a ruined crofter's cottage near the Bridge of Orchy; the hoops of that bridge; and the path of an old road, curving away into the distance and shining with wetness. There was, too, the motif of the delta: in the antlers of the deer, in the branching forms of the pale-green lichen that cloaked the trees and boulders, in the shape of Loch Laidon, in the crevasses and fissures in the peat, and in the forms of the few stag-headed old Scots pines.

As we walked, I thought about my map, which was beginning to shape itself, clarifying location by location. I tried to imagine the wild places I had not yet reached, each remarkable for its particular arrangements of space and species, its angles of rock and light. The map I was making would never attain completion, but I was happy with its partiality. It could not include every wild place, nor did I want it to. For such a map, which sought to equal the land itself, would be like the one Borges wrote of in his cautionary tale 'On Exactitude in Science'. The story is set in an Empire in which the art of cartography has attained such perfection 'that the map of a single Province occupied the entirety of a City'. Over time, Borges continued, even the accuracy of these province-sized maps was no longer satisfactory, and so the Cartographer's Guild created a map of the Empire 'whose size was that of the Empire, and which coincided point for point with it'. The map was, of course, unusable and oppressive. So it was 'delivered up to the Inclemencies of Sun and Winters. In the Deserts of the West, still today, there are Tattered Ruins of that Map, inhabited by Animals and Beggars.'

I wondered how my map might seem to someone reading it a century hence: what changes would have been wrought in the human relationship with the wild over that time. Maybe Forster's obituary would have come true by then; maybe wildness would have become extinct in these islands, perhaps in the world. If so, my map could

seem quaint and outdated to its reader: a relic, the expression of a set of
hopes and fears from an earlier world and mind. Perhaps, if it were read
at all, it would be read fondly, in the way we now regard early mariners'
maps as embodiments of dreams and worries – those hills of gold drawn
in a continent's interior, those sea-monsters cavorting in the margins of
the known.

In 1960, the historian and novelist Wallace Stegner wrote what
would become known as 'The Wilderness Letter'. It was sent as an
appeal to an official involved in a federal policy review of America's
'Outdoor Recreation Resources', and would later be published in a collection of Stegner's essays. In it, Stegner argued that a wild place was
worth much more than could ever be revealed by a cost–benefit analysis of its recreational economic value, or its minerals and resources.
No, he explained, we need wild places because they remind us of a
world beyond the human. Forests, plains, prairies, deserts, mountains:
the experience of these landscapes can give people 'a sense of bigness
outside themselves that has now in some way been lost'.

But such landscapes, Stegner wrote, were diminishing in number.
The 'remnants of the natural world' were 'being progressively eroded'.
The cost of this erosion was incalculable. For if the wild places were
all to be lost, we would never again 'have the chance to see ourselves
single, separate, vertical and individual in the world, part of the environment of trees and rocks and soil, brother to the other animals, part
of the natural world and competent to belong in it'. We would be
'committed wholly, without chance for even momentary reflection and
rest, to a headlong drive into our technological termite-life, the Brave
New World of a completely man-controlled environment'.

I had read Stegner's essay the week before coming to Rannoch, and

out in the Moor's space his ideas seemed to reverberate even more powerfully. 'We simply need wild country available to us,' he concluded,
'even if we never do more than drive to its edge and look in. For it can
be a means of reassuring ourselves of our sanity as creatures, a part of
the geography of hope.'

Around noon, we emerged at the road on the western side of the
Moor, and I stood there, peat-spattered and tired, on the edge of the
asphalt, my thumbs tucked into the straps of my rucksack, as big freezer
lorries thundered past, carrying fresh vegetables northwards to the Great
Glen and beyond. We were bog-people, stepped from one time into
another. The angles and the straight lines of the vehicles that flashed
past, and the garishness of their colours, seemed bizarre after the long
hours on the Moor: strange as spaceships.

In lay-bys further up the road, I could see that cars had pulled over,
and groups of people – twos, threes – were standing and staring out
across the Moor, turning at times, and speaking quietly to one another.

5

Forest

When I returned home from the Moor, I put the dolphin-shaped piece of wildwood pine on a shelf above my desk: another found object to set among my growing collection. Stones mostly, which were forming a small storm-beach, but also a feather from a kestrel, a few blades of blond moor grass and a willow catkin, whose sides had flexed open to spill fluorescent yellow pollen. I placed the pine fragment at one end of the loose line of objects, and it watched me with its knot-eye while I worked. Its grain flowed like water, and its surface was riddled with tiny boreholes: entrances to an inscrutable complex of corridors and passageways, which prompted dreams of miniaturisation, of exploring the labyrinth inside the wood-shard.

My habit of gathering stones and other talismans was a family one. My parents were collectors. Shelves and window-sills in my house were covered in shells, pebbles, twists of driftwood from rivers and sea. For as long as I could remember, we had picked things up as we walked. Humdrum, everyday rites, practised by millions of people. Sometimes the collection was for a purpose: my father had specialised in making reed boats, and hours of my childhood had been spent on riverbanks and lake shores, constructing these craft, often to elaborate specifications – catamarans with pebbles for ballast and hazel leaves for sails, pinned in place with hawthorns or blackthorns – before setting them sailing in ones, pairs, flotillas.

Now, though, collecting offered a way both to remember and to join up my wild places. Fifteenth-century mapmakers developed the concept of the 'isolarion': the type of map that describes specific areas in detail, but does not provide a clarifying overview of how these places are related to one another. At this early stage of my journeys, I still did not know what family resemblances would emerge between the places I would reach, what unexpected patterns and echoes might occur. The objects seemed to hold my landscapes together, without binding them too tightly.

They also offered hints and clues. The pine shard suggested where I should go to next. It had come from the preserved root of an ancient tree, thousands of years old, that would itself have been part of the great northern pinewoods which covered the Scottish Highlands until around 3000 BC. Almost nothing still remains of this magnificent prehistoric forest – which vanished largely due to climatic causes; smothered by the blanket peat bogs that spread during the cold and wet Atlantic period – except for a few relict fragments here and there. The most extensive of these is the *Coille Dubh* – the Black Wood – which lies just to the east of Rannoch Moor.

To move to the Black Wood after the Moor would be to follow a logic of opposition: from the wet to the wood, from the bog to the pine, from openness to enclosure. It would also be to travel backwards in time, for several thousand years earlier the Moor would have resembled the Wood. So in early December, three weeks after the first redwings had arrived in East Anglia, and when the hawthorns near my house were glossy with plump fruit, I travelled north again.

I entered the Black Wood one morning, from its long loch-bound northern limit, passing under the eaves of the outer trees. Winter had lent an edge to the air, and the sky was a single blue. Light fell from a plain sun, and blowing sideways through the light was a cold wind. I carried no map of the Wood with me because it is impossible to get lost there. Its thousands of acres are spread over the northern slopes of a range of ancient, glacier-ground mountains: even in the worst of weathers, gravity will lead one out of the Black Wood, for all its fall-lines lead back to the loch-side, and safety.

I wandered in the Wood all that day, tacking back and forth, following rides, moving through its dozens of covert worlds: its dense and almost lightless thickets, its corridors and passageways, its sudden glades and clearings. I leapt streams, passed over sponge-bogs of sodden peat, soft cushions of haircap mosses. There were big standing groves of green juniper, alders, rowans and the odd dark cherry. The pines, with their reptilian bark, gave off a spicy resinous smell, and their branches wore green and silver lichens of fantastical shapes: antlers, shells, seaweeds, bones, rags. Between the trees grew heather and bracken. I climbed a whippy rowan, scattering its orange berries in all directions, and a tall old birch that shivered under my weight near its summit.

At times the forest was so thick that any sense of direction came only from the sense of slope. Then – as at the bealach above Coruisk – a vista would open, framed by branches, to show ground far above or glinting water far below. Often, the only noise I could hear was the creak of boughs rubbing against each other in the wind, like pipes heating up in a house, and I thought back to my Cambridgeshire beechwood.

Around dusk, there was a drop in the wind, and coppery clouds pulled slowly overhead, their high cold bosses still struck with the light of the low sun. Then it started to snow – light flakes ticking down through the air, settling on every upturned surface. A flake fell on the dark cloth of my jacket, and melted into it, like a ghost passing through a wall.

Snow! I had loved old woods in snow for as long as I could remember. Winter woods were realms of austere beauty and tremendous adventure to me: the snow-bound chase out of which the wolves run in John Masefield's *The Box of Delights*, the frozen forests of the Snow Queen's Narnia, and the wildwood in the Wirral through which Sir Gawain travels on Christmas Eve, during his quest to find the Green Knight, after sleeping out on bare rock and under waterfalls. 'A thick forest, wild and drear . . . of great hoar oaks, a hundred together, of hazel and hawthorn with their trailing boughs intertwined, and rough ragged moss spreading everywhere.' Roger and I had once tried to work out the route Gawain would have taken through the Wirral to reach the Green Knight's Chapel. As far as we were able to tell, he would now be able to make the whole journey by A-road in a single day, sleeping in a bed-and-breakfast if he wanted to make a weekend of it.

In a clearing, I found a big storm-felled birch, prostrate but alive. It had been blown over two or three years earlier, I guessed, from the extent of the growth since then: an ordered row of healthy branches which shot upwards from the main trunk. Flat brown semicircular fungi clustered on the trunk's southerly flank, like embedded coins. I walked round to the root bole. As the tree had fallen, it had torn up in its roots a circular cliff of mud. The upper rim of roots had dried as hard as rock, and had turfed itself over, providing a roof of a foot or more. The snow was coming faster now. I cleared an area at the foot of the bole, cast around for fallen pine branches, and layered them so that they formed a springy mattress. Then I leaned larger boughs against the sides of the bole to provide a rough triangular porch.

I was glad of the shelter, even within the wider shelter of the forest. From inside the den, warm in my sleeping-bag, I watched the snow fall beyond the roof, more heavily and more softly, and it seemed strange that so much motion could provoke so little sound. In those minutes before sleep, I felt accommodated by the forest, and watched it move into night: the dark settling like a fur on every object, the dropping snow, the quick adroit movements of birds between trees. I thought of what Nan Shepherd, the Scottish novelist and poet, had once written of the Cairngorms: 'No one knows the mountain completely who has not slept on it. As one slips over into sleep, the mind grows limpid; the body melts; perception alone remains. These moments of quiescent perceptiveness before sleep are among the most rewarding of the day. I am emptied of preoccupation, there is nothing between me and the earth and sky.'

To understand the wild you must first understand the wood. For civilisation, as the historian Robert Pogue Harrison writes, 'literally cleared its space in the midst of forests'. For millennia, 'a sylvan fringe of darkness defined the limits of its cultivation, the margins of its cities, the boundaries of its domain, but also the extravagance of its imagination'. Although the disappearance of the true wildwood occurred in the Neolithic period, before humanity began to record its own history, creation myths in almost all cultures look fabulously back to a forested earth. In the ancient Sumerian epic of Gilgamesh, the quest-story which begins world literature, Gilgamesh sets out on his journey from Uruk to

the Cedar Mountain, where he has been charged to slay Huwawa, the
guardian of the forest. The Roman Empire also defined itself against the
forests in which its capital city was first established, and out of which its
founders, the wolf-suckled twins, emerged. It was the Roman Empire
which would proceed to destroy the dense forests of the ancient world.

The association of the wild and the wood also runs deep in etymology. The two words are thought to have grown out of the root word
wald and the Old Teutonic root *walthus*, meaning 'forest'. *Walthus*
entered Old English in its variant forms of 'weald', 'wald' and 'wold',
which were used to designate both 'a wild place' and 'a wooded place',
in which wild creatures – wolves, foxes, bears – survived. The wild and
the wood also graft together in the Latin word *silva*, which means
'forest', and from which emerged the idea of 'savage', with all its con-
notations of ferality.

The wood and the wild are connected, too, because as the forest has
declined, so too has the world's wildness. Eight thousand years ago,
early in the Holocene, Britain was a dominion of trees. Forest spread
across it from coast to coast. The cover was not continuous: records of
pollen, weather, and contemporary studies of the behaviour of colonis-
ing trees in the presence of wild herbivores, now suggest that the forest
was broken and in places savannah-like, with glades and open areas of
grassland present long before the first human beings arrived. But its
extent was vast.

There have been many periods in the history of these islands when
this wood – the deepwood, as I came to think of it during my time in
the *Coille Dubh*, or the wildwood as the botanist Oliver Rackham calls
it – was all. The most recent of these periods, and the wood-reign out
of which humans would emerge, came in the final centuries of the last

Ice Age, when the glaciers, which for thousands of years had covered all but the southern parts of the land, began their retreat.

To conceive of the history of these millennia, you have to reset the chronometers of your imagination, and to think in ice-time and in tree-time. You have to imagine the air temperature rising over years. The fall of heavy warm rain on the grey backs of the glaciers. The blue glacial prows that marked the outworks of the ice, some of them hundreds of feet high, beginning their northwards retreat. The noise of those centuries, near the frontline of the glaciers, would have been prodigious: the screams of rending ice, the roars of calving ice.

The glaciers receded. Fifty miles a century, roughly speaking – half a mile a year. They left behind them a transformed terrain: diminished hills and deepened valleys. Furling out from their snouts were blue meltwater rivers, which harrowed channels through the raw earth, and filled lakes the size of counties.

At the height of the last glacial period, the ice had been so dense and extensive that its weight depressed the land beneath it into the earth's mantle. Think of that: it caused an entire country to sink down into the earth. Conversely, so it was that when the ice melted and its weight was lifted from the land, the bones of the earth rose – in some places by hundreds of feet. Geologists call this effect 'isostatic rebound'. The rebound was most pronounced in the north of Britain, where the ice had been most massive; on the south coast, by way of counteraction, the coastline dipped.

As the ice melted, and the land tilted, the oceans grew. For glaciation had stored a significant proportion of the world's water. The run-off from the melting ice across the northern hemisphere joined the oceans, raising sea-levels by nearly 400 feet in places, and transforming the

map of the world. Among those transformations was the cutting, sluicing and filling of the channel between what is now England and what
is now France. The ancient land-bridge of chalk, weald sands and clay
was gouged out by rivers. As the sea-levels continued to rise, the water
flooded up the river valleys, ate at the hills, and eventually overran the
bridge entirely. Britain was islanded: the archipelago was made.

The ice retreated up through the land – lobes, fingers, sheets,
reversing irregularly, northering. The land it left behind was at first
entirely barren. Bare drifts of till, comminuted rock, a glittering domain
of boulders, pebbles, sand and clay, rich in metals that had been filtered
and sorted by the ice's latticework. Pools of silver water gleaming in
the hollows. Sphagnum bogs thickening in the pools, and the bogs
becoming stew-pots for mats of heath. Meanwhile, on the knolls
left barest by the ice, on fertile mineral soil freshly broken by the
glaciers and not yet rain-leached, the deepwood began to found
itself. Dwarf forests first, of willows, birch and pine, relatively arctic
trees, easily dispersed, finding shelter from the glacial winds in
depressions and niches.

The wood deepened, keeping a steady distance from the ice: alders in
thick stands along the river valleys, willow on the boggy ground, oak,
lime, hazel, ash and hornbeam, and through it all a scrub, filling the
aisles of the wood and thronging its borders.

In this way, there emerged a youthful, supple forest, new-born out of
the glaciers. The blue ice gave to the green wood. Where the wood
caught fire and burned, as it did at times, the energy of suns was
returned to the air.

I woke in my Black Wood den early the next morning, after a long and broken night. The snow had stopped falling, and lay everywhere in voluminous drifts. It was so soft and light that nothing could move trackless upon it. It kept all marks. Even loose leaves that had dropped on to the snow had settled down into depressions of themselves. As I walked, it flattened and creaked beneath my feet. The wood's few sounds were muffled, as though their edges had been rounded off. Where streams of meltwater ran in gulleys, little hills of snow had formed on the stones and branches and islands in the streams, around which the water ran in intricate deltas. The forestry tracks, which I came upon here and there, had been smoothed into white avenues.

Half-buried in the root bole of a fallen pine, I found a flat oblong stone, made of fine alternating strata of white and fume-blue. I worked it out from the earth, and brushed it clean of frosted mud. It fitted my palm. I closed my fingers around it and moved on, feeling it give weight to my hand. The sky was clear and pale, and the light took a cold brightness from the settled snow. I walked through the forest, heading southwards and upwards, towards the crags that rose to 2,000 feet above the trees.

I reached the south-western edge of the wood around ten o'clock, and began the climb to the summit of the crags. The snow lay ridged upon the heather stalks, and the ascent was hard and slippery. Triangular patterns of ice had formed on the peat-mud's surface. The bigger pools had frozen in shaded concentric layers, so that they seemed charts of their own depths. There was a bite to the air, and I was glad of my wool jumper.

I reached the summit, sat on a boulder and looked down upon the white landscape. The breeze carried up bird calls from the forest below.

Light flurries of snow were being blown across the hillside below me, and I could see other such flurries moving miles to the north and west. In their intervals, the sun was rich and hot, firing through blue-gold breaks in the cloud. White peaks receded to the north. Invisible to my south was Schiehallion, a peak whose form so closely resembled an isosceles pyramid that in 1774 the astronomer and mapmaker Nevil Maskelyne had made it the subject of an experiment to determine the Earth's density.

Only the long loch remained snowless, but by reflection it too had taken on the silver-white colour of the day. On a rounded hill above the loch, patches of plantation forest had been clear-cut, so that the hill resembled a skull that had been shaved in preparation for an operation.

The human shallowing of the deepwood began around 4000 BC, with the dawn of settled agriculture. During this Neolithic period, human intervention supplanted climatic change as the chief influence on the forest's nature. By tool, by browsing animal and where possible by fire (for relatively little of the vegetation of Britain and Ireland was flammable), those first farmers began to drive back the forest, freeing up areas of tillable land, then hoeing and hand-ploughing the cleared ground to found pasture. During the Bronze Age, woodsmanship techniques became more sophisticated, and wood was used to make trackways across fen and bog, to create artificial islands or crannogs, to construct wattle huts and to smelt bronze, as well as for religious purposes including the erection of so-called 'woodhenges': formations of buried upright tree-trunks.

The deepwood has been in decline since the beginning of the Neolithic. It is thought that England reached the hinge-point of being half woodland during the second millennium BC, in the Bronze Age. The Domesday Book records the forested area of England to compose about 15 per cent of the total land surface. In the two and a half centuries that followed, an expanding population put more pressure on the forest. By 1497 – the year John Cabot sailed from Bristol to America and saw 'closely packed, deep, dark forests standing silent and unbroken along the coasts' – the tree cover of Britain and Ireland had largely been replaced by field, pasture, meadow, moor, heath and bog.

Trees were also required for combustion and construction. Ships and houses were to be built, and timber was needed in considerable quantities to make the charcoal used to smelt iron. 'Before this nation . . . there were many great woods full of all sorts of wild beasts,' observed the finely named John Manwood – an expert on forest law, and Elizabeth's judicial officer in charge of the New Forest – in 1592, 'but after the same came to be inhabited, the woods were, by degrees, destroyed, especially near the houses, and as the land increased in people, thus the woods and coverts were daily destroyed . . .' So thoroughgoing was the deforestation in Scotland, that by the seventeenth century Scotland was a net importer of timber. In Ireland squirrels became extinct. Gone were the chieftain elms and the giant ashes, gone the stately pines.

It was in the twentieth century that the deepwood came to its true end. During its course, forests were depleted at unprecedented speed across the western hemisphere. In Britain and Ireland, the two wars led to almost unregulated clear-felling. Half a million acres of broadleaf forest were felled in the years 1914 to 1918 to meet war needs.

Techniques of woodsmanship and forest husbandry – regular cutting, coppicing and pollarding – that had been developed over centuries lapsed from practice. In the thirty years after 1945, the 'locust years', nearly half of the remaining ancient semi-natural forest remained was lost to plantation, development and the plough.

The deepwood is vanished in these islands – much, indeed, had vanished before history began – but we are still haunted by the idea of it. The deepwood flourishes in our architecture, art and above all in our literature. Unnumbered quests and voyages have taken place through and over the deepwood, and fairy tales and dream-plays have been staged in its glades and copses. Woods have always been a place of in-betweenness, somewhere one might slip from one world to another, or one time to a former: in Kipling's story 'Puck of Pook's Hill', it is by right of 'Oak and Ash and Thorn' that the children are granted their ability to voyage back into English history.

There is no mystery in this association of woods and otherworlds, for as anyone who has walked in woods knows, they are places of correspondence, of call and answer. Visual affinities of colour, relief and texture abound. A fallen branch echoes the deltoid form of the streambed into which it has come to rest. Chrome yellow autumn elm leaves find their colour rhyme in the eye-ring of a blackbird. Different aspects of the forest link unexpectedly with each other, and so it is that within the stories of forests, different times and worlds can be joined.

Woods and forests have been essential to the imagination of these islands, and of countries throughout the world, for centuries. It is for this reason that when woods are felled, when they are suppressed by tarmac and concrete and asphalt, it is not only unique species and habitats that disappear, but also unique memories, unique forms of thought. Woods, like other wild places, can kindle new ways of being or cognition in people, can urge their minds differently.

Before coming to the Black Wood, I had read as widely in tree lore as possible. As well as the many accounts I encountered of damage to trees and woodlands – of what in German is called *Waldsterben*, or 'forest-death' – I also met with and noted down stories of astonishment at woods and trees. Stories of how Chinese woodsmen of the T'ang and S'ung dynasties – in obedience to the Taoist philosophy of a continuity of nature between human and other species – would bow to the trees which they felled, and offer a promise that the trees would be used well, in buildings that would dignify the wood once it had become timber. The story of Xerxes, the Persian king who so loved sycamores that, when marching to war with the Greeks, he halted his army of many thousands of men in order that they might contemplate and admire one outstanding specimen. Thoreau's story of how he felt so attached to the trees in the woods around his home-town of Concord, Massachusetts, that he would call regularly on them, gladly tramping 'eight or ten miles through the deepest snow to keep an appointment with a beech-tree, or a yellow-birch, or an old acquaintance among the pines'. When Willa Cather moved to the prairies of Nebraska, she missed the wooded hills of her native Virginia. Pining for trees, she would sometimes travel south 'to our German neighbours, to admire their catalpa grove, or to see the big elm tree that grew out of a crack in the earth. Trees were so rare in that country that we used to feel anxious about them, and visit them as if they were persons.'

My favourite story concerned the French airman and writer Antoine Saint-Exupéry, who in 1933 flew several Libyan tribal leaders from their homes in the desert to tropical Senegal. As they climbed out of the aeroplane and saw the jungle stretching away from the edge of the landing-strip, Saint-Exupéry recorded, they 'wept at the sight of the trees', never having encountered such beings before.

Single trees are extraordinary; trees in number more extraordinary still. To walk in a wood is to find fault with Socrates's declaration that 'Trees and open country cannot teach me anything, whereas men in town do.' Time is kept and curated in different ways by trees, and so it is experienced in different ways when one is among them. The discretion of trees, and their patience, are both affecting. It is beyond our capacity to comprehend that the American hardwood forest waited seventy million years for people to come and live in it, though the effort of comprehension is itself worthwhile. It is valuable and disturbing to know that grand oak trees can take three hundred years to grow, three hundred years to live and three hundred years to die. Such knowledge, seriously considered, changes the grain of the mind.

Thought, like memory, inhabits external things as much as the inner regions of the human brain. When the physical correspondents of thought disappear, then thought, or its possibility, is also lost. When woods and trees are destroyed – incidentally, deliberately – imagination and memory go with them. W. H. Auden knew this. 'A culture,' he wrote warningly in 1953, 'is no better than its woods.'

The truth of Auden's proposition would be proved only a few years after he made it. In the late 1960s, a virulent strain of Dutch elm disease arrived on the south coast of England, brought in with a shipment of rock elm logs from the United States. From its beachhead near

Southampton, the disease spread rapidly inland and outwards. Within two or three summers there were few sizeable elms left alive in the south of the country. Within ten years, around thirty million had died: 1976, the year of drought, was the peak of the epidemic, but millions more trees have perished since then. Though the elm has not become extinct, it has been devastated, and with it has gone one of the most distinctive presences of the English landscape.

Among the many admirers of the elm was John Constable. Constable loved trees as he loved people. His friend and biographer C. R. Leslie wrote that he had often seen Constable 'admire a fine tree with an ecstasy of delight like that with which he would catch up a beautiful child in his arms'. And of all trees, Constable loved the elm best.

In Dedham Vale on the border of Essex and Suffolk, where Constable lived, there were elms twice as old in years as they were high in feet – and they were hundreds of feet high. Smaller elms grew through and into the hedgerows, lined the banks of the Stour, and flanked Dedham's churches. Sentinel elms were planted to mark the old ways, the drovers' roads, so that they could be followed in mist: trees as way-finders, map-markers.

Constable sketched and studied the elms intently. He recorded the elmy underworld, the shady green-gold circle of leaves beneath the first boughs, and he recorded the canopy, which on the biggest elms could spread over a quarter of an acre of sky.

In 1821, he painted an elm on Hampstead Heath in which the foliage of the tree is forgotten; the canvas instead concentrates on the trunk of the tree, the point at which it meets the earth. The tree is an English elm: we know this, for its bark has cracked into polygonal patterns, where the bark of the wych-elm and the Huntingdon elm would have fractured more linearly, into long crevasses and furrows, and the bark of the smooth-leaved elm would have formed a regular meshwork of angled ridges and valleys.

Bark is a subtle, supple substance, easily overlooked. It can be thought of as the tree's skin; like skin, it carries the marks of folding and of expansion, a stretching which snaps it into flakes or plates or lenticles. If you were to take slow-motion footage of elm bark over a year, you would be able to see it moving, working, living: crevasses gaping, calluses forming, the constant springing open and closing over of fissures. As Constable knew, a world can reveal itself in a tree's bark. Lean in close to bark, and you will find a landscape which you might enter, through whose ravines and edges you might make day-long journeys.

Constable's painting of the Hampstead Heath elm is a study of permanence and transience. There is permanence in the root-work of the tree, its delving into the ground in which it has dwelt for decades and should dwell for decades to come. There is transience in the light, falling generously and temporarily upon the grass behind. And there is transience in the foreknowledge we now have of the fate of this elm.

During the Dutch elm disease epidemic, Constable's nameless elm died, along with the other elms on Hampstead Heath, and the elms that lined the Stour, or raised their single verticals on the skyline of the Dedham Vale. His Hampstead elm would have died as all the others died: first its finely serrated leaves, with their racing-green uppers and silver-green undersides, would have curled and browned and crisped. Then the branches would have wilted and drooped. Then the bark itself would have hardened and scabbed off, to reveal bare trunk wood beneath, which would have been so smooth, pale and sheeny that it recalled bone.

Dutch elm disease is a fungus that diffuses itself with distinctive efficiency. Its spores are spread by its vector, the native elm bark beetle, *Scolytus scolytus*. The beetles lay their eggs in the bark of dying elms and the larvae form networks of tunnels, which are known as galleries, under the dead bark. The fungi produce sticky spores on the walls of these galleries, so when the larvae mature into adult beetles and emerge they are already contaminated with spores. They fly to healthy elms and feed off their living bark, depositing the spores of the fungus. The fungus spreads quickly through the root systems of a tree, causing the capillaries to tighten. The tree's water-conduction system fails; it dies of thirst. So the beetles seek and destroy each tree in turn, sparing the oak to the elm's left, the ash to its right.

The patterns left by the beetles beneath the bark are eerily beautiful. The beetles bore out nuptial chambers in which they breed, and feeding galleries radiate off this central channel, tunnelled out by the larvae. The resulting forms resemble radiations from a dark sun, or the imprint of a winged or tentacled creature. The bark beetles have been called 'engravers', for the affinity between the distinctive linear pattern they leave on the inside of the bark and the work of a skilled mason lettering a headstone.

The devastation of the elm, when it came, seemed to some a prophecy fulfilled. For the elm had long been associated with death. In country lore, it was known as the tree of ill-omen. It was ascribed a maliciousness; if you loitered beneath it, branches would drop on to you from the canopy. The tree's habit of throwing out one strong side branch also made it a popular gallows tree. Elmwood was for a long time the staple wood of the coffin-maker. These associations with death were turned true by history. So synonymous is the elm with death now in England, that one cannot help but look at Constable's paintings as elegies for the elm – studies in the future pluperfect.

So the elms died, and the bark of the land was changed by their dying. Familiar horizons were transformed. People found it difficult to orient and steer themselves in landscape they had known for decades. Yet the elm is not extinct. Small trees live on in hedgerows, suckering out versions of themselves, spreading laterally, keeping their heads down: any tree that grows above twelve feet tends to become infected. Although the elm's associations with death are formidable, so too is its capacity for survival.

Just before leaving for the Black Wood, I had gone over to Suffolk to see Roger, and to talk to him about forests, and about the elm in particular. I had not been born until 1976, the drought year, and I wanted to know what it had been like to live through the ravagings of Dutch elm disease, to watch the countryside change so drastically.

Roger's knowledge of trees and silviculture was immense, gleaned from a lifetime spent not only reading about wood but also working with it: planting, pleaching, coppicing, laying and turning. His sense of trees, like his sense of life, was strongly communal. He disapproved of the habit of fetishising single trees – chieftain pines or king oaks. Trees to him were mutual organisms, best understood when considered in their relationships with one another. Put differently, trees were human to Roger, and humans tree-like, in hundreds of complicated and profoundly felt ways. Since finishing *Waterlog*, he had been at work on *Wildwood*, a book about woods and trees. Researching it, he had travelled to Kyrgyzstan and Kazakhstan, Australia, Tasmania, and throughout Europe and Britain. As the years passed, the project branched out, digressing into studies of the hula-hoop craze, the manufacture of pencils, the history of the Green Man, Roger's anarchist ancestors, the architecture of Bender shelters . . .

Roger, like my mother and father, was a collector. He collected knowledge, he collected books, he collected friends, and he collected things. His mind and his house were both prolifically stocked. Every shelf and sideboard in Walnut Tree Farm was thronged with objects that Roger had found on his travels, or that his many friends had carried back from theirs: birds' nests, flint hagstones, buzzard feathers, clumps of sheep's wool, a chert arrowhead, a wooden propeller from an early plane, stamped with an untraceable serial number. Over the years, I had brought him several stones, and he had brought me others in return: mineral postcards, hand delivered.

Almost everything in the farm was second-hand, collected: its framework comprised salvaged oak beams from a demolished barn, and on its floor of salvaged flagstones stood salvaged stand-alone dressers, bookshelves and chests of drawers. Roger was an inveterate scavenger: visiting farm sales and auction sheds, rummaging junk shops, skips and tips – but also forests and riverbanks – for what might be unexpectedly useful or unexpectedly beautiful. His finds were spread around the house and meadows. At the back of the house was one of his favourite trophies: a big cast-iron bath, in which he liked to wallow during the summer months, filled with water that he heated by snaking out a hosepipe on the brick terrace and leaving it to bask in the sun.

When I went to see Roger that day, we ate lunch together in his kitchen and drank glasses of apple juice. He talked about the vanishing of the elm, about trees he had known that had died – including the great English elm at Rookery Farm in Norfolk, under which he had taught *Howard's End* to his Lower Sixth students in 1976. The following year, the tree was infected with the disease, and began to perish; two years later, leafless and grey, it was felled.

After we had finished eating, Roger said he had a new scavenging prize, of which he was proud. He took me out into his steepled barn. In the dim cold light, I could see a series of fat metal tubes of differing lengths laid out on a worktop. Roger looked expectant. I looked puzzled. They were organ-pipes from a local Suffolk church, he explained, which had been about to go for scrap, until he had heard about them and bought them off the church. Excitedly, he showed me how he had fitted a steam-hose to the narrowed bottom of the middle-C pipe, and lidded the top end, in this way making a chamber in which he could steam lengths of wood into pliability for furniture making.

Then he took me over to another workbench, where he picked up an elmwood bowl he had turned from the trunk of an elm felled by the storm of October 1987. Elm is a magnificent timbering wood, he told me that day, because it continues to live and breathe long after it has been carpentered into a table or floor. Its vitality, he said, is exceptional among woods. He said, too, that the elm would return to England: that I should not worry, that in due course, probably after humans were gone or had retreated, the elms would rise again.

From my crag-top perch above the Black Wood, I looked back down on to the forest below me, and watched the trees move differently in the wind. The big oaks held their round shape, their branches describing orbits around a fixed point, their leaves bustling in circles. The thinner younger pines quivered and swung in arcs and lines. I wondered if it would be possible to traverse the Black Wood without touching the ground, keeping only to the canopy, in the manner of Cosimo.

Away to my west were the first reaches of Rannoch Moor, which showed white and silver, widening off beyond sight. To the north, over the road on the far side of the loch, the hillsides were thick with conifer plantations. The trees, set in their dark regular straight-sided patterns, appeared unnatural, as though their outlines had been cut with a jigsaw. Even at this distance, I could see the churned-up ground of the clear-cut zones, where, through the settled snow, the black sump-holes, the stubs of trunks and the tracks of machinery were still visible. It looked like a war-zone. I stood, and shook the snow from my feet, and began the descent back down the hillside and into the moving wood.

The poet and musician Ivor Gurney was born and brought up in rural Gloucestershire at around the end of the nineteenth century. For his family, as for many at that time, the long country walk was a habit and a pleasure. Like the poet Edward Thomas – whom Gurney admired – he grew up as a natural historian, exploring Gloucestershire's river-banks, woods and hedges.

The loving intensity of Gurney's relationship with the Gloucestershire landscape rings throughout the poetry and letters he wrote as a young man, and the journals he kept. He observed how the fields enjoyed a 'clear shining after rain', and wrote of the wide River Severn 'homing to the sea'. Of all aspects of the countryside it was woodland he loved best, with its 'avenues of green and gold'. A composer as well as a poet, timber and timbre were to Gurney closely grown together: among the many poems he set to music were his own 'Song of the Summer Woods' and A. E. Housman's 'Loveliest of Trees'.

In 1915, Gurney joined up to fight in the Great War. His first posting was to Sarras, on the Ypres Salient. When Gurney arrived at Ypres, the Salient had been a battle area for two years, and the landscape he found there was a dark travesty of the countryside he had left behind. Before the war, Sarras with its rivers, orchards, woods and pastures might have resembled Gurney's Gloucestershire. But two years of conflict had transformed it. Mud, midway between fluid and solid, threatened to drown men and entomb them simultaneously. On the military maps of the area that Gurney used, some of the old names of the landscape remained. But many of the new names spoke of the avoidance of death, or of its arrival. Shrapnel Corner, Crump Farm, Hellfire Corner, Halfway House, Dead Dog Farm, Battle Wood, Sanctuary Wood. The woods were no longer there, however; these were ghost names only. The trees had been felled for revetting, or blasted from the earth by shells. The only evidence of the forests that remained were upright bare dead trunks, stripped of leaves, branches and bark by shrapnel and gunfire. At their bases, human bones protruded from the mud like roots, and blood salted the earth.

To Gurney, writing home, it seemed he had come to an anti-landscape, whose featurelessness was a form of assault: 'Masses of unburied dead strewn over the battle fields; no sign of organised trenches, but merely shell holes joined up to one another . . . and no landmarks anywhere.' The Salient denied the permanence, the rich and complicated pasts of the trees that Gurney cherished: their consoling constancy, their rootedness.

In the trenches, he was seized often by what he called a 'hot heart desire' for his Gloucestershire landscape. He was 'clutched at and heart-grieved' by 'desperate home thoughts' of 'Cotswold, her spinnies'. 'We suffer pain out here,' he wrote home, 'and for myself it sometimes comes that death would be preferable to such a life.'

But Gurney survived the war. He was injured – shot in the chest, and gassed – and invalided home. Shortly after the Armistice, he entered upon a period of frenzied creativity. Between 1919 and 1922, he wrote some nine hundred poems and two hundred and fifty songs. Walking and inspiration became intertwined for Gurney. He strode the coun-tryside both day and night, often for hours. The letters he sent during these years speak of how much he 'needed' the night-walking in par-ticular. At night, he was able to follow what he called 'the white ways . . . unvisited by most', which was, he said, a form of 'discovery'. 'O that night!', he wrote to a friend. 'Meteors flashed like sudden inspira-tions of song down the sky. The air was too still to set firs or beeches sighing, but – O the depth of it!' He spoke of 'brambles beautiful in wind', of the 'black greenery of beech against the moon', of how a low moon threw into relief the 'still sky-rims . . . high above the valley', and of 'bronzed cloud-bars at cold dawn'. 'Earth, air, and water,' he wrote late in that period of his life, 'are the true sources of song or speaking.'

By 1922, Gurney's mental state, always precarious, had tilted into unbalance. He took to eating in binges, and then fasting for days. He lost weight quickly, and his behaviour become increasingly unpre-dictable. His family reluctantly committed him to the care of the asylum system. He went first to an institution in Gloucester, and then to one at Dartford in Kent. In both asylums, he was not permitted to walk outside the perimeter of the grounds.

It was to the Dartford asylum that Helen Thomas, the widow of Edward Thomas – who had been killed at the Battle of Arras – travelled on several occasions in the late 1920s to visit Gurney. She later reported that, when she first saw him, his madness was so acute that he was able to communicate only briefly with her, and showed little interest in her presence, or her association with Edward.

The next time she travelled to Dartford, however, Helen took with her one of her husband's Ordnance Survey maps of the Gloucestershire landscape through which both Thomas and Gurney had walked. She recalled afterwards that Gurney, on being shown the map, took it at once from her, and spread it out on his bed, in his hot little white-tiled room in the asylum, with the sunlight falling in patterns upon the floor. Then the two of them kneeled together by the bed and traced out, with their fingers, walks that they and Edward had taken in the past.

For an hour or more this dream-walking went on, Gurney seeing not the map, but looking through its prompts to see land itself. 'He spent that hour,' Helen remembered, 'revisiting his beloved home . . . spotting . . . a track, a hill, or a wood, and seeing it all in his mind's eye, a mental vision sharper and more actual for his heightened intensity. He trod, in a way we who were sane could not emulate, the lanes and fields he knew and loved so well, his guide being his finger tracing the way on the map . . . He had Edward as his companion in this strange perambulation . . . I became for a while the element which brought Edward back to life for him and the country where the two could wander together.'

Helen returned to visit Gurney several times after this, and on each occasion she brought the map that had been made soft and creased by her husband's hands, and she and Gurney knelt at the bed and together walked through their imagined country.

I left the Black Wood late in the afternoon of that winter day, returning to the northern brink of the Wood. As I stepped from the trees, I heard a clatter, like the sound of gravel being thrown on to a wooden table. Six crows, two of them juveniles, were at play, hopping from the low branches of a pine down on to the snow and then flapping back up again, chattering to one another in a familial manner. On the ground, they walked with their distinctive nodding motion, their feet wide apart, as if trying to keep their balance. They tilted their heads, and watched me watching them. The light of the snow gave a faint indigo sheen to their feathers and lent beads of whiteness to their eyes.

Crows, like all corvids – ravens, jackdaws, rooks, magpies – are relatively recent arrivals in Britain. It is thought they established themselves here once the clearance of the deepwood was begun by human hand, during the Neolithic period: an ancient inter-animation of the human and the wild. Dense wood is no good to crows – they are creatures of mixed cover and openness.

As I stood there, the two young crows walked out into an area of fresh snow, and began to circle one another playfully, each keeping a steady distance from the other, like opposing magnets, or kings on a chessboard.

6

River-mouth

Enlli, Coruisk, Rannoch and the Black Wood. Island, valley, moor and forest. Each landscape had taken me by surprise, had behaved in ways I had not foreseen or sometimes even wanted. But I had also learned from each place, had been brought to think by each in unexpected accents and shapes. Connections and patterns were emerging, too, supplied by the land itself. It was starting to seem that certain landscapes might hold certain thoughts, as they held certain stones or plants.

I still, though, wanted to get further north, to keep following my original magnetic orientation, to push on up into the bleak and stripped-back territories that had long held such a power to move me. So a few weeks after returning from the Black Wood, I left Cambridge again, training north, reading Auden as I went: boreal poems about night sailings, the blizzard's march, windy dwellings under headlands.

My intention was to make a single winter journey along the uppermost edge of Scotland, where it faces north on to the Pentland Firth. At that latitude, I would be closer to the Arctic Circle than to the south coast of England. I wanted to follow the hard rimrocks – the Moine schist, the Cambrian quartzite, the Lewisian gneiss – that had kept this storm-crashed coast from ceding to the sea, and in this way to join up some of the reputedly wildest places of the mainland: Cape Wrath, its most north-westerly point; Ben Hope, the most northerly of all mountains; and Strathnaver, the most beautiful and melancholy of Scotland's river glens. After all that, I thought, I would surely be ready to come south again . . .

I began in Strathnaver. Twenty-seven miles long, Strathnaver follows the sinuous path of the Naver as it flows from its source in the shadow of Ben Klibreck to its mouth in the Pentland Firth. The strath is wide and flat at its base, with fertile meadows, and protected by hill ridges to east and west.

The night before reaching the strath, I stopped at a hotel on a lonely stretch of road near Altnaharra. I ate a quiet meal, and then, ordering a drink, fell into conversation with a big man, dressed in camouflage trousers and a thick military-green jumper. His name was Angus and he was a forester. For the past few years, his job had been to cut down the conifers which had been recklessly planted over the peatbogs of Sutherland and Caithness during the 1980s, by landowners keen to profit quickly from the tax-breaks that the Conservative government had given to such forestry projects.

The peatbogs, known as the Flows, cover hundreds of square miles of the far north of Scotland. Like other peatlands, they are astonishing landscapes; their protection status is now equivalent to that accorded the Serengeti. And like all peatlands, they are vulnerable. Many of Britain and Ireland's peatlands have vanished. The vast Bog of Allen, thousands of years in the making, was turfed into power-stations and burnt almost out of existence within two decades. The Lancashire Mosses were drained off and farmed. And the Flows were planted with thirsty and fast-growing conifers, which smothered and drained the bog, killing its mosses and destroying the rare species of birds, plants and insects that had thrived there.

The Flows had, just, been saved from extinction. The land had been expensively bought back, and steps were now being taken to restore it to its pre-plantation state. The first stage was to cut down the conifers. 'Sitka shit', Angus called them. He was paid twenty-five pence per tree felled. He loved his work, he said, even with the midges that emerged in their billions during the summer months, even with the deer-ticks that now carried Lyme disease. He had been born in Sutherland, but had married a French woman, and after living in the Auvergne for ten years they had moved back to Scotland, because he found he missed the landscape too much to keep away. Sometimes, in winter, he said, he went out deep into the forests, made a shelter, shot a deer, and stayed for a few days or a week. It saved the long walks in and out.

That evening, after an hour or so of talking, I made to leave, wanting to get to sleep. Before coming to the hotel, I had identified a place to spend the night: in a roadside sitka plantation, where the tightly meshed canopy of needles would keep light rain off me. I didn't tell Angus I was going to sleep in a plantation; I thought he might disapprove, and I was a touch embarrassed.

As I stood to go, Angus asked if I wanted to come fishing for sea-trout with him the next day, in the estuary of the Naver. I said that I would, very much. He gave me directions to his house, which he told me he had built himself. It was impossible not to find it, he explained, for it was the only house on the waterward side of the long road that ran along the shore of Loch Naver. I should come there first thing, and we would drive together up the strath to the river-mouth, where the free fishing was.

Near the estuary, he said, there was a grave set up on a ridge, looking out over it. A child, Elsa Danckwerts, had died of leukaemia in 1902, and her parents, who were Dutch immigrants, had chosen to bury her there, overlooking the sea. The gravestone was a sight in itself, let alone the view from it. He also said that as we drove, he would tell me about the Clearance history of the glen – for the valley was the scene of one of the darkest episodes in Scottish history.

On a warm Sunday morning in May 1819, the Reverend Donald Sage took the pulpit for the last time at the little church of Langdale in Strathnaver. It was a beautiful day, and the trees, the mountains and the river, he later remembered, 'with which all our associations of "home" and "native land" were so fondly linked, appeared to unite their attractions to bid us farewell'.

Sage ministered to many of the small parishes – Achness and Kildonan and Syre – that lay in the long river valleys which stretched between the Pentland Firth on the northern coast, south-west to Caithness and the North Sea coast. That Sunday would be his last in the Langdale church, he knew, because he and his congregation had been warned that the Clearance of the townships of Strathnaver would begin again soon. Men working for the Countess of Sutherland, who owned the valley, would come in numbers and compel the inhabitants from their homes, so that the land could be turned over to the more lucrative rearing of sheep.

The accounts of what happened in Strathnaver over the following weeks and months are contradictory and disputed. It is known that a total of 1,200 people, almost the entire population of its townships, were evicted from the strath that year, by a combination of threats and false promises. It is known that the Clearances were driven by nothing more or less urgent than greed for profit on the part of the landowners. It is known that, by May of 1820, a crow had built its nest inside the abandoned church at Langdale.

What is unclear is the degree of violence used. Donald MacLeod, an inhabitant of the Rosal township in Strathnaver, recorded that on the day of one of the Clearances, he walked at eleven o'clock at night to a hill above the strath, and looked back. In the darkness, he wrote, he could still hear the cries of women and children, the barking of dogs and the lowing of cattle. He could see, too, the buildings of that district, over two hundred of them, burning, either in full flame or collapsed into glowing timbers. The Countess's men had come on horseback and on foot, he said, bearing brands, mattocks and sledgehammers, and with these they had broken up and burnt the schoolhouses, kilns, corn-mills, stables, barns and byres, as well as dozens of houses.

Strathnaver was cleared in two campaigns, 1814 and 1819. The displaced inhabitants were mostly driven north, to the coast. There they were expected to make new lives on the Pentland Firth, where the topsoil was thin, sandy and salt-blasted. Even the journey to the inhospitable coast was arduous; there were deaths along the way from fatigue and exposure. One man, Donald Mackay, whose two daughters were weak with disease and malnourishment, was so desperate to get them aboard a small sloop travelling to Caithness that he carried them on his back, one at a time, to the coast. He laid the first down in the open air on the beach, then walked back, and picked up the other. In this way, he walked twenty-five miles.

Those who completed the exodus to the coast faced great hard-ship. Unacquainted with the skills of the sea, many came close to starvation, and were reduced to gleaning for cockles on the shoreline, or eating nettle broth thickened with oatmeal. Such exigencies must have been painful to the refugees, for they had been turned out of one of the reputedly most idyllic of all Scottish glens.

But, over the course of five years – by emigration, conscription, death and displacement – Strathnaver, like so many of the valleys of Scotland, was all but emptied of its people. During the Clearances, wrote Alexander MacKenzie in 1881, the families of the northern glens were 'utterly rooted and burnt out', and parish after parish was 'con-verted into a solitary wilderness'.

From the road, Angus's house had a tight, low look. Its single grey pebble-dashed storey seemed crouched down into the land. But its position was magnificent. Immediately behind it stretched the loch, which was flashing in the clear dawn light. Stands of silver birches flut-tered in the wind, their trunks as bright as whitewash. And rising to the south was Ben Klibreck, still backlit, its outline long and curvaceous. On either side of the house's driveway sat a massive glacial boulder, on which a complex map-work of snail trails glimmered.

We drove up the strath road in Angus's car, with black fishing-rods sticking out of each back window like aerials. He pointed out land-marks as we drove: houses abandoned during the Clearances and never reoccupied, lazy beds, old fish ponds, Bronze Age hut circles. After forty minutes or so, we reached the river's mouth, and parked near a girdered steel bridge, which had recently been painted a gleaming black. I got out. The air was cold in the nose, and smelt different from the loch air: sharper, saltier.

A path led over the steep rocky ground to the western side of the bridge. We followed it, and stepped down on to the wide golden flats that banked the river. The sand was airy, and I sank in it up to my ankles.

An exquisite optical effect had been created by the combination of dry air and strong wind. Billions of particles of loose sand were being blown across the flats, giving expression to the wind, moving with such coherence and fluency that they seemed to form a rippling second skin, silky and supple, which shifted so quickly over the set sand beneath it that it was hard to conceive of the two as of the same substance and different only in their motions.

We trudged downstream through the shifting sand, the river to our right, towards the sea. At one point, we disturbed an otter, which loped and skittered away over the rocks, then poured itself into the brown water, where it was instantly invisible. The winter sunlight was so bright that it lay in ingots on the riverbed.

Angus gestured to the easternmost of the headlands, at the entrance to the estuary. Up there, he said, were the ruins of a nineteenth-century look-out point. During the spawning season, men would sit there, watching for incoming shoals of salmon. The salmon were then so many in number, he said, that when they shoaled they would form dark masses under water, big enough to be visible from the look-out. The watchers would shout, and boats would be launched to haul a net across the mouth of the estuary. Those days were gone, though: the river was poor in salmon now.

He told me that the first settlements had been established in Strathnaver more than six thousand years previously, and that there had been human presence of some kind here more or less ever since. Marks of these successive occupations were to be found everywhere in the strath. The Neoliths had buried their most important dead in chambered cairns whose ruins were still visible. There were rings and rows of standing stones, erected in the Bronze Age. Up round the corner of the bay – he gestured north and west – was a Christian settlement, established by Cormaic, a colleague of St Columba. The settlement was on an island: Eilean Neave, the Island of the Saints.

Then he pointed up at an outcrop ridge of sand and rock, which ran lateral to the river, hackled with green marram grass. Up there was a broch, he said, the remains of an Iron Age broch. Its walls were fifteen feet thick! In those days, he said with a slow smile, they knew how to keep the wind out of a building.

For the rest of that sunlit morning we fished the western bank of the river, moving silently for hours, rods held low and angled down to the water, while above us two buzzards turned in tight spirals.

Two centuries previously, the exiled people of Strathnaver would have passed along that bank of the river. They would have reached this rivermouth exhausted and frightened. The dunes which stood so splendidly to either side of the estuary would, to them, have been the gateway to a new and hard coastal land.

It is difficult, even now, to travel through the cleared glens of Scotland and miss the evidence of earlier calamity. Difficult, too, not to be disturbed by it, not to find one's own relationship with the land changed by the knowledge of what once occurred here. The pasts of these places complicate and darken their present wildness; caution against romanticism and blitheness. To be in such landscapes is to be caught in a double-bind: how is it possible to love them in the present, but also to acknowledge their troubled histories?

Sorley MacLean, the poet who led the revival of Gaelic verse in the twentieth century, knew this bind well. MacLean was born on the island of Raasay, on the west coast of Scotland, in 1911. During the Clearances, Raasay's population had been almost eradicated. Dozens of families emigrated, and dozens were forcibly evicted. Those who stayed were pushed to the rocky northern end of the island, making room in the more fertile south for the Cheviot sheep. All four of MacLean's grandparents were forced from their farms. The abandoned dwellings and steadings were boarded up, or left to dissolve into the land, gathered back by moss and ivy.

Several of MacLean's finest poems are set on Raasay, and the island's wildness was, to MacLean, partly a consequence of loss: its spaciousness declared an absence, and its solitude a calamity. Nowhere is this more apparent than in his dream-poem, 'Hallaig', which is set in the cleared Raasay township of that name, and in the woods that surrounded it.

Wood was central to Raasay's pre-Clearance culture. The surprisingly extensive forests of the island were worked by its inhabitants. Their boats were made of oak and pine, with oars and rudders of ash. Hawthorn and holly were used for hedging. Houses were made with beams of oak and thatch-supports of hazel. Baskets were woven of willow, and bowls were turned out of elder, and then polished up until the hooped patterns of grain could be seen on the wood. Life demanded the indefinite flourishing of the trees, and so the woods were worked and sustained. But when the people were cleared, the grazing of the sheep that took their place repressed the woods and prevented their regeneration. The woods departed, as the people had departed before them.

For MacLean, the woods that remained on the island were precious and beautiful. He wrote once of standing in a storm in a pinewood, near the 'green unpressed sea', and feeling the moving trees as 'wind-headed' and 'giddy' about him: 'the great wood in motion, / fresh in its spirit'. But the woods were also, for MacLean, eloquent of the island's tragedy. They were uncanny realms, where time flickered back and forth, where past and present became confused. In the Raasay forests, he wrote, 'the dead have been seen alive', and the disappeared 'are with us still'. So it is that in 'Hallaig', the cleared generations return as ghosts in the forms of trees. The poem is set at twilight, and in it, MacLean imagines a crowd of young Raasay girls, strolling along 'lightsome and unheartbroken' out of the wooded hills of the island – 'a flickering birch, a hazel, a rowan'.

We caught sea-trout; Angus took four, I took one. Small silver fish, little more than a pound each, which glittered in the light. Angus left me early in the afternoon, taking his catch back to his family. I thanked him for his kindness, and watched him walk away over the soft sand towards the bridge.

I turned and made my way to the ridge that Angus had pointed out to me earlier, with the broch on its summit. I climbed its steep side, scrambling up over sand that gave way beneath my feet in little spills, grasping fistfuls of sharp grass for support, until I reached rock.

Near the end of the ridge, I came to the broch. Its massively thick walls were well preserved, or had been re-created: they formed a rough stone ring, about thirty feet in internal diameter, with an entrance passage opening to the north-west. The ground around the broch still bore the marks of a ditch and a rampart, and, on the lower ground just to the west, I could see the imprints of what might have been hut circles.

I stepped inside, and was surprised by the sudden calm. Rounded black stones, striated with quartz, lay about on the mossy floor like cannonballs. A dark charcoal ring marked the site of an old fire. I knelt by one wall, and scraped away a patch of moss and sand at its base. The stones descended as far as I could dig. The floor on which I was standing was the result of centuries of sand-drift. I remembered how, in certain parts of the Sahara, people did not try to keep the sand out of their houses, but would instead invite it in. They spread it thickly across the floors, then laid hand-woven rugs over it, and in this way used it to soften their sleep.

Later that afternoon, I left the broch and went walking, to see what the land and the water held. At the edge of the river, where the bank angled down into the water, the tides had cut the sand into stepped terraces.

Down on the shore, I found a limb of pale dry driftwood, rubbed by the sea back to its grain lines. I saw the tracks of an otter, perhaps the one we had seen, pressed into the wet sand as cleanly as a pastry cut, with a forwards fling of sand from the tip of each sharp toe-mark, showing that it had been moving at speed. I came across a set of animal bones, scattered in a rune I could not read. I picked up other things, carried them back to the broch, and laid them on its floor. A worn black stone, two inches long, shaped roughly like a seal; basalt, I guessed. A little rhomboid stone, whose grey and white strata recalled the grain of the driftwood and the sand terrace. A hank of dried seaweed. A wing feather from a buzzard, tawny and cream, barred with five dark diagonals. When I teased two of its vanes apart, they unzipped with a soft tearing noise. I arranged the objects into lines and patterns, changed their order. I would give the seal stone to my friend Leo, I thought, the seaweed to Roger, and I would keep the other objects for my storm-beach.

As the day's light lessened, I walked back down to the river's mouth, and in the shallow waters of the estuary, where the salt and the fresh wove with one another, and the river lost itself gently into the increased space of the ocean, I swam briefly. Though I could not see how the two waters mingled, I could feel it all about me: the subtle jostle of currents, and the numberless small collisions of wave and ripple.

Later that evening, my skin still tingling from the coldness of the swim, I moved stones to make a ring near the broch, and within the stones I lit a driftwood fire, and cooked my sea-trout over the embers.

As the trout baked, its skin shrank, darkened and rucked up. Rain fell briefly, sizzling on the fire, and mottling the smaller rocks so that they resembled curlew eggs. Later, a flight of little birds flashed overhead like a shower of arrows. Far to the north, out in the Firth, the fixed constellation of a ship's lights – white–red–white – slipped past. When I had eaten, I returned to the broch, lay back on the soft sand in my sleeping-bag, and gazed up at the circle of stars chosen by the broch's walls. The sky was clear, and the stars were pointed and precise.

Lying there on the drifted sand, under the white stars, I thought about how the vision of wildness with which I had begun my journeys – inhuman, northern, remote – was starting to crumble from contact with the ground itself. No such chaste land exists in Britain or Ireland, and no such myth of purity can hold. Thousands of years of human living and dying have destroyed the possibility of the pristine wild. Every islet and mountain-top, every secret valley or woodland, has been visited, dwelled in, worked, or marked at some point in the past five millennia. The human and the wild cannot be partitioned.

Since the Celtic Christians, culture has endured in wild places and the wild has endured in culture. Landmarks and dwellings – shelter-stones, petroglyphs, cairns, stone walls, bothies, shielings, villages, townships – are to be found within wild places. Journeys have taken place into the wild, or across it. And it has been the subject of stories, songs, legends and poems – including MacLean's hauntingly reciprocal sense of the relationship between people and trees.

Nowhere was this more evident than in Strathnaver. The many human pasts of the glen were deeply involved with its wildness: as much as the otter prints, the old shoals of salmon moving inland off the ocean or the ice-scars on the rocks. Somehow, I thought, the river and the land seemed to caution against categorical thinking, against partitions. Everywhere that day I had encountered blend-ings and mixings: the blown sand moving over the set sand, the sea water mingling inscrutably with the fresh. I recalled something the writer Fraser Harrison had said: 'Our perception of land is no more stable than our perception of landscape. At first sight, it seems that land is the solid sand over which the mirage of landscape plays, yet it turns out that land too has its own evanescence . . . "Place" is a restlessly changeable phenomenon.'

Just such a restless mingling of history and presence existed in Strathnaver. The wildness of the river and its borderlands were regarded so differently by a forester felling trees, by the captain of a fishing-boat plying the hard waters of the Firth, by an Iron Age settler, by a Christian monk, by parents who had lost their daughter, or by a dispossessed people, trekking northwards into alien country. Or, of course, by a traveller passing through for a few days.

Then there were the unreadable priorities of the landscape's non-human inhabitants, its fish and birds and animals, all moving in patterns older than history. How did the land look to these creatures, I wondered, how did they steer themselves within it? The otter, tracing scent maps, trotting over the stones, slipping freely between its three elements of water, air and earth. The salmon nosing up the river-mouth, navigating back to their birth-grounds, guided by a chemical memory and by the stars. Or the buzzards who had hung over for most of that long day, prospecting in their idle spirals, gazing down upon the terrain as an arrangement of planes and forms, and vigilant for movement within those forms.

Later that night, I woke with a dry throat, and took a long drink from my flask. The night had made the water cold. It was after one in the morning. I stood, and looked out over the broch's walls, out past the look-out point, to the empty northern firth, and to the river, dispersing tirelessly into the sea. The light of the high moon was curdling on the estuary in white streamers and curls, and dark moon-shadows were cast tightly beneath the stones and rocks. The wind was still strong, and where moonlight fell on the flats I could just make out the shifting skin of the blown sand.

7

Cape

The name Cape Wrath is from the Old Norse. 'Wrath' means not 'anger', but 'turning-point'. When Viking raiders, setting off on long Atlantic voyages of exploration and plunder, rounded the Cape's distinctive cliffs they knew their home had been truly left behind. For the Norsemen, it was a marker in the ocean world, and they named it as such.

The Cape was a pivot in my journeys, too. My aim was to reach it, to spend a night or nights out in the wild land around it, and then to climb Ben Hope and sleep on its summit. After Hope, I would turn back south, and start to work down through Ireland and the west of England: heading back into easier land and softer seasons.

I left Strathnaver very early one morning. I drove through the neat village of Tongue, where I stopped to buy provisions, round the fretted shores of Loch Eriboll, where salmon-farm cages floated in the bay, and past Foinaven's hulk. Then, on narrower roads, I reached the nearly treeless land around Kinlochbervie, where the road ended and the path to Sandwood Bay and Cape Wrath began.

Sandwood Bay is the long sickle-shaped beach which lies to the south of Cape Wrath. It was regularly used as a safe harbour by Viking expeditions, who would run their longboats up on to the beach to escape storm waves, or in order to restock their freshwater supplies from Sandwood Loch, which gathers just inland from the Bay. The name is also from the Old Norse: Sandwood, from *sandvatn*, meaning sand-water.

I left the road-head and walked for five brisk miles over moorland to the Bay. Then on across hours of rough and sunlit ground – the sea, docile and silvered, always on my left – towards the Cape. From the miles I walked during that day, I recall a buzzard's shadow cast on the heather, flicking up and down as it passed over undulating ground. I remember stopping at a nameless stream, in whose water small black trout sped and darted, and picking up the bleached skull of a gull. When I rotated it in my hands, I could hear the silty run of sand grains through its chambers. At the same stream I found a near-perfect sphere of cloudy quartz.

Just south of the Cape, I stopped on a promontory which looked west into the bright extensive air. I drank cold water from a cup. The headland of the Cape rose nearly 400 feet out of the sea, the white light-house reached sixty feet above it. The army's live-firing range, away to the east, was silent. The air was so clear that I could see out to sea for dozens of miles. The dark horizon line was as plain as a strap.

On the north-western coasts of Britain and Ireland, the air has a remarkable transparency, for it is almost free of particulate matter. Little loose dust rises from the wet land, and the winds blow prevailingly off the sea. Through such air, photons can proceed without obstacle. The light moves, unscattered, and falls upon the forms and objects of those regions with candour. Standing within such a light, you feel thankful for its openness. There is a sense of something having been freely given, without its store having been diminished.

The clear quality of the light in the north-west has attracted artists and writers. It is also spoken of with exactitude and love by those who have lived and worked in these regions. Many of the people displaced during the Clearances, who had spent so much of their lives within this light, recalled it longingly after they had left.

I looked out to sea and watched the waves build as they approached the land, curling up out of the water along their length, like flicked ropes. The air above the sea was live with scores of birds: fulmars planing the wind in white curves, stubby guillemots like winged cigars, whirring along just above the waves, gulls making their weightless turns and angles, and giving their quick cries. So much life was at work in this place! I picked out one fulmar and followed its motion for a few minutes, watching the laterals of its gliding wings, wondering what sort of pattern its complex flight-path would make if it could be plotted. Out of sight to the east were the Clo Mor Cliffs, home to a far bigger seabird colony: tens of thousands of puffins, razorbills, guillemots, fulmars and kittiwakes.

But I knew that the Clo Mor colony, like numerous other seabird colonies – on little Rona, on steep-sided Hirta, Sula Sgeir, Foula and Fair Isle and on Skomer and Skokholm off the Dyfed coast – was under severe stress. After a century's increase, seabird numbers had begun to dip, and in some places, populations were close to collapse. Sustained over-fishing was affecting the numbers of sand-eels, the silver fish that are the staple of many seabirds. The warming of the seas brought about by climate change was also driving the sand-eels further and further north. The sand-eel scarcity was beginning to have a serious impact on the colonies. Chicks were dying or being left by the thousand, as the adult birds – guillemots and razorbills in particular – were obliged to push further north in search of dwindling food stocks. On cliffs along the coasts, nests were being abandoned, and homes left empty.

After half an hour on the Cape, watching the birds turn and the waves rise, I walked back south towards the Bay. The weather began to change rapidly. The bright containing light flattened out, and a brown storm light replaced it – a strange greasy shining out of the clear Atlantic sky. Then, distantly, sails of black rain came into view out to sea, and moved inland. Ghosts of longboats. The air the storm drove before it smelt salty and wet. The sea became quiet, its movements curved and gluey. Long compact waves rose foamlessly up and over the rocks at the base of the cliffs above which I walked. As the black sails reached the shore, I heard the fizz of rain on sea: rods of water driving down into planes of water.

My map showed that inland of me was a dwelling of some sort, marked Strathchailleach, which might provide shelter, so two miles to the north of the Bay, I cut eastwards, feeling tired. The ground dropped into a wide valley down which a brown stream meandered. On the outside edge of its loops, big chocolatey peat banks were exposed. Held within the loops were green semicircles of lush grass. Set on one of these was a cottage: white gable ends, grey walls, a corrugated iron roof, rusted red.

I lifted the heavy latch, pushed the door open, ducked under the low lintel and stepped into a corridor. The air was damp and peaty. The door swung shut behind me, and the latch dropped back into place. Darkness. Rain firing off the roof. I could see two thin boxes of light: doors. I walked to one of them, groped for a handle, opened it towards me, and light fell in a slab on to the floor of the corridor, as though it had been leaning against the other side. A typed note in a plastic bag was pinned to the wall: it said that the cottage was 'a simple shelter maintained in remote country for the use and benefit of all who love wild and lonely places'.

The door I had opened gave on to an end room with a sooty fireplace and a rough wooden table. The room was lit by a single four-paned window, sunk far back into the wall. I laid an arm on the cold window-ledge to measure the thickness of the wall; it was the depth of my arm from elbow to fingertip.

Rough painted murals covered the interior of the room, their bright colours glowing even through the soot. A sea eagle stooping on a mallard drake. Viking longboats with dark sails pulling on to a beach. A deer. A wild cat, scowling. On the single bookshelf were a copy of the Bible and *Salar the Salmon* by Henry Williamson. Tucked between the books was a thick sheaf of typed papers, the topmost of which was headed 'Strathchailleach'.

By the fireplace I found a candle and a box of matches. I lit the candle, dripped a puddle of wax on to the table and held the candle end in the wet wax until it set and stuck, at an angle. In a bucket I found slabs of dry heathery peat. I crumbled them into a pile of tinder, and lit it. The smell of burning peat filled the room, and pale grey smoke stung my eyes and settled in my hair.

When the fire was going steadily, I sat down at the table to read the papers. 'Travel as far north-west on the British mainland as the public roads will allow,' the first page began, 'then carry on, along wild mountain tracks, over a sweeping river and across a wide swathe of barren moorland, and you will reach the cottage of Strathchailleach . . .' The papers told the story of the cottage and its former inhabitant. It had been lived in for three decades by James McRory-Smith, or Sandy, as he was called by those few who knew him. He had been a riveter by trade, working the Clyde shipyards. Then his wife had died in a car accident. He had left his trade, abandoned his home in Glasgow, and moved haphazardly north, until he reached Strathchailleach, then an uninhabited crofter's cottage, some time in the late 1960s. In the hearth of the back room he lit a peat fire, which he would keep almost continuously stoked for the next thirty years.

I wondered about McRory-Smith's journey north. What questions had he asked of those he had met on his way? What ghosts had he been in flight from, or in search of, that had brought him to this land? What had decided him that he should settle here? Perhaps it was only that there was nowhere further north to go.

During the years he lived in the cottage, McRory-Smith gathered driftwood from Sandwood beach. He fished the lochans and the rivers, where in autumn and winter the salmon rammed upstream to spawn. He cut three decades' worth of peat from the brown banks to the west of the cottage. Now and again he walked the fourteen-mile round trip to the nearest village, to pick up supplies, buy batteries for his radio and collect his pension. During the long winter nights, when the temperature in the cottage dropped far below zero, he painted the murals, and listened to the radio. He was often unwelcoming to visitors: here was no example of the hermit made saintly by the wild. He struck me as an irascible, contorted opposite of the monks of Enlli, a man who came to this wild place not in search of solace but in flight from grief.

In 1981, Strathchailleach was hit by a winter storm so forceful that it collapsed the western gable wall. McRory-Smith retreated into the back room and waited out the storm, until he could go for help. With assistance, he rebuilt the west wall, and he continued to live in the cottage until shortly before his death in 1999.

McRory-Smith's story put me in mind of George Orwell. Between 1946 and 1948, Orwell spent six months of each year living and working in Barnhill, an exceptionally isolated stone-built cottage set on the tawny moors of the northern tip of the Scottish island of Jura. To reach the cottage from London was a forty-eight-hour journey, ending with a seven-mile walk from Ardlussa, the village at the head of the island's only motorable road. Flowering rushes flourished on the path between Ardlussa and Barnhill, and after his first visit to the cottage, Orwell bought a scythe with which to cut them back as he walked. What a morbid sight he must have made to any other traveller who met him on that lonely road at dusk! A tall thin cadaverous man, moving slowly forwards along the path, swinging his scythe through the fast-growing rushes . . .

At Barnhill, Orwell kept a small orchard and vegetable garden and farmed livestock: sheep, cows, a pig. The sea was only a few hundred yards to the east, over a low rise of moor. A few miles to the north was the Sound of Jura where, during the changes of the tides, the great Corryvreckan Whirlpool sucked and spun. Orwell fished the sea, the lochs and the rivers, and on warm days he swam in the lochs and in the Sound itself. Inside the house, he kept a peat fire burning, and he lit his rooms with paraffin lamps whose flames quickly sooted up the walls.

It was during those years, seated at a big scarred wooden table, between walks and work on the land, that Orwell wrote his most visionary book: *Nineteen Eighty-Four*. It is clear that Orwell needed to be in that wild landscape to create his novel; that there was a reciprocality between the self-willed land in which he was living and the autonomy of spirit about which he was writing. On Jura he found himself able to think and see differently, roused by the country – harsh, graceful, aerial, marine – that surrounded him.

The price of this vision, though, was his life. For Jura killed Orwell in the end. His fragile lungs, unable to stand the island's dampnesses and colds, succumbed to tuberculosis, of which he died in 1950.

The pitch of the noise of the rain on the cottage's roof changed suddenly, became sharper. I opened the front door and looked to the sky. A hailstorm had swept in off the sea. Beads of ice were hitting the roof and then rolling down the corrugations in neat scuttling processions, so that in the gutter beneath each furrow a pile of hail was building.

I went back into the end room, knelt down in front of the peat fire and blew on it. The fire ate deeper into the peat slabs, and raced along the heather stalks so that they glowed like fuses. And as I blew, too, films of ash peeled themselves off the surface of the peat, and yawed up the flue, lifted by the hot air. They were patterned in grey and black, so that it seemed briefly as though dozens of little maps were lifting off from the peat's surface, and vanishing up into the darkness of the flue.

Since the start of my journeys, I had been studying cartography. I had read book after book, spoken to surveyors and mapmakers, and tried to understand the rudiments of different projection techniques – Azimuthal, Gnomonic, Pseudoconical. The language of geodesy sounded like the language of spells.

Before it was a field science, cartography was an art: this was the first thing I had understood. We are now used to regarding cartography as an endeavour of exacting precision, whose ambition is the elimination of subjectivity from the representation of a given place. Such a presumption is hard to set aside, for we are accustomed to trust maps, to invest confidently in the data with which they present us. But in its pre-modern expressions, mapmaking was a pursuit that mingled knowledge and supposition, that told stories about places, that admitted fear, love, memory and amazement into its projections.

Broadly speaking, there are two types of map: the grid and the story. A grid map places an abstract geometric meshwork upon a space, within which any item or individual can be co-ordinated. The invention of the grid map, which occurred more or less coevally with the rise of modern science in the sixteenth century, lent a new authority to cartography. The power of grid maps is that they make it possible for any individual or object to be located within an abstract totality of space. But their virtue is also their danger: that they reduce the world only to data, that they record space independent of being.

Story maps, by contrast, represent a place as it is perceived by an individual or by a culture moving through it. They are records of specific journeys, rather than describing a space within which innumerable journeys might take place. They are organised around the passage of the traveller, and their perimeters are the perimeters of the sight or experience of that traveller. Event and place are not fully distinguished, for they are often of the same substance.

The earliest sorts of maps would have been story maps. Spoken cartographies, describing landscapes and the events that took place in them. Maps that could be learned, amended and passed on between people and down through generations. This distinctive crag, that tree-line, this bend in the river, the rock at which this accident

occurred, that tree where the hive was found: such features would have
been descriptively plotted to make a route that was also a story. Perhaps
there were written maps, too, portable or permanent, now lost to us. In
Bedolina, on the Lombardy plain of Italy, one of the oldest written
maps of the world exists: a complex petroglyph, clearly topographical in
nature, incised upon an angled boulder whose surface has been
smoothed by the retreat of the glaciers to make an ideal writing sheet.
It shows human figures, animals, settlements, dwellings, paths both
zigzag (uphill) and straight (along the flat). The map is palimpsestic in
nature: the first markings are thought to have been made in the Bronze
Age, around 1200 BC, and the most recent – the houses – during the
Iron Age, around 900 BC. The map is vast, extending fifteen feet wide
and over seven feet high.

In the long history of way-finding, the grid map is a relatively new
development. But its dominance is now almost total. From the fif-
teenth century onwards, new instruments of measurement (the
compass, the sextant, the theodolite and eventually the chronometer,
which allowed the determination of longitude), and new methods of
analysis (orthogonal sectioning, triangulation techniques) came into
being; advances that permitted a conceptual lattice to be extended over
the earth's surface.

Before this newly rigorous cartography, the more impressionistic and
itinerant mapping practices of pre-scientific cultures quickly fell back.
By the late eighteenth century, the potency of the grid map was so evident that the two young republics of that era founded themselves
geographically upon its principles. Thomas Jefferson's cartographers
divided the hinterland territories of America into the rectilinear forms
of township, county and state which persist today, and the French

Republic despatched two of its finest astronomer-cartographers to determine the extent of the meridian arc between Dunkirk and Barcelona, and thus to re-establish the French metric system upon the fundamental unit of the metre – which was to be one ten-millionth of the distance of that section of the meridian.

The grid map has proved an exceptionally efficient method for converting place into resource, and for devising large-scale approaches to a landscape. It is a technique that has brought uncountable benefits and advances with it. But so authoritative is the grid method, so apparently irrefutable the knowledge that it dispenses about a place, that it has all but eliminated our sense of the worth of map-as-story: of cartography that is self-made, felt, sensuous. The grid's rigorous geometry celebrates precision, and suppresses touch, feel and provisionality.

It is not that we should desire the abolition of the grid map – I travelled with them throughout my journeys – only that we should not forget story maps, for they exemplify a largely lost way of proceeding within a landscape. As the American poet Robert Penn Warren beautifully observed, 'our maps have grown less speculative, less interested in the elemental possibilities of the Earth's skin, and that suggests that the Earth has lost its capacity to keep secrets. We tend to look at them for what we want to avoid, rather than what, in good fortune, we might discover. There is not much mystery in a landscape we cannot enter.'

Cultures that grow up in close correspondence with a particular terrain often develop idiosyncratic methods of representing that terrain. These can be drastic and punitive. Certain Inca tribes would bind the heads of their babies with cloth, so that their skulls grew into the rough shape of the mountains from which they were thought to be descended. Other methods were more benign and practical. In 1826, at Cape Prince of Wales in the Canadian Arctic, a British naval officer encountered a hunting party of Inuit. Unable to communicate directly with the officer, but comprehending his desire for orientation, the Inuit created a map on the beach, using sticks and pebbles 'in a very ingenious and intelligible manner' to build a scaled replica of the region. The Inuit people are also known to have carved three-dimensional maps of coastlines from wood. In this way, the maps were portable, resistant to cold and, if they were dropped into water, would float and could be retrieved.

The Inuit have also developed a portfolio of sky maps and cloud atlases: a knowledge of the moods of the sky so precise that it allows them to infer the quality of the ice beneath the clouds, as well as future weathers. The Koyukon people of north-west interior Alaska use intricate stories to map their landscape: narration as navigation. According to the anthropologist Richard Nelson, who lived closely with the Koyukon, the landscape is to them:

> filled with networks of paths, names, and associations. People know every feature of the landscape in minute detail. The lakes, river bends, hills and creeks are named and imbued with personal and cultural meaning. People move in a world that constantly watches – a forest of eyes. A person moving through nature, however wild, remote . . . is never truly alone. The surroundings are aware, sensate, personified. They feel.

Such maps are, it is true, inaccurate by the standards of modern surveying. But they are alert to aspects of the land to which such surveying might be blind. For in such maps, human memory and natural form rebound endlessly upon one another.

They are deep maps, too, that register history, and that acknowledge the way memory and landscape layer and interleave. They are living conceptions, idiosyncratically created, proved upon the pulses of a place, born of experience and of attention. The map of a seabed intuited by a fisherman who has fished the same ocean for so long that he knows, though he has never seen, the differing textures and substances of its floor, the contours of its hills and valleys, and can tell the changes wrought upon its face by storms. Or those river-pilots who know the waters and currents and sandbanks so well that they can steer through them in darkness, or blindfolded. I had read of a man called Cathel Morrison, a crofter and conservationist who had been born and brought up near Sandwood Bay, and who had, throughout his life, watched the changing positions of the Bay's dunes, tracking their strange migrations by sketch map, fixed-point photograph and memory.

Maps such as these, held in the mind, are alert to a landscape's volatility as well as its fixtures. They tell of the inches and tints of things. They are born of a sophisticated literacy of place, rather than aspiring solely to the neutral organisation of data. We cannot navigate and place ourselves only with maps that make the landscape dream-proof, impervious to the imagination. Such maps – and the road-map is first among them – encourage the elimination of wonder from our relationship with the world. And once wonder has been chased from our thinking about the land, then we are lost.

The day's light was tending to nothing as I walked the final miles from the cottage back to the bay. I had cut peat bricks from the nearby bank to replace what I had burnt, stacked them to dry, and then left the cottage. It would have been a fine place to sleep, but I wanted to spend the night among the dunes of Sandwood, to be out in the rain and the storm. What was it that Robert Scott had written to his wife, Kathleen, as he lay dying in his small tent in Antarctica, only eleven miles from One Ton Depot and safety, knowing he would never see his family again? 'How much better this has been than lounging about in too great comfort at home.' It was the most heartless sentence I had ever read! But for all my disapproval, there was something there, some selfish love of asperity, that I guiltily recognised. And that evening, my inner Scott was telling me that I should leave the cottage and spend the night out in the sea storm.

I reached the bay's brink, and picked my way down through the crags that fortify its northern end, passing small waterfalls growing turbulent with storm water. The wind had become gusty, and kept cuffing me off balance. Sleet and rain still fell at a cold slant. A mile to the south of the bay, there was a sun flare over a salient of dark rock. Moor grass shook at my feet.

The river that bounded the bay beneath the crags had risen sharply. I had crossed it easily earlier in the day. It was now thirty feet wide, and the water was torrid.

I stood there, considering how to cross, when, unexpectedly, because I had not seen another person for two days, a woman stepped from behind one of the dunes and came to stand opposite me, on the far side of the river. I waved at her with one hand, using the other to shield my eyes from the flying sand. She waved back. Sand grains were moving over every surface in a loose laminar flow.

I sat on a rock, took off my boots and socks, and waded into the river. The water was so cold that my feet quickly numbed. It felt as though I were walking on short stilts. There was the distant sensation of slippery rocks, of boulders shifting beneath feet, and I remembered the deer crossing the Abhainn Bà on Rannoch Moor.

When I reached the sand on the far side of the river, the woman walked forward to meet me, holding out a stiff arm for balance. I clasped it around the wrist, and came out of the water, and, unsteady, caught at her shoulder with my other hand.

We stood in that odd half-embrace, shifting our feet uneasily to keep our balance in the wind and on the soft sand, as though performing an awkward ballroom dance. I leaned close to her ear, and spoke in a shout. She did the same to me. The wind tore at our words. We swapped information. The river leading north-east from the loch's inland end was torrential – uncrossable without a rope and a partner. The big waterfall to the north was being blown back up the cliff by the wind. She said that according to the forecast she had heard, the storm was due to be short-lived, but severe. As we spoke, I noticed, over her shoulder, far out on the grey horizon, the low flat form of a cargo ship, still and turreted as a castle.

We left each other. She to go back south towards Kinlochbervie, and I to find a sleeping place among the dunes. I watched her walk away for thirty or forty yards, being steadily gathered up by the sand-storm, her outline becoming grainier, as though she were being tuned out, until suddenly, with a snap, she was no longer there, and I stood unaccompanied on the beach.

A dark sky over shining acres of sand, the sun an orange stoke-hole to the west, and a huge onshore wind. I watched the storm gather in the last light. Above the wind noise, I could hear the chitter of blown sand and the rounded boom of heavy waves striking the cliffs to the north of the bay.

I walked up the long beach, passing between the big dunes that had formed there, and that grew, shifted or shrank with each great storm. The wind coming off the sea was so strong that, running and leaping with it at my back, I found I could take giant moon-steps, six or seven feet at a time, landing heel-first in the soft sand. It felt as though a hand were lifting me up and then setting me down with each long pace. I ran half the depth of the beach in this way, and then turned and walked back into the wind, leaning against it, down towards the water's edge.

All along the shoreline, sea-foam, thick and yellow as cream, had gathered in trembling drifts, ten feet deep and hundreds wide. The wind was scooping up loose balls of foam, and blowing them across the sand, and as they tumbled and scudded over the beach, they diminished in size, dwindling until, like a magician's trick, they vanished.

I spent that long night in a valley between two big dunes, close to the shore where the waves broke and the foam thickened, but safely up beyond the tideline. My bivouac bag kept me dry, and my sleeping-bag kept me warm. I dug a dip in the sand for my shoulders and one for my hips, and patted up a shallow pillow for my head. The dune valley sloped down a little towards the water, so that from where I lay I could see out to the sea, its black skin heaving and white waves curling out of the darkness to break along the beach.

The noise of the storm made sleep difficult. But I was happy to be there, sleepless inside the storm. For it was an extraordinary night. In its first few hours, the darkness was so absolute that it seemed to have become a black fluid, within which existed turbulent forms that could be sensed but not seen: funnels, tubes, spindles and whorls, gusting sheets of wind and unexpected eddies of storm energy. Around midnight I felt myself inside what might have been the storm's hollow. There was a brief passage of calm, and then the inner edge of the storm rushed in, and the night fell back into unrest.

I finally slept, and when I woke, just after dawn, the storm had passed, the wind had settled, and with it the sand: a moist layer coated me, and when I moved it cracked into parched-earth patterns. I shook myself off, climbed to the top of a dune, and sat on the marram grass, eating an apple and some chocolate.

On the beach, a new line of drift debris – thick kelp stems with flaring arms like ganglia, driftwood, more plastic bottles – marked the reach of the storm-driven tide. Water was still fresh on the drifted objects, and they gleamed. The early small sun hung over the high ground, and I could feel its weak heat on the edges of my face. Thirsty, I climbed down from the dune, and walked to the bay's southern end, where I found a small rainwater stream, catching its way down a slope. I washed my face and, where the water pooled, leaned forward and drank. Then I set off back towards Kinlochbervie and Ben Hope.

8

Summit

A snowy owl taking flight from the quartz and granulite summit of Ben Hope, set on a meridian course north, would bank out over the Pentland Firth, pass to the east of the Faeroes, cross the Arctic Circle, and enter the Greenland Sea. It would fly above the pack ice that locks the channel between Spitzbergen and Greenland. It would pass, as all things meridian must, over the Pole. From there, without changing direction, it would fly south past the ice-bound island of Vrangelya in the Chukotse Sea. Only after many hours would it reach ground as high as Hope again: a nameless peak in the mountains of north-western Siberia, where the temperature is so cold that steel splits and larch trees shower sparks at the touch of an axe. As I drove east to the mountain from Kinlochbervie, I imagined Ben Hope and this nameless peak rhyming in their altitude, across thousands of miles of cold space, each northering towards the other.

I had been told that if you climb Ben Hope on the summer solstice, and spend a clear night on its summit, you will never lose sight of the sun. The combination of elevation and northerliness means that the uppermost rim of the sun never dips fully below the horizon. A truly white night. In the autumn, too, it was said to be a fine place for watching the aurora borealis, which shimmered like aerial phosphorescence, green and red. But I was most drawn to Hope in its winter moods. For several years I had wanted to climb it when snow was on the ground, and spend a cold night on its summit: the sense of polar space opening out beyond me, the scents of berg and frazil washing down off the invisible Arctic Ocean.

Hope is a mountain which holds the solstitial opposites of north: it knows both the affirmation of the never-vanishing sun and the indifference of the eighteen-hour night. There could be, I thought, no other place in Britain or Ireland where you could better feel a sense of 'bigness outside yourself', in Stegner's phrase. That 'bigness' had been there on Rannoch Moor and at Sandwood, and I had felt a chronic version of it in Coruisk. But I wondered if, once I began to move south, it would fall away, become unlocatable.

I drove through sleet, then sunshine, then squalls, with raindrops the size of berries pelting on to the windscreen. No weather system remained dominant for more than an hour. By early afternoon I was at Hope's south-western foot. Clouds bearing cargoes of snow pushed past to the north-east. Snow was falling lightly over Foinaven, to the west across moor. The sky above me was clear, a pale winter white. I looked up at Hope, remembering its shape from the maps I had studied.

The geography of Hope is exquisite: a steep summit cone, shapely and symmetrical when seen from the sea. A sharp curving north ridge, on which peregrines nest, forms a glacis protecting the mountain's northern approach, and keeps secret the watery land on Hope's eastern flank – a region of fourteen lost lochs and lochans. To the south, the mountain's long plateau-ridge, the Leitir Mhuiseil, streams out, tapering for three miles, trimmed on its western flank with a band of silver-grey schist and flashed here and there with quartz.

I started up Hope as the day's light began to dim, feeling excited, almost jaunty, to be out there alone. Following a stream-cut, I passed big boulders worked by the water into curious shapes. As I climbed, the view over the surrounding landscape opened. Hundreds of empty miles of watery land radiating out in each direction, big peaks here and there – Klibreck, Loyal, holding snow in their eastern corries – and Loch Hope leading the eye north, past the mountain's cliff ramparts, and out to the spaciousness of the Firth.

Reaching the upper brink of the Leitir Mhuiseil, I saw three deer standing watchfully on the ridge's rim. They observed my approach, then turned in synchrony and rode their long legs off and out of sight. I sat by a stream, and drank handfuls of cold water. Westwards, the late sun was breaking through the cloud cover here and there, so that the day's light fanned slowly upon the moors. I could see white bows of blown snow, strung by sharp straight rays of sunshine, and I counted four separate storms spaced across the earth. To the east, though, night was coming: the edges of that world were in a cooling blue of shadow and dusk and chill.

Hope did not give itself up easily. The ascent was nearly from sea-level, and the huge summit cone, crag-bound, was steadily steep. By the time I reached the top, the air around me was dark and gritty, and the wind colder. The summit was bare, stripped by gales and frost-weathering. Rime ice had formed in feathery windrows on shattered grey rocks, which were also marked with lichens the colour of lime and tangerine. Between the rocks, snow lay in stripes and furrows, dry and granular as sand. Working quickly, with numbing hands, and a growing sense of worry – was this too cold a place, too hard a place, to spend the night? – I moved rocks to clear a lozenge-shaped space of rough flatness, and arranged them into a low curving wall, a foot or so high.

That night the winds began a slow swing from west to north, bringing snow showers scattering against the canvas of my bivouac bag, and raking the summit rocks with hail. A moon was up there somewhere, breaking through the cloud cover. It was far too cold to sleep. I lay like a compass needle, head to the north, on my front, looking towards the sea, watching patches of silver open and close over the distant waters, trying to keep warm.

At two o'clock, still sleepless, I left the shelter, crossed back to the main top, and began to pace out the reach of the mountain's curving summit plateau. The cloud cover had thinned. Moonlight came and went in squalls. Each rock wore a carapace of ice, which cracked and skittered off in shards at the slightest contact. Little hail drifts had built up in the lee of the rocks; otherwise the wind had stripped away all the unfrozen snow. The air smelt bright.

I walked out to where the mountain's eastern ridge began, and from there looked down into the lost lochs, which were holding moonlight like snow. Moving across to the south-western tip of the plateau, I sensed more than saw the massive complex of Foinaven miles away, its snow-shires flashing silver, the rest of its black bulk invisible in the dark. The cold was pressing, constant, and I began to shiver; not a surface tremble, but a deep convulsive shaking. In that deep winter darkness, my sunny East Anglian beechwood felt suddenly hugely distant, the landscape of another continent or era, not just another country.

This was one of the least accommodating places to which I had ever come. The sea, the stone, the night and the weather all pursued their processes and kept their habits, as they had done for millennia, and would do for millennia to follow. The fall of moonlight on to water, the lateral motion of blown snow through air, these were of the place's making only. This was a terrain that had been thrown up by fire and survived ice. There was nothing, save the wall of rocks I had made and the summit cairn, to suggest history. Nothing human. I turned east and south, straining to see if there was any flicker of light in the hundreds of miles of darkness around me. Even a glimpse of something lit, however distant and unreachable, would have been reassurance of a sort. Nothing. No glimmer.

There could have been nowhere that conformed more purely to the vision of wildness with which I had begun my journeys. I had been drawn here by a spatial logic, a desire to reach this coincident point of high altitude and high latitude. But now I could not wait to leave it. It was an amplified version of the discomfort I had unexpectedly felt at the Inaccessible Pinnacle in Coruisk.

If I could have safely descended from the summit of Hope in the darkness, I would have done so. The comfortless snow-shires, the frozen rocks: this place was not hostile to my presence, far from it. Just entirely, gradelessly indifferent. Up there, I felt no companionship with the land, no epiphany of relation like that I had experienced in the Black Wood. Here, there was no question of relation. This place refused any imputation of meaning.

All travellers to wild places will have felt some version of this, a brief blazing perception of the world's disinterest. In small measures it exhilarates. But in full form it annihilates. Nan Shepherd found this out on the Cairngorm plateau, another bare, stripped, Arctic zone. 'Like all profound mysteries, it is so simple that it frightens me,' she had written of the water that rises on the plateau. 'The water wells from the rock, and flows away. For unnumbered years it has welled from the rock, and flowed away. It does nothing, absolutely nothing, but be itself. One cannot know the rivers till one has seen them at their sources; but this journey is not to be undertaken lightly. One walks among elementals, and elementals are not governable.'

Musicians speak of the 'reverberation time' of a note or chord: the time it takes that sound to diminish by a certain number of decibels. The reverberation time of that black and silver night on Hope would be endless for me. Standing there, I knew that the memory of it might fade but it would never entirely disappear. I wondered if there would be any such places south of there, or if this was to be in some way the end of my journeys.

At some point, the winds dropped, and the temperature rose by a degree or two. I returned to the shallow stone shelter and was able at last to sleep, for perhaps two hours, little more, longing for dawn and escape from the summit. When I woke at first light, cold to the core, the air was windless. My rucksack was frozen, the canvas rigid and pale as though it had been fired in a kiln. I found and kept a fragment of quartz granulite, irregular in its shape: sharp-edged, frost-shattered. Then I set off down the mountain, and it seemed as I did so that descent in any direction from that summit would be a voyage south.

9

Grave

The day before I reached the Burren, the worst storms to hit Ireland and Scotland for ten years passed over the countries. The accounts that emerged after the wind had lessened had about them the sound of a scourge. A fishing-boat with nineteen crew had foundered off the coast of Skye. Three people had been killed inland, two more were missing. A lorry-driver had died after his vehicle was blown off the Foyle Bridge in Londonderry. Many trees had been flattened, with the slow pressing down that big wind effects on forests: the trees supporting each other in their mutual falls, their canopies tangled, their limbs interlocked. On North Rona, in the Western Isles, the gusts reached 124 miles per hour: quick enough to peel iron from the roofs of barns and sheds, to pick up people and livestock. On South Uist, five members of a family were compelled to leave their home by rising waters: trying to cross a causeway to safety on Benbecula, they were swept to their deaths by storm waves.

The afternoon following the ebb of the storms, standing out on the flat rocks on one of the western headlands of the Burren, I could still see traces of this recent ferocity. The sea was rough, with angry wave sets champing at the rocks. A wide current flowed alarmingly fast along the headland – a northerly tide-rip so quick that it moved even surface objects at about 300 feet a minute. The sky was steep and black with rain. Surf brawled over offshore reefs.

The Burren rises, silver, in the north of County Clare, on the mid-west coast of Ireland. Its name comes from the Gaelic *boireann*, meaning 'rocky place', and the region is so called because most of its surface is made up of smoothed limestone, intercut with bands of clay and shale. The limestone forms a vast escarpment, between the granite of Galway and the sandstones of Liscannor. From there it extends north-west, dipping beneath the Atlantic, to resurge thirty miles off-shore as three islands: Árainn, Inis Meáin and Inis Oírr, or the Aran Islands, as they are called in English. Seen from a distance, on a sunlit day, the limestone of the region gleams silver and grey, and the Burren seems to have been cast in pewter.

One of the two most remarkable aspects of the Burren is its flora. Arctic, Alpine and Mediterranean plants all live within its 150 square miles. Nowhere else in Europe do species of such contrasting hardi-hoods coexist. The spring gentian, more usually found in the high meadows of the Alps, blooms within inches of the dense-flowered orchid, a native of Italy and Spain; the hoary rock rose and the mountain aven prosper near the maidenhead fern, a favourite Victorian house plant. That such botanical paradoxes are possible is a function of the Gulf Stream, of limestone's ability to absorb heat in the summer and release it in the winter, and of the Burren's exceptional light levels.

It was this unique climatic and botanical entanglement that had drawn me to the Burren. With its familial resemblances north to Scotland and south towards England, it seemed like the ideal landscape to come to after Hope.

The Burren's other distinction is as a landscape of the dead. It has been occupied more or less continuously for 5,000 years. The abundant calcium makes for good bones on grazing livestock, and the soil that gets caught in the rifts of the limestone makes the land richer and more amenable to cultivation than the bare granite regions that surround it. And five millennia of human activity in the Burren also means that buried in it are 5,000 years' worth of the dead. Walking its grey reaches, you find memorials to the dead everywhere: stone circles, dolmens, wedge-tombs, headstones, crosses, burial grounds consecrated and unconsecrated. It is a landscape of funerary monuments. Almost every era – Neolithic, Bronze Age, Iron Age, medieval and modern – has interred its people here, and has marked their resting places in stone. The past has a thickness in the Burren. Human time there is the historical equivalent of limestone: it has experienced a long slow settle into density.

Few of the Burren's dead died peacefully. In the 1650s, Oliver Cromwell's troops laid western Ireland waste. Clare was among the devastated counties, the Burren among the plundered regions. Two centuries later, the Great Famine fell upon Ireland. Clare was again one of the counties worst affected. Villages emptied during the Famine by starvation and emigration still stand in the Burren: roofless gables, sightless windows. Some of the thousands of paths and walls that mark the landscape were built by the victims of the Famine. Relief administrators, unwilling to provide aid for free, made starving people labour on purposeless projects in exchange for food tokens. Men who could hardly stand unaided were set to work building roads which led nowhere, and walls which protected nothing.

When Cromwell came across the Irish Sea with his army, to begin his brutal purge of Catholics and Royalists, he entrusted the wrecking of North Clare and the Burren to General Edmund Ludlow. Years later, looking back on that campaign, Ludlow would dismiss the Burren in a phrase that has sounded down through its history. The Burren was, Ludlow wrote, 'a savage country', in which 'there is not water enough to drown a man, wood enough to hang one, nor earth to bury him'. What a way of looking at any landscape: to read it only for how it might collaborate in murder. Ludlow was wrong, as well as grotesque. He had been an inattentive mover through that country. For the Burren, I would learn during my days there, is filled with all the things Ludlow missed. It is filled with water, wood, earth and the dead, and all are part of its wildness.

I travelled to the Burren in midwinter with Roger. He had reached a pause in his writing, and now that I was not heading so far north, he was keen to join me on some of my journeys, and perhaps do some woodland research along the way. When I asked if he wanted to come with me to the Burren – an area renowned for its dwarf hazel forests – he agreed immediately. I was very pleased at the prospect of Roger's company; I had been alone for too long in the north.

We drove up towards the Burren from Shannon. The radio broadcasts spoke of climate change: another pessimistic report on sea-level increases had been released. It made me feel even more guilty than usual about driving, made the road seem an even less desirable place to be. There are few planning restrictions on roadside signs in Ireland, and every hundred yards was a gaudy placard in the shape of a shamrock or horseshoe, enticing motorists to turn off to a visitor attraction or a bar. Traffic was slow, and the trees by the roadside appeared stunted by pollution rather than by wind, their leaves grey with road pall.

As we neared the outer reaches of the Burren, though, the roads narrowed and became lined with healthy fuchsia hedges: in autumn, little pink lantern-flowers would hang brightly among the dark green leaves. The light assumed a clearer tone: reactive to the expanse of grey stone beneath it and to the tremendous mirror of the sea beyond that.

Our base in the Burren was an old low-slung house in its centre, belonging to a friend of Roger's. The house blended New Age and old age. Guarding the front door was a row of ancient hawthorns, quiffed eastwards by the onshore winds, from which silver wind-chimes hung and rang in the ceaseless breeze. Behind a gnarled gorse bush in the garden stood a three-foot plaster statue of Jesus, his right hand raised in permanent and startling blessing.

The evening of our arrival, we moved round the house, looking out of the windows on every side. Visible in the grey dusky light, midway up the glass of each window, was a flat horizon-line of dark rock. It felt as though we were in a diving-bell, part-submerged and gazing out at the water as it encircled us. That night, we sat in half-darkness round a peat-fire, reading out passages from books to each other and talking. I told Roger about my night on the summit of Hope, about the sudden fear I had felt instead of the exultation I had expected, about the intractability of that place.

At dawn the next morning, we began our explorations, carrying with us a map of the area made by the cartographer and landscape historian, Tim Robinson, who lived up the coast in Roundstone. Roger had been unusually and mysteriously ill in the month before we left, and he was still weak, so we moved gently, walking for slow miles across the limestone, pacing out the Burren's reaches, trying to begin to understand this heavily encrypted landscape.

The solubility of limestone, its acquiescence to water, means that the Burren – like its sister limestone lands in the Peak District and the Yorkshire Dales – is rich with clandestine places: runnels, crevasses, dens, caves, hollows, gullies. It is a landscape that has the vast, involuted surface area of a coastline, or a lung's interior. Things pool and hide in limestone, including meaning: it forms a lateral landscape, but not a shallow one.

The soft worn beauty of limestone has also made it a commodity. From the middle of the nineteenth century onwards, a trade in the stone grew; it was desirable for rockeries and municipal flower-beds. Legal and illegal quarrying means that in Britain, where a scant 6,000 acres of surface limestone pavement exist, only around 200 acres remain undamaged.

Limestone, I found during my time in the Burren, demands of the walker a new type of movement: the impulse to be diverted, to wander and allow the logic of one's motion to be determined by happenstance and sudden disclosure. We learned, or were taught by the ground, how to walk without premeditation: turning corners when they came, following bends in valleys, our paths set by the ancient contingencies of geology and the immediate contingencies of footfall, our expectations quickened – ready for surprise when it happened.

It happened often. Birds sprang from invisible crannies in the stone: a woodcock rolling away through the low air, a snipe exploding out of a scrubby hollow. Hares pelted up from their forms. On a summit, out of sight of the sea, we found a cow's skull, green with mould, and then, scattered over half an acre, like the wreckage of an air crash, the rest of its skeleton. In gullies we found groves of ancient hawthorns and black-thorns, lichen flourishing on their thin trunks, giving them the look of shaggy centaur's legs.

Once, in a rain-filled midday dusk, we watched a peregrine fly from an escarpment of wet limestone cliffs facing the Atlantic. It launched from its rock sill, flapped its wings clumsily twice, three times, seemed as if it would sink, and then lifted and flew out and over the wooded hillside until it was only a black star in the grey sky.

Early on another day, we crested a pass to find three hundred acres of bright water shining in the valley beneath us, unmarked on our map. It was a *turlough* – one of the temporary lakes which form in limestone country after heavy rain, when the water level rises up from beneath the rock, like a bath filling from its own plughole. This *turlough* had overwhelmed the valley, and we could see dozens of trees standing in their own reflections, like playing-card kings. A sparrowhawk circled above the water, covering miles in minutes.

Hours further on, at the junction of three remote valleys, we discov-ered a silver acre of limestone pavement. These pavements, like those of the Yorkshire Dales, are divided into clints (the glacially polished hori-zontal surfaces) and grykes (the vertical fissures which divide the clints, and which have been worn out by water erosion). The openness and polish of the pavements lend them an air of expectancy, as though some entertainment or spectacle is soon to be convened there. They make you think of plazas or town squares in winter, empty except for pigeons and shadows. Roger spoke of their resemblance to the Dancing Ledge on the Dorset coast: the broad sea-smoothed rock plinth where the men of Swanage used to take their ladies to dance and more, while the waves broke and the sun set. I remembered the hard igneous summit of Hope, and felt surprisingly happy to be on this softer stone.

We stepped down on to the pavement from the hillside, and as we did so three feral goats – chocolate-and-cream coats, fish-hook horns – graciously ceded the space to us, and began to climb the steep moor on the other side. We picked our way over the grykes, their rims weathered into curves, into the centre of the pavement. Their form was exquisitely complex, and the ridges and valleys induced brief losses of scale, so that they could have been satellite maps of mountain ranges or river deltas.

Near the centre of the pavement, we reached a large gryke running north to south. We lay belly-down on the limestone and peered over its edge. And found ourselves looking into a jungle. Tiny groves of ferns, mosses and flowers were there in the crevasse – hundreds of plants, just in the few yards we could see, thriving in the shelter of the gryke: cranesbills, plantains, avens, ferns, many more I could not identify, growing opportunistically on wind-blown soil. The plants thronged every available niche, embracing one another into indistinguishability. Even on this winter day, the sense of life was immense. What the gryke would look like in the blossom month of May, I could not imagine.

This, Roger suddenly said as we lay there looking down into it, is a wild place. It is as beautiful and complex, perhaps more so, than any glen or bay or peak. Miniature, yes, but fabulously wild.

After we had crossed the pavement, we found, beneath a steep lime-stone escarpment, the remains of a ring fort. All that was left of it were concentric ridges under the grass, made visible by their shadow more than their substance, arranged around a sunken central pit. We stepped over the berm and down into the fort's interior, and stood, turning, looking down the three valleys that radiated from it.

The fort would probably have been built, like the hundreds of others in the region, around 3,500 years ago, by settlers who moved out to the coastal regions from the wooded interiors of the country. The name we now give these structures is misleading: the 'forts' were primarily domestic rather than military in purpose, with each one being the centre of a small community, and denoting a dominion or territory of about one square mile.

There was so little to indicate the fort, just the vestiges of its form, but stepping down into it I felt the swift deepening of time, the sharp sense of the preterite, which occasionally comes in such places. We stood quietly together inside the fort's circle, working out the sight-lines down the valleys, trying to imagine how the people who lived and worshipped here had perceived this landscape. The long late sunlight lay on the settlement like cloth, shaping itself to the grass and the stone.

In the aboriginal culture of New Guinea, landscape possesses two distinct surfaces of existence. The archaeologist Christopher Tilley describes them well: 'One is fixed, the land of the dead, ancestral forces; the other, the land of the living, is mobile, but always gravitating in relation to the first. There is an invisible and underlying order of spirit beings, including totemic ancestors and ghosts of the dead.' The Burren, it seemed that sunlit afternoon, also possessed these different orders of existence, moving in relation to one another. They worked like skins, differently holed and punctured, sliding over one another. At certain times and in certain places the holes aligned, and one could see through the present land, the land of the living, backwards into another time, to a ghost landscape, the land of the dead.

The wild and the dead have long been involved with each other. Although we are now accustomed to orderly burial in sacralised ground – acre on acre of ranked graves – this has not always been the way. The wild has often been a place to which the dead are returned, slipped into earth as if into water.

On 18 April 1430, John Reve, a glover from the village of Beccles in Suffolk, was summoned to the bishop's palace in Norwich to account for his heretical belief in the rightness of burial in wild places. Reve's defence was recorded. 'I have held, believed and affirmed,' he declared courageously to the tribunal, 'that it is as great merit, reward and profit to all Christ's people to be buried in middens, meadows or in the wild fields as it is to be buried in churches or churchyards.'

Reve's moving belief in the righteousness of wild burial would find many later historical counterparts, both within and without the Christian tradition. Seventeenth-century Quakers took to burying their dead in orchards and gardens as a mark of dissent, while the Marquis de Sade ordered in his will that, at his death, his body be collected on a cart by the local woodseller, taken to the woodlands on the Marquis's estate, and there interred in a freshly dug grave. 'Once the grave has been filled in,' he stipulated, 'it will be planted with acorns so that in time to come the site being covered over and the copse being once again as thickly wooded as it was before, the traces of my grave will disappear from the surface of the earth.'

Wildness and death are strongly linked in my family. My great-grandfather, who moved to Switzerland in an attempt to cure his bronchitis, was buried in the Veytaux cemetery on the shores of Lake Geneva: his grave has a view up a steep valley towards the Rochers de Naye, the distinctively indented rock ridge that rises above the Lake.

My maternal grandparents had four children. One of them, Charmian, was born with spina bifida. She died on 25 October 1954, after a month of life: her body was cremated at Honor Oak Crematorium, and her ashes were scattered on One Tree Hill in the North Kent Downs, looking out over the Weald – Weald, from the Old English for 'forest', or in its sixteenth-century version, 'wild'. My father has asked me to spread his ashes on the slopes of Beinn Alligin, a mountain in the Torridon range on the north-west coast of Scotland. Alligin is a fortress of old red sandstone: it rises over 3,000 feet almost straight out of the Atlantic. To its north stretches the treeless expanse of the Flowerdale Forest, one of the largest areas of unroaded terrain in Britain and Ireland.

An Irish friend once told me a story about how his aunt had upset the family. One summer, a salesman had come knocking on the door when everyone else but she was out. She had let him in, heard him talk and bought his product, which was a grave plot. The family were worried that she had been gulled, and they wanted her to get her money back. But she would not do so. The grave site was on a cliff-top, she said, a rare site, and she showed them the map. It had a beautiful view over the Atlantic. It would be a good place, she said, to spend the rest of eternity.

So many of the wilder landscapes of Britain and Ireland are filled with graves, marked and unmarked. So many ancient burial places are located within sight of a river or on bluffs and promontories overlooking the sea. There are the chambers at Maes Howe on Orkney, the barrows of the southern counties of England – Wiltshire, Dorset – and the circles and stone-lines which brood on the moors of Devon and Cornwall, and on the Scilly Isles. In Northumbria, there are communal graves on Dod Hill, Redesdale and Bellshiel Law dating from 2000 BC.

At Sutton Hoo in Suffolk, a burial site from around AD 500 is set on a bluff above the River Deben, and contains the bodies of the Wuffingas, an elite cadre of noblemen who ruled the area at that time. The name Hoo is derived from the Old English word *haugh*, meaning 'high place'.

To travel to somewhere like Maes Howe or Sutton Hoo, or to walk between the graves out in the wild reaches of the Burren, is to find yourself unaccountably uplifted. There are beliefs expressed here, you think, which might be learned from. A sense of orientation, perhaps, or connection. The exhilaration you feel has something to do with the innocence of the assumptions embodied in such a grave site, with its unbashful vision of a continuity between life, death and place. That, and the simple fact that so many people, of so many ages, should have set their dead to gaze out over space.

We moved through dozens of weathers in our time in the Burren. Black angled rain, bleaks of cloud, sunsets that turned the watery hollows of the limestone to mercury or blood. A dusk that came in the form of a grey line of cloud with a sharp straight edge, drawn over from the east like a swimming-pool cover. On a beach where the sand swirled in a yellow and grey Messerschmidt two-tone, we watched ten-foot combers queuing up and breaking perfectly along their length as they neared the beach.

I came to feel, during the days we spent there, that the significant form of the Burren was the circle. It was there in the ring forts, there in the mountains, with their stepped profiles. And there, too, in the closed chemical loop of stone and bone that made the

Burren: the limestone of which it was composed being itself the consequence of the settling out of boned and unboned bodies; the
richness of the limestone attracting humans to the landscape; and
then the death and burial of those humans. Bone returning to stone.

The Burren, like the Yorkshire Dales, is an antique sea. Hundreds of
millions of years ago its limestone was the bed of a shallow tropical
ocean, upon which the bodies of oysters, sea-snails, ammonites, belem-
nites, coccoliths, sea lilies and corals rocked gently down in their
billions, to form a limy silt. Each fragment of the Burren is a mau-
soleum, each hill a necropolis of unthinkable dimensions, containing
more dead organisms than there are humans who have ever lived.

To be in the Burren is to be reminded that physical matter is
simultaneously indestructible and entirely transmutable: that it can swap
states drastically, from vegetable to mineral or from liquid to solid. To
attempt to hold these two contradictory ideas, of permanence and
mutability, in the brain at the same time is usefully difficult, for it
makes the individual feel at once valuable and superfluous. You become
aware of yourself as constituted of nothing more than endlessly
convertible matter – but also of always being perpetuated in some
form. Such knowledge grants us a kind of comfortless immortality: an
understanding that our bodies belong to a limitless cycle of dispersal
and reconstitution.

Of all the stones of the archipelago, limestone has always been the
best accomplice to metaphysics. W. H. Auden, who so loved the karst
shires of the Northern Pennines, adored limestone. What most moved
him about it was the way it eroded. Limestone's solubility in water
means that any fault-lines in the original rock get slowly deepened by a
process of soft liquid wear. In this way, the form into which limestone

grows over time is determined by its first flaws. For Auden, this was a human as well as a geological quality: he found in limestone an honesty – an acknowledgement that we are as defined by our faults as by our substance.

One afternoon, walking back through a silky cold sunlight after a day out on the limestone pavements, Roger and I met a man, perhaps sixty years old, with a thick brown moustache, and a shotgun crooked in his arm. He had, he said, taken three woodcock. They were stowed in the game pockets of his jacket; I could see the shapes of their long hard beaks showing through the cloth. Bright red domed beads of blood stood out on the waxy sleeves of his jacket, and in one I could see a fish-eye reflection of me and the land behind. He was a Clare man, he said, and had been shooting here for more than forty years. He spoke of the changes over the time he had known the area; of the return of the hazel scrub during the past decade, a sign that the land was not being farmed as hard, that more food was being transported into the area from outside. I asked him about the hares of the Burren, for we had seen several of them that day, long-legged and long-eared, sitting like sentries, or sprinting gracefully off around a hillside. He said that hares were a special animal here. Thirty years back, when times were hard, his father had shot hares, and they had eaten them as a family, but now no one did, because they were scarcer, but also because they were considered to be animals of poetry. There would be uproar in the gun clubs if anyone was heard to have shot a hare.

The hares were still chased, though, by men on foot and with dogs, he said, but they were always left to run free at the end of the chase. He turned and pointed to the far end of a long low hill of grey karst to our east, softened by purple hazel scrub, and said that a running hare, leaving from the spot on which we three were standing, would make for that end of the hill, and then – he swept his finger along the horizon of the hill, and we followed its indication – race all the way along its top, before coming back, in an arc of nine or ten miles' distance, to exactly the point from which it had set off. He spoke beautifully about the form of this run, and the instinct which brought the hare back to its starting point, so turning arc into circle.

On our last night in the Burren, the sky cleared and the air cooled. The moon was a waxing crescent, bone-coloured, about a third of full, and bright enough to see by. The stars were myriad. I wanted to be out in the Burren by night, so I left the house and went walking alone in the clear winter darkness. I hoped I could find my way back to a big ring fort we had reached on our first day – the triple-ramparted Cathair Chomain. It was close to freezing, and my breath fletched in the air. Roosting birds, unidentifiable in the dark, rose from the ground with flaring wings and eyes like jewels. The only sound I could hear was the stony krekking of a raven. Every now and then a car passed distantly along the single road that crosses the Burren's centre, its headlight cones floating in the darkness.

I walked slowly, following short sunken valleys, picking my way carefully over the limestone pavements, scrambling up little rock cliffs, and pushing through the dense dwarf hazel thickets, beneath whose shoulder-high canopy the moonlight had little reach. I was feeling proud of my nimbleness – until I slipped and banged my right shin so hard I had to sit and wait for the pain to ebb.

Eventually I reached the fort, navigating by a mixture of map, memory and luck. Three rings of pale stone, partly grown over by grass, and the central enclosed circle a jungle of thorn and briar. I sat between the first and second walls, under the guardian arm of an old elder, which had curled round and down upon itself to form a nearly closed hoop. Beneath it, I found and kept a little squashed sphere of limestone, which was soapy to the touch.

I stayed for a while, there in the elder's kind crook, on the cold grass, watching the stars shed their impassive light. I thought about the historical shadows that had fallen across my journeys, up in the cleared glens of Scotland and now here in the Burren. I had expected to find evidence of contemporary damage, contemporary menace, but I had not thought to encounter these older darknesses. I had passed through lands that were saturated with invisible people, with lives lived and lost, deaths happy and unhappy, and the spectral business of these wild places had become less and less ignorable. My idea of wildness as something inhuman, outside history, had come to seem nonsensical, even irresponsible.

But I also thought about what Roger had said as we peered into the thriving floral world of the gryke. His comment about its wildness had jolted my mind unexpectedly, brought previously unrelated thoughts into configuration and thrown others apart. It had made me see how wedded my old sense of the wild was to an ideal of tutelary harshness – to the scourges of rock, altitude and ice. Down in the gryke, though, I had seen another wildness at work: an exuberant vegetable life, lusty, chaotic and vigorous. There was a difference of time-scheme between these kinds of wildness, too. My sense of a landscape's wildness had always been affected by the gravitational pull of its geological past – by the unstillable reverberations of its earlier makings by ice and fire. The wildness of the gryke, though, was to do with nowness, with process. It existed in a constant and fecund present.

When the cold became too much to bear, I got up and set off to steer a safe course home. The stars performed their slow whirls around the pole, as I moved in the dark past orthostat, capstone, ruin and famine grave.

The main material causes of the Irish Famine are well established: a rickety system of estate management based on absentee landlordism, and a monoculture potato diet among the peasantry. There was, too, the rapidity and virulence of the potato blight itself, which moved with appalling speed, afflicting entire fields overnight. Potatoes, usually rummaged firm and gold from the ground, came up stinking and mushed. Despair spread with the blight, and with the hunger came epidemic disease: dysentery, typhoid.

In 1847, the height of the Famine, at least a quarter of a million people died. In the thirty years from 1841 to 1871, Ireland's population was nearly halved by death and emigration, from around 8,175,000 to 4,412,000. The most conservative estimates of the dead of these years, taken from the Census, suggest that between one and one and a half million people perished. The highest mortality rates were in the western and north-western regions. Connaught, the province comprising Galway, Leitrim, Sligo, Roscommon and Mayo, lost over a quarter of its population.

Death rarely came rapidly. Starvation could take months to kill a person. An American missionary, Asenath Nicholson, who travelled through Ireland during the Famine, distributing Bibles and food, wrote of how, as flesh fell slowly from the bones, hope left the mind, until the starvation victim moved into a state of depressed inanity. She recorded that, in the 'second stage of dying', the starving would stand in the same spot for hours, 'giving a vacant stare, and not until peremptorily driven away will they move'. Those even closer to death, Nicholson wrote, could be told because of the way their heads bent forwards; they would walk 'with long strides, and pass you unheedingly'. In the workhouses, children lay for days before they died, eerily motionless. 'In the very act of death still not a tear nor a cry,' observed an English clergyman, Sidney Osborne, visiting a Limerick workhouse. 'I have scarcely ever seen one try to change his or her position . . . two, three, or four in a bed, there they lie and die, if suffering still ever silent, unmoved.' William Carleton, in *The Black Prophet*, his Famine novel of 1847, described the 'fearful desolation' he had encountered in the western parishes: gaunt figures, 'their eyes wild and hollow, and their gait feeble and tottering', the roads black with funerals, the death-bells pealing forth in every parish 'in slow but dismal tones', and how in the soup shops 'wild crowds' swarmed, 'ragged, sickly, and wasted away to skin and bone'.

In the worst affected villages, there was no one well enough to dig graves, and so bodies were stacked in ricks. Where interment could take place, the dead were buried in pits, thousands of which were dug, and from which bones are still turned up. In the coastal parishes, the burying grounds were often excavated on the borders of the sea, where the soil was loosest, and the dead were piled into the earth on top of one another. In the shallower pits, as the corpses swelled, the topmost layer of dead would be pushed to the surface. Feral tribes of dogs roamed and fed on the corpses. The animals came to look, said one witness, 'so fat and shining', plumped as they were on human flesh. Dogs ate the dead, and the living ate the dogs.

People began to commit crimes deliberately, so that they could be transported to penal colonies – to anywhere but foodless Ireland. A British magistrate who visited Skibbereen in County Cork, on Christmas Eve 1846, found himself in a world dreamed up by Bosch or Goya. 'In a few minutes [I was] surrounded by at least two hundred phantoms, such frightful spectres as no man can describe. By far the greater number were delirious, either from famine or from fever. Their demoniac yells are still ringing in my ears, and their horrible images are fixed upon my brain.'

Many of those who died in the western counties, however, did so in their rural huts and cabins, quietly. In a dark expression of the politeness and dignity which characterised much behaviour during the Famine, the last to die in a family would often save the strength to reach, close and fasten the door of the cabin, so that the corpses would not be visible to passers-by. The cabin would then be pulled down upon them for a grave.

In August, months after my journey to the Burren with Roger, I returned alone to the west of Ireland: to County Galway in Connacht, just to the north of the Burren. Trying to get a perspective on the land, I climbed Bin Chuanna, the highest peak in the Garraun range. Chuanna rises above the Killary peninsula, on whose westernmost tip

Ludwig Wittgenstein lived near the end of his life, in a house built to store Famine relief aid, when he was trying to finish his *Philosophical Investigations*.

I ascended Chuanna on a windy bright day. Partway up its pathless north face, a heron launched itself from high rocks above me – a fold-away construction of struts and canvas, snapping and locking itself into position just in time to keep air-bound – before beating seawards on its curved wings, away towards Rosroe. Around noon, I reached the summit: a rough broken tableland of flat rocks, perhaps a quarter of an acre in area, and planed smooth by the old ice. There was a single small cairn, and on its top sat a horned sheep's skull. I picked up the skull, and as I did so water streamed from its ragged nose-holes in sudden liquid tusks, and ran on to my hand and up my sleeve. I put it back on the cairn top, having turned it so that it faced eastwards and inland, looking over miles of empty land glinting with lakes, on which thousands of wild geese over-wintered each year. The sun came out, breaking fitfully through the clouds and warming my hands and face. Seawards, I looked across the intricate tasselwork of inlet and peninsula. Close at hand, sheets of mica scattered the sunshine, so that even the dry rocks shone in the light. I found a rough pyramid of quartz, and took it for my storm-beach.

From Chuanna's summit I followed the course of a nameless stream back off the mountain's western side. The stream flowed into a loch, and the loch formed a river, so I continued to follow the river until, late in the afternoon, I reached the sea: a semicircular white sand beach, a mile or so to the south of Rosroe, its curve perhaps half a mile long from tip round to tip.

When I stooped and caught up a handful of the sand, I saw that many of its particles were sickle-shaped fragments of shell, pale and small as cuticles, which recalled in their form the larger curve of the bay. Here and there people were sitting on the sand, or wading in the shallows. At either end of the semicircle, arcing out in a chain into the sea, was a run of two or three small islands, perhaps twenty yards apart from one another, separated by channels of blue water through which the ebbing tide ran.

The sun fell brightly on those islands, so I thought that I would swim across and explore them. I walked round the beach as it curved south and west, until I reached its outermost point, a small triangular headland of golden sand, formed by the meeting of two sets of waves which came together transversely from north and south, making parallelogram patterns of water, diagonals sifting into diamonds.

I waded out into the first of the tidal channels, carrying my rucksack above my head, feeling the firm ripples of sand upon the soles of my feet, and the transways strikes of the little waves on my shins. Small unspecifiable fish darted away from my feet, and once a little dab or plaice raised itself up in a puff of sand and glided off. The channel deepened quickly. Soon I was up to my chest in the water, whose colour had changed from the friendly green of shallow sandy water to a chillier blue. I could feel, too, that it was flowing faster, and that the warmth of the shallower water had become riddled with bands and tubes of cold.

I reached the first of the islands, and then walked out into the second of the channels. This one was deeper, and at its centre the water reached up to my chest, and the currents swayed me off balance, so I was relieved when it shallowed again, and I walked out on to a golden beach, leaving slight footprints on the hard scoured sand.

I sat down on the beach for a while, and let the sun and the wind dry me, and then I set out to explore my Crusoe island. There was not much to it. It was about twenty yards across and thirty wide, rising to ten feet or so above sea-level, rock-bound on its seaward side, and topped by green machair and golden sand. I checked the high-water wrack lines as I walked, which lay like rusty contours around the island. They suggested that it would not be overwhelmed, even in a storm. The forecast was good, and the island was a wild and beautiful place, so I decided to sleep there.

As afternoon graded into evening, I sat with my back against a tall rock and watched the Atlantic, while the rock pulsed the day's stored heat into me. I ate sardines and rye bread, and cut hunks of cheese with my knife. Gentle water glittered in the bay. As the sun lowered, the air became colder, and the turn and rise of the tide deepened and quickened the water in the channels which I had earlier crossed. I felt a calm settle into me; there was no way of leaving the island now, and no easy way on to it, and the impossibility of either escape or disturbance had a tranquillising effect, quite different to the alarm I had felt on the summit of Hope. This was a happy marooning. What was it that W. H. Murray had written? 'Find beauty; be still.'

Some time later, the sun set into the western sea, laying out a swaying ferrous path which reached the shore of the island. Almost immediately, the stars began to prick into sight: the sky was cloudless and clear of light pollution. I counted them as they appeared, until they came too quickly to count, filling the sky in bright complex specklings, so that the air seemed to become soft and mobile with them.

I slept unexpectedly well in my dip of sand on the summit of the island, and did not wake until after dawn. I felt a rush of surprise and then of happiness to be where I was. I had slept on an island! The dream of every child who has read *Swallows and Amazons*. This gentle place had allowed me to use it as home, and although I knew that such anthropomorphic fancies were absurd, I felt briefly as though I had been guarded or cradled in some way by the place. It was the obverse and balance to the sensation of being on the summit of Ben Hope. This island was the salutary wild; that summit the indifferent wild. Each was remarkable, though, and I was grateful to have known them both.

The sea on both sides of the island shifted evenly, its surface smooth and shining, its interior clear. Looking at the channels, I saw that I had an hour or so before the tide would let me cross back to the mainland again. I undressed, and padded across the black rocks on the bayward side of the island. Their stone was cold underfoot. I slipped gently into the water, breathing sharply at its coldness, then lolled back in it, and let the low humped waves, which were barely perceptible except as shrugs of the water, raise me up and lower me down again, as though I were being courteously lifted to make way for something passing underneath me.

Around eight o'clock that morning, when the sun had risen above the eastern mountains, I walked down the sloping beach and into the tidal channel, and began to wade back across it, feeling the water heavy against my legs, smelling the salt rising off the warming surface, back across to the sickle-shaped beach.

Later that morning I drove north to the town of Westport and climbed Croagh Patrick, the sacred mountain which rises there, from land once

called Mureisc Aigli, the Sea-Marsh of the Eagle. My hope had been to
spend the night on Patrick's summit, where there had once stood a
Celtic hill-fort and, later, a drystone oratory. But it happened that I had
inadvertently chosen a holy day, the Feast of the Ascension, for my
climb, and the path up the mountain was busy with hundreds of pilgrims – ordinary men, women and children from the surrounding
towns and counties, who had come to test the strength of their Catholic
faith against the mountain, for reasons I could not fathom. I started up
the mountain among them, listening to them talk. Many of the men
had chosen to walk barefoot and bare-chested, and most of these had
blood seeping from the wounds the mountain's rocks had left on their
feet.

I had not expected the pilgrims, nor had I expected the litter on
Patrick's summit: chocolate-bar wrappers stuffed into rock crevices, rotting banana skins lying outside the door to the new oratory. It was an
uneasy mix of the sacred and the profane; I left it to the pilgrims.

After my magical coastal night, though, I still wanted to sleep at altitude, and so I drove back down to the southern flank of Mweelrea,
the great mountain that rises above Doo Lough – the Black Lough. As
I had passed Mweelrea earlier, I had spotted a hanging corrie, nameless
and difficult of access, overlooking the Lough, and had thought that
it might make a good place to spend the night.

I reached the corrie as dusk was falling, cresting its lip about 1,000
feet above the valley floor, to find myself in a wide, sunken bowl of grass
and boulders, with encircling rock walls that rose 600 feet or so on
every side and were washed by a series of fine waterfalls.

Few people would have been into this corrie before, I guessed. There
was no reason to come this way: no water to fish, no easy route through

it up on to Mweelrea itself. The corrie was its own lost world, with only one way in and one out. What a place it was to be in that dusk, with the waterfalls misting in the thickening light.

Within an hour, pale cloud had gathered around the mountain above, and clothed the summits of the crag curtain, so that through the dusk the waterfalls appeared to drop coldly and sourcelessly from the sky. The silence in the corrie, save for the waterfalls' white noise, was absolute. I could see down into part of the valley beneath, and to Doo Lough, whose surface had become still and uniform as a sheet of dark iron.

The valley I overlooked that evening was allegedly the site of one of the worst episodes of the Famine. At Louisburgh, the town to the north of the valley, in the cold spring of 1849, a crowd of around 600 people gathered. Many were close to death from starvation; all were hoping to find food at one of the relief stations that had been established in Louisburgh. Food, or an admission ticket to the Westport work-house, which would at least guarantee them some sustenance. But the Relieving Officer of Louisburgh told the crowd that he could not supply them either with food or with tickets. He said that they should instead apply to the two Poor Law Guardians of the region, Colonel Hograve and Mr Lecky, who were due to meet the following day at Delphi Lodge, the big house at the southern end of the valley, ten miles away, beyond Doo Lough.

Two accounts exist of what then happened, of contrasting gravity. The more distressing is collected in James Berry's *Tales of the West of Ireland*. According to Berry, that night, the crowd slept in the streets of Louisburgh. It was a clear night, and the temperature dipped conse-quently low. The next morning, an estimated 200 people were found dead where they lay. The survivors began the long walk south, up over the Stroppabue Pass, and down round Doo Lough. There was no road at that point, and they walked on sheep tracks. Nor were there bridges over the rivers, and at two points the marchers had to ford the Glankeen River, which was turbulent with water from the previous days' rain.

When they finally arrived at Delphi, the Guardians were still at lunch, and sent word that the people should wait. So they sat down among the trees at the brink of the estate, where several died of exhaustion. When Hograve and Lecky had at last finished their lunch, they went down to where the people were, and told them that neither food relief nor workhouse tickets would be forthcoming, and that the people should return to Louisburgh.

The survivors set off northwards, retracing the path they had just so effortfully taken. The weather had worsened by this point, with the wind veering round to the north-west, bringing hail and sleet. Their clothes, soaked by stream-fording and sleet, froze quickly about their limbs to the 'stiffness of sheet iron'. Many died where they fell by the side of the track, killed by hypothermia and exhaustion. When those that were left reached the crest of the pass, at Stroppabue, above the Doo Lough, the wind was of such strength, and the people of such weakness, that scores were buffeted into the water of the Lough, where they drowned.

The next morning, Berry recorded, the path from the Glankeen back to Houston's house was covered with corpses 'as numerous as the sheaves of corn in an autumn field'. The Relieving Officer at Louisburgh, having heard of the tragedy, gathered together a group of near-starving men, and they walked along the corpse-strewn track, interring the dead where they lay. When the burial party reached Doo

Lough, where so many had died, there was not enough earth to bury the bodies, except in the little glen or ravine which ran down the brow of the cliff between Stroppabue and Doo Lough. 'So,' recorded Berry, 'they had to gather all the corpses and carry them to the little glen where they buried them in pits just as on a battlefield, and there they lie sleeping where the sighing of the winds through the tall, wild ferns which wave above their nameless graves forever sings their requiem.'

When I woke in the corrie above Doo Lough that night, at some point in the small hours, the cloud had passed away, and the moon was pouring its light down on to the valley. I was thirsty, so I took my metal cup and walked to the side of the corrie, and held the cup beneath the spill of one of the waterfalls. The water hit the tin and set it ringing like a bell. I drank the cold clear rainwater, and looked down over the dark valley. The shadows of the mountains on either side of the lough were cast over its floor in clear black shapes. The starlight fell upon the scene, old light from dead stars, and where it fell, the boulders and swells of the landscape cast dark moon-shadows, and I could see the night wind rippling over the grass of the valley, stirring it into ghostly presence.

10
Ridge

For four days in late March, snow settled unexpectedly across Britain, taking it by surprise. Spring had arrived a week previously: black buds had popped green on the ash trees, and I had seen brown hares making curved runs in the Suffolk fields as I drove across to see Roger in Mellis. But then the wind changed direction, northerlies brought freezing temperatures, and spring stopped. Gritter lorries moved over the roads, whirring out fans of salt and stone. Children made an ice slide on a quiet road near my house, and queued up in jostling lines, polishing the ice to the consistency of milk-bottle glass. John, who had sailed me out to Enlli, wrote from his home in Hope Valley in the Peak District, to say he had spent two days out tracking hares. He spoke of big beluga drifts of snow, and of the hares, still in their white fur, moving unhurriedly between them.

I had been hoping that spring would hold, for I wanted to see the fizz and riot of the land coming to life again after winter, to feel some of the warmth I had glimpsed in the gryke but that I had so far missed on my journeys. My plan had been to go to the Forest of Bowland in Lancashire, where I could explore the rich green valleys of the Ribble and the Lune, and sleep out on riverbanks. Roger was going to join me. But the return of the snow changed things. I decided instead that I would go alone for a proper night walk in the Cumbrian mountains.

Snow perpetuates the effect of moonlight, which means that on a clear night, in winter hills, you can see for a distance of up to thirty miles or so. I know this because I have experienced it several times before. Several, but not many, because in order to go night-walking in winter mountains, you require the following rare combination of circumstances: a full moon, a hard frost, a clear sky and a willingness to get frozen to the bone.

I watched the forecasts. They anticipated that a further 'snow-bomb' – the remnant of a polar low, dragged south by other fronts – would hit north-west England, before quickly giving way to a high. When the snow-bomb landed, temperatures over the hills were expected to drop as low as –15°C, with winds gusting at speeds of up to fifty miles per hour. It seemed too much to hope that I would be rewarded with such conditions . . . But the chance was there, and so I left Cambridge and travelled up to Buttermere, in the mid-western fells of the Lake District: back on to the hard rocks, the granite and the tuff.

'Is the Lake District another bourgeois invention, like the piano?' Auden had asked in 1953. Certainly, with its tea shops and eroded footpaths, it could feel like that; as though it had been loved into tameness by its millions of visitors. But I hoped that, out by night in the snow, I might catch at some of its remaining wildness.

Noctambulism is usually taken to mean sleepwalking. This is inaccurate: it smudges the word into somnambulism. Noctambulism means walking at night, and you are therefore etymologically permitted to do it asleep or awake. Generally, people noctambulise because they are in search of melancholy, or rather a particular type of imaginative melancholy. Franz Kafka wrote of feeling like a ghost among men – 'weightless, boneless, bodiless' – when he walked at night.

I had found another reason for being out at night, however, and that is the wildness which the dark confers on even a mundane landscape. Sailors speak of the uncanniness of seeing a well-known country from the sea; the way that such a perspective can make the most homely coastline seem strange. Something similar happens to a landscape in darkness. Coleridge once compared walking at night in his part of the Lake District to a newly blind man feeling the face of a child: the same loving attention, the same deduction by form and shape, the same familiar unfamiliarity. At night, new orders of connection assert themselves: sonic, olfactory, tactile. The sensorium is transformed. Associations swarm out of the darkness. You become even more aware of landscape as a medley of effects, a mingling of geology, memory, movement, life. The landforms remain, but they exist as presences: inferred, less substantial, more powerful. You inhabit a new topology. Out at night, you understand that wildness is not only a permanent property of land – it is also a quality which can settle on a place with a snowfall, or with the close of day.

Over the past two centuries in particular, however, we have learned how to deplete darkness. *Homo sapiens* evolved as a diurnal species, adapted to excel in sunlit conditions, and ill-equipped to manoeuvre at night. For this reason, among others, we have developed elaborate ways of lighting our lives, of neutralising the claims of darkness upon us, and of thwarting the circadian rhythm.

The extent of artificial lighting in the modernised regions of the earth is now so great that it produces a super-flux of illumination easily visible from space. This light, inefficiently directed, escapes upwards before being scattered by small particles in the air – such as water droplets and dust – into a generalised photonic haze known as sky glow. If you look at a satellite image of Europe taken on a cloudless night, you will see a lustrous continent. Italy is a sequined boot. Spain is trimmed with coastal light, and its interior sparkles. Britain burns brightest of all. The only significant areas of unlit land are at the desert margins of the continent, and along its mountainous spine

The stars cannot compete with this terrestrial glare, and are often invisible, even on cloudless nights. Cities exist in a permanent sodium twilight. Towns stain their skies orange. The release of this light also disrupts habits of nature. Migrating birds collide with illuminated buildings, thinking them to be daytime sky. The leaf-fall and flowering patterns of trees – reflexes controlled by perceptions of day length – are disrupted. Glow-worm numbers are declining because their pilot lights, the means by which they attract mates, are no longer bright enough to be visible at night.

By the time I reached the mountains, it was late afternoon. The snow-line was regular at 1,000 feet, dividing the world into grey and white, lower and upper. It was clear from the mood of the sky that another big fall was coming. Dark clouds had started to hood the earth from the east, and the brown burnt light of imminent snow was tinting the air. Scatters of thin sleet were falling. My cheeks and nose buzzed with the cold.

The path to the upper ground switchbacked from the lake shore through tall oak woods. Old coarse snow lay in rows between the trees, and in rings around their bases. Where I brushed against branches and leaves, snow spilled on to me like sugar. I met three other people, all of whom were descending. On each occasion we spoke briefly, acknowledged the extraordinariness of the land in this weather, and went our ways.

After half an hour, I reached the wide valley that holds Bleaberry Tarn, and behind which rises the line of peaks including Red Pike, High Stile and High Crag. Looking to my east and north, all I could see were white mountains. Distant snowfields, on mountains whose names I did not know, gave off bright concussions of late light. The wind was cold, and blowing into me. It was already so strong that I had to lean into it at a five-degree vaudeville tilt.

Above the hanging valley, the path was thick with hard compacted snow, its stones grouted with ice. To the right of the path, I noticed an irregular trail of tiny red crooked poles, an inch high at most, standing out from the snow like stalagmites. Two days previously, when the snow first fell, someone must have dripped blood as they walked, and the blood had frozen as it trickled down into the snow. Since then, a steady wind had chafed away the loose snow, so that what remained standing were the poles, each one a drip of blood.

By the time I reached the ridge, at over 2,000 feet, the snow had thickened to a blizzard. Visibility was no more than a few feet. The white land had folded into the white sky, and it was becoming hard even to stand up in the wind. I would need to find somewhere to sleep out the worst of the storm, so I cast about for sheltered flat ground, but could see none.

Then I came across a tarn, roughly circular in shape, perhaps ten yards in diameter, pooled between two small crags, and frozen solid. The tarn ice was the milky grey-white colour of cataracts, and rough and dented in texture. I padded out to its centre, and jumped gently a couple of times. It did not creak. I wondered where the fish were. The tarn was, if not a good place to wait out the storm, at least the best on offer. It was flat, and the two crags gave some shelter from the wind. My sleeping-bag and bivouac bag would keep me warm enough. And I liked the thought of sleeping there on the ice: it would be like falling asleep on a silver shield or a lens. I hoped that when I woke, the weather would have cleared enough for some night-walking.

The painter Samuel Palmer and the poet Edward Thomas both knew and loved the wilding quality of darkness. In twilight, dawn and full night, Palmer would walk the countryside around the village of Shoreham, in Kent, where he and a tribe of fellow painters known as the Ancients lived in the 1820s and 1830s. Sometimes, when they walked together by night, they would sing the witches' songs from *Macbeth*. Palmer's watercolours and etchings brim with his astonishment at the Kent countryside.

Learning from the work of his acknowledged master, Blake, Palmer developed an artistic language that allowed him to record that astonishment: how leaves seem to dance before the eyes at dusk, or the indigo of early-morning and late-evening skies, or the vast creamy intensity of a harvest moon. To him, even the heavily farmed landscape of Kent teemed with a marvellous wildness, which expressed itself in energies, orders and rhythms. To Palmer, the growth of an apple from a branch was cause for wonder, as were the ripe synchronous patterns of a cornfield in a windy dawn, or the mackerel mottling of moonlit clouds.

Edward Thomas was, from a young age, a walker, both by night and day. In his mid-twenties, when he was suffering from depression, he would often set off on long walking tours, alone, in the march-lands of Wales and England. Like so many melancholics, he developed his own rituals of relief, in the hope that these might abate his suffering, and that he might out-march the causes of his sadness.

He left a record of one of these tours in his extraordinary short book of 1905, *Wales*. It reads like a dream-story or song; an entranced account of the months Thomas spent exploring the wild places of that country – its rivers, mountains, estuaries, forests and lakes. As he moved between these places, he spoke to those he met along his way; he noted down the stories they told him, and the songs which on occasion they sang him. He wrote his book using a wild goose feather he had found on the sands of Kenfig, and cut into a quill pen.

In *Wales*, Thomas exults in the joy of walking fast in darkness, the joy of seeing the summits of the hills 'continually writing a wild legend on the cloudy sky' by day. He describes how, at night, the land becomes cast into 'no colour', and then how, when the sunlight returns, the world awakens again to its hues. Once, on the winter hills, the temperature falls so low that he has to stop and warm himself in the moist breath of a flock of sheep. And one dawn, having walked in the mountains through the night, he comes to a narrow pass between two peaks, and stops for shelter in a little copse of oak and hazel. The mist has risen from the low ground around him, and in the dying moonlight, he wrote, he sees 'a thousand white islands of cloud and mountain'.

Up in the mountains at night, Thomas remarks near the end of *Wales*, 'It becomes clear, as it is not in a city, that the world is old and troubled, and that light and warmth and fellowship are good.' A year after the declaration of the First World War, Thomas enlisted. He joined the Artists' Rifles – a large volunteer battalion for the London and Middlesex areas – and was posted first to Hare Hall Training Camp in Essex, where he worked as a map-reading instructor, using the skills of land knowledge he had learned as a walker. In January 1917, he was posted to the Western Front. He wrote to his wife Helen on 29 January, the day before he left England, to say that once he was 'over there', he would 'say no more goodbyes'. From the letters and the journal he wrote while at the Front, it is clear that Thomas often recalled his walking days, and that the memories of those years of openness, and of freedom to move, were a steady consolation to him, until he was killed by a shell-blast on the first day of the Battle of Arras, just after dawn.

Up on the ridge, the blizzard blew for two hours. I lay low, got cold, watched the red reeds that poked up from the ice flicker in the wind. Hail fell in different shapes, first like pills, then in a long shower of rugged spheres the size of peppercorns. Over half an hour, the hail turned to snow, which had the texture of salt and fell hissing on to the ice. I had begun to feel cold, deep down, as though ice were forming inside me, floes of it cruising my core, pressure ridges riding up through my arms and legs, white sheaths forming around my bones.

I must have slept, though, for some hours later I woke to find that the snow had stopped and the cloud cover had thinned away, and a late-winter moon was visible above the mountains: just a little off full, with a hangnail missing on the right side, and stars swarming round it. I got up, and did a little dance on the tarn, partly to get warm, and partly because if I looked backwards over my shoulder while I danced, I could see my moon-shadow jigging with me on the snow.

I appreciated the effort that the moonlight had made to reach me. It had left the sun at around 186,000 miles per second, and had then proceeded through space for eight minutes, or ninety-three million miles, and had then upped off the moon's surface and proceeded through space for another 1.3 seconds, or 240,000 miles, before pushing through troposphere, stratosphere and atmosphere, and descending on me: trillions of lunar photons pelting on to my face and the snow about me, giving me an eyeful of silver, and helping my moon-shadow to dance.

I had woken into a metal world. The smooth unflawed slopes of snow on the mountains across the valley were iron. The deeper moon-shadows had a tinge of steel blue to them. Otherwise, there was no true colour. Everything was greys, black, sharp silver-white. Inclined sheets of ice gleamed like tin. The hailstones lay about like shot, millions of them, grouped up against each rock and clustered in snow hollows. The air smelt of minerals and frost. Where I had been lying on the tarn, the ice had melted, so that there was a shallow indent, shaped like a sarcophagus, shadowed out by the moonlight.

To the south, the mountain ridge curved gently round for two miles. It was as narrow as a pavement at times, at others as wide as a road, with three craggy butte summits in its course. To the east and west, the steep-sided valleys, unreachable by the moonlight, were in such deep black shadow that the mountains seemed footless in the world.

I began walking the ridge. The windless cold burnt the edges of my face. These were the only sounds I could hear: the swish of my breathing, the crunch my foot made when it broke through a crust of hard snow, and the wood-like groans of ice sinking as I stepped down on it. I passed an ice dune which was as smooth and glassy as the sill of a weir. My shadow fell for yards behind me. Once, stopping on a crag-top, I watched two stars fall in near parallel down the long black slope of the sky.

When I came to a big frozen pool of water, I took a sharp stone and cut a cone-shaped hole in the white ice where it seemed thinnest. Dark water glugged up into the hole, and I knelt, dipped my mouth to the ice and drank. I caught up a handful of snow, and patted and shaped it in my hands as I walked, so that it shrank and hardened into a small white stone of ice.

Where the ground steepened, I moved from rock to rock to gain purchase. On the thinner sections I walked out to the east, so I could look along the cornice line, which was fine and delicate, and proceeded in a supple curve along the ridge edge and over the moon trench, as if it had been engineered.

Several small clouds drifted through the sky. When one of them passed before the moon, the world's filter changed. First my hands were silver and the ground was black. Then my hands were black and the ground silver. So we switched, as I walked, from negative to positive to negative, as the clouds passed before the moon.

The human eye possesses two types of photo-receptive cells: rods and cones. The cone cells cluster in the fovea, the central area of the retina.

Further out from the fovea, the density of cone cells diminishes, and rod cells come to predominate. Cone cells are responsible for our acute vision, and for colour perception. But they work well only under bright light conditions. When light levels drop, the eye switches to rod cells.

In 1979, three scientists, Lamb, Baylor and Yau, proved that a rod cell could be tripped into action by the impact of a single photon. They used a suction electrode to record the membrane current of pieces of toad retina with high rod-cell density. They then fired single photons at the retinal pieces. The membrane current showed pronounced fluctuations. It is agreed that this is among the most beautiful experiments in the field of optics.

It takes rod cells up to two hours to adapt most fully to the dark. Once the body detects reduced light levels, it begins generating a photosensitive chemical called rhodopsin, which builds up in the rod cells in a process known as dark adaptation.

So it is that at night, we in fact become more optically sensitive. Night sight, though it lacks the sharpness of day sight, is a heightened form of vision. I have found that on very clear nights, even at sea-level, it is possible to sit and read a book.

Rod cells work with efficiency in low light levels. However, they do not perceive colour – only white, black and the greyscale between. Greyscale is their approximation of colour: 'ghosting in' is what optic scientists call the effect of rod-cell perception. It is for this reason that the world seems drained of colour by moonlight, expressing itself instead in subtle but melancholy shades.

The brightest of all nightscapes is to be found when a full moon shines on winter mountains. Such a landscape offers the maximum reflection, being white, planar, tilted and polished. The only difficulty for the night-walker comes when you move into the moon-shadow of a big outcrop, or through a valley, where moon-shadow falls from all sides and the valley floor receives almost no light at all. The steep-sidedness of the valley is exaggerated: you have the sensation of being at the bottom of a deep gorge, and you long to reach the silver tideline of the moonlight again.

To be out by night in a forest, by a river, on a moor, in a field, or even in a city garden, is to know it differently. Colour seems absent, and you are obliged to judge distance and appearance by shade and tone: night sight requires an attentiveness and a care of address undemanded by sunlight.

The astonishment of the night-walker also has to do with the unconverted and limitless nature of the night sky, which in clear weather is given a depth by the stars that far exceeds the depth given to the diurnal sky by clouds. On a cloudless night, looking upwards, you experience a sudden flipped vertigo, the sensation that your feet might latch off from the earth and you might plummet upwards into space. Star-gazing gives us access to orders of events, and scales of time and space, which are beyond our capacity to imagine: it is unsurprising that dreams of humility and reverence have been directed towards the moon and the stars for as long as human culture has recorded itself.

Our disenchantment of the night through artificial lighting may appear, if it is noticed at all, as a regrettable but eventually trivial side-effect of contemporary life. That winter hour, though, up on the summit ridge with the stars falling plainly far above, it seemed to me that our estrangement from the dark was a great and serious loss. We are, as a species, finding it increasingly hard to imagine that we are part of something which is larger than our own capacity. We have come to accept a heresy of aloofness, a humanist belief in human difference, and we suppress wherever possible the checks and balances on us – the reminders that the world is greater than us or that we are contained within it. On almost every front, we have begun a turning away from a felt relationship with the natural world.

The blinding of the stars is only one aspect of this retreat from the real. In so many ways, there has been a prising away of life from place, an abstraction of experience into different kinds of touchlessness. We experience, as no historical period has before, disembodiment and dematerialisation. The almost infinite connectivity of the technological world, for all the benefits that it has brought, has exacted a toll in the coin of contact. We have in many ways forgotten what the world feels like. And so new maladies of the soul have emerged, unhappinesses which are complicated products of the distance we have set between ourselves and the world. We have come increasingly to forget that our minds are shaped by the bodily experience of being in the world – its spaces, textures, sounds, smells and habits – as well as by genetic traits we inherit and ideologies we absorb. A constant and formidably defining exchange occurs between the physical forms of the world around us, and the cast of our inner world of imagination. The feel of a hot dry wind on the face, the smell of distant rain carried as a scent stream in the air, the touch of a bird's sharp foot on one's outstretched palm: such encounters shape our beings and our imaginations in ways which are beyond analysis, but also beyond doubt. There is something uncomplicatedly true in the sensation of laying hands upon sun-warmed rock, or watching a dense mutating flock of birds, or seeing snow fall irrefutably upon one's upturned palm.

The mountaineer Gaston Rebuffat identified a retreat from the real as under way fifty years ago, in his memoir *Starlight and Storm*. And Rebuffat knew the real. He had spent his life in mountains by night and by day. He had bivouacked on north faces, in rock niches, in snow holes, and walked and climbed in all weathers and all hours. Starlight and storm, for Rebuffat, were indispensable energies, for they returned to those who moved through them a sense of the world's own forces and processes. 'In this modern age, very little remains that is real,' he wrote in 1956.

> Night has been banished, so have the cold, the wind, and the stars. They have all been neutralized: the rhythm of life itself is obscured. Everything goes so fast, and makes so much noise, and men hurry by without heeding the grass by the roadside, its colour, its smell . . . But what a strange encounter then is that between man and the high places of his planet! Up there he is surrounded by silence. If there is a slope of snow steep as a glass window, he climbs it, leaving behind him a strange trail.

After an hour's slow walking, I reached the flat-topped final summit of the ridge. Leading off it to the south-east was a steep little ice couloir, only twenty or thirty feet long, curved up at either edge, and sheeny with clear ice. It led down to a saddle and a small lower top. I sat down and heeled my way to the rim of the couloir, then luged down it, using my feet as brakes, striking ice chips with them, and feeling the cold black air crack against my face as I slid, so that it seemed as though I were passing through shattering plates of ice, until I slowed to a halt. Then I cleared some space among the rocks of the outcrop, pitched my bivouac, and tried to sleep.

Before sunrise I got up, stretched, stamped my feet and blew into my cupped hands. Then I walked over to the hard drifts of snow on the eastern side of the outcrop, and cut a snow seat, in which I sat and watched as dawn, polar and silent, broke over the white mountains.

The first sign was a pale blue band, like a strip of fine steel, tight across the eastern horizon. The band began to glow a dull orange. As the light came, a new country shaped itself out of the darkness. The hills stood clear. Webs of long, wisped cirrus clouds, in a loose cross-hatched network, became visible in the sky. Then the sun rose, elliptical at first, and red. I sat and watched that dawn, looking out over a land which was and was not England, with the cold creeping into me, and the white mountains receding into the white sky. For reasons I could not determine, it felt quite different here, on this snowy peak, from the summit of Hope: perhaps it was just the proximity of houses, towns, people, only an hour or so away from me, or perhaps the magical otherworldliness of the night walk, whose beauty I knew I would never forget.

About half an hour later, the sky was a steady tall blue. I stood up, feeling the stiffness of the cold deep inside the joints of my legs, but also the early sunlight warm on my cheeks and fingers, and started to descend the mountain. As I got lower, the land began to free itself from the cold. Wafers of ice snapped underfoot. I could hear melt-water chuckling beneath the hard snow billows. Here and there, yellow tussocks of grass showed through the white. I was walking out of winter.

From a black rock wall spilled a waterfall which was only part frozen: a hard portcullis of ice, beautifully mottled by dark figures of thaw, and water falling from it. The water's turbulence was surprising and swift after the night world. I stood for a while watching it, and then drank from the stone cistern it had carved out beneath it, and snapped off an icicle to eat as I walked. Nearby, I found a gourd-shaped hole in a rock, in which water had gathered, and frozen. I pried at the edges of the ice, and found I could lift out the top two inches, revealing clear water beneath. The ice was as thick as the glass of a submarine's window, and I held it to my eyes, and briefly watched the blurred world through it. Then I drank the sweet cold water beneath it, and set off down the mountain, picking my path through the steep uneven ground.

The shoreline forest, as I came back through it, was busy with birdsong. I felt tired, but did not want to sleep. Near the head of the lake, just downstream of a small stone-and-timber bridge, where the river widened, there was a deep pool, glassy and clear, banked by grass.

I sat on the grass, and watched light crimp on the water's surface, and flex on the stones that cobbled the stream-bed. I lay flat on the bank, rolled up my sleeve, and reached down to the bottom of the stream, where the water was weaving and unweaving the light, and picked a white stone, hooped once round with blue. I sat on the bank, holding the stone, and tried to list to myself the motions that were acting upon it at that moment: the earth's 700-miles-per-hour spin around its axis, its 67,000-miles-per-hour orbit about the sun, its slow precessional straightening within inertial space, and containing all of that, the galaxy's own inestimable movement outwards in the deep night of the universe. I tried to imagine into the stone, as well, the continuous barrage of photons – star photons and moon photons and sun photons – those spinning massless particles which were arriving upon the stone in their trillions, hitting it at 186,000 miles-per-second, as they were hitting me, and even with the stone still solid in my hand, I felt briefly passed through, made more of gaps than of joins.

I took off my clothes and waded into the water. It felt as though cold iron rings were being slid up my legs. Dipping down, I sat in the water up to my neck, huffing to myself with the cold. The current pushed gently at my back. I listened to the whistles and calls of a farmer, and saw sheep streaming like snow across the green fields on the lake's far shore. In an eddy pool a few yards downstream, between two dark boulders, the curved rims of sunken plates of ice showed themselves above the surface. The sun was now full in the eastern sky, and in the west was the ghost of the moon, so that they lay opposed to each other above the white mountains: the sun burning orange, the moon its cold copy.

In the first years of the nineteenth century, Samuel Taylor Coleridge fell into a depression deeper than any he would experience in his long and depressive life. Sick in body, and in love with a woman who was not his wife, he was brushed by what he called 'the dusky Wing' of melancholy.

He was at that time living in Keswick in the Lake District, and it was to the wild land surrounding his home that he turned for solace. He began to walk: alone, for increasingly long distances, regardless of the weather, and sometimes at night. Starting in the summer of 1802, and extending through to the winter of 1803, he went on a series of wild walks, each lasting several days, moving between the waterfalls, woods, crags and summits of the surrounding fells. He carried a green oilskin knapsack, into which he packed a spare shirt, two pairs of stockings, some paper and six pens, a copy of the poems of Voss, some tea and some sugar, and an improvised walking-stick, made by stripping the besom from a broom. As he walked, he studied intently the patterns made by the landscape: the behaviour of falling water, the cloud structures in the storm skies, the eddies of leaves disturbed by wind.

There was no obvious logic to the routes Coleridge chose to walk during that restless year: he went, on the whole, where inclination and chance took him. But one preoccupation does emerge out of the haphazardness – a fascination for waterfalls. If there was any purpose in his mind, it seems to have been to join up the waterfalls of the land around him; to walk between what he called these 'great water-slopes', and so make a waterfall map of the 'wild Heart of the mountains'.

Turbulence calmed Coleridge during these months. Storms settled him, the tumult of waterfalls stilled his worries. One day, up on the summit of Scafell, he was caught by a 'Thunder-shower', and took 'imperfect Shelter' in a sheepfold. He hunched behind one of its stone walls as the thunder crashed exhilaratingly about him. 'Such Echoes! O God! what thoughts were mine! O how I wished for Health & Strength that I might wander about for a Month together, in the stormiest month of the year, among these Places, so lonely & savage & full of sounds!'

On another day, in a 'hard storm of rain', he moved between several of the 'water-slopes' of the Lake District: Lodore Falls, Scale Force, Moss Force – waterfalls which he knew would be 'wonderful

Creature[s] . . . in a hard rain'. Reaching Moss Force, he found it in full cry, 'a great Torrent from the Top of the Mountain to the Bottom', and, watching those 'great Masses of Water' gout after one another into the chicane, they seemed suddenly to Coleridge to resemble 'a vast crowd of huge white Bears, rushing, one over the other, against the wind—their long white hair shattering abroad in the wind'. Lodore Falls appeared to him like 'the Precipitation of the fallen Angels from Heaven'. Some days later, still exhilarated, he sat in Greta Hall in Keswick, and wrote a letter to Sara Hutchinson describing his adventures. 'What a sight it is to look down on such a Cataract!' he exclaimed, '—the wheels, that circumvolve in it—the leaping up & plunging forward of that infinity of Pearls & Glass Bulbs—the continual change of the *Matter*, the perpetual *Sameness* of the *Form*.'

In the letters, poems and journal entries that Coleridge wrote over the course of those months, we can see him beginning to think out a new vision of the wild, a vision which at times approaches the level of a theology. One idea above all emerges: that the self-willed forms of wild nature can call out fresh correspondences of spirit in a person. Wildness, in Coleridge's account, is an energy which blows through one's being, causing the self to shift into new patterns, opening up alternative perceptions of life.

Unmistakably, the wild land of the Lake District acted for good upon Coleridge. As he moved between the crags and cataracts, over the fells and the moors, and through the pathless wilds, a sense of joy – joy, the 'beautiful and beauty-making power' as he had longingly called it during the dark spring of 1802 – began to seep back into him. Walking over soft mossy ground on the slopes of Red Pike – 'a dolphin-shaped Peak of a deep red' that rises to the south-west of Buttermere – he gave 'many a hop, skip, & jump'. Up on the mountains that year, he found not the 'Darkness & Dimness & a bewildering Shame, and Pain that is utterly Lord over us' which had characterised his depression, but instead a 'fantastic Pleasure, that draws the Soul along swimming through the air in many shapes, even as a Flight of Starlings in a Wind!'

The cold clear weather held for the day after my night walk over Red Pike. I had been reading Coleridge's letters, and so, inspirited by his vision of a waterfall map, I set off in the late afternoon for a valley south-east of Buttermere that held a long series of waterfalls.

I neared the waterfalls at dusk. Crows wheeled over the crags that flanked the valley, their backs showing an unexpected silver as they caught the last of the light. The land boomed with stillness. Standing water and moving water alike were frozen. Grass crunched brittlely underfoot. Here and there were big sycamores and oaks, their leaves candied with frost. Ice lidded the puddles on the path. I tapped at one with my foot, and the ice fractured like a mirror, falling in angled shards into the dry hollow beneath. Always to my left was the frozen river, the dusk light glaring off its ice. In such circumstances, the eye was grateful for any movement or colour: the faint indigo of the dusk sky, or a crow flying straight up the valley, black and intentful against the white land.

In this valley, that runs roughly from north to south, the river, gathering its water from the surrounding hills, falls 400 feet over the course of a mile, in a long cadence of waterfalls, rapids and pools. The river's action has bored millions of years down into the hard Ordovician rock to create plunge pools which froth when the water is running. In high winter, though, the river can freeze. That evening, the pools were plateaux of ice, finished with a white ceramic glaze. The rapids had set into a smooth milky flow, as though they had been photographed on a long exposure. The waterfalls had hardened into complicated bulbs and fists. Between the rocks on the river's banks, blue ice gleamed in webbed lines. Where the river dropped down over a rough ledge of worn rock, it had frozen into a glassy curve.

I had come to the valley that evening because I loved the river, and because I wanted to watch cold night fall from the valley's head. But as I walked further up the path, it occurred to me that the frozen river was itself a track: that there was no reason why on this rare night I could not use its glowing surface as my way.

Just north of a set of rapids, I stepped on to the ice, and began to move upstream, against the flow. In places where air had been trapped in the ice's making, it depressed gently, white cracks streaking radially out from beneath my feet, the ice settling down into its own narrow spaces and chambers, so that it seemed as if I were leaving wide stars when I walked. Where the river's slope steepened, I leaned forwards and steadied myself, using hands and fingertips to gain purchase on the ice, feeling the florets of this solid water. At the short steeper falls, I moved from rock to rock where it was possible, and where it was not, I went to the angled banks of the river, and found a way up there, before returning to the ice.

By the time I reached the lowest of the main falls, where the valley kinked round to north-north-west, the light was candling only the rowans which leaned from the upper crags. The valley had set into silver, black and white. The cold air burnt as I breathed it down into my body.

Up near where the falls began, on one of the last plateaux of ice, at the foot of a crag, I lay down and put my ear to the river's hard brim, and I could hear dark loose water glugging somewhere far beneath the surface. And when I put my eye to the ice and gazed down into it, I could just see formations of rods and quills, which caught the last light and concentrated it into bright spines and feathered cones, and between them I could also see numberless air bubbles, which in their silver chains resembled constellations.

11

Holloway

For months after the Cumbrian night walk, I was unable to travel, kept in Cambridge by work and my young daughter. I watched spring come and go in the city – crocuses bursting on the Backs, white cherries blossoming on the avenues, blackcaps singing their hearts out – frustrated not to be getting away, up to the Ribble and the Lune. I walked or ran up to the beechwood several times, and climbed my tree. Then one day in early June, Roger rang. I was pleased to hear from him, because I had been having some difficulty getting through to him at Walnut Tree Farm. Squirrels, he said. Squirrels had been the problem. His phone line had first gone crackly, then dead, and he had called in the engineers. The engineers had found that squirrels had been nibbling the phone line. Apparently, Roger explained, this was becoming quite a common occurrence. Squirrels are highly intelligent, agile enough to tightrope-walk along telephone wires, and poor conductors of electricity. Somehow they have realised that by biting through to the bare wires and short-circuiting the fifty volts that run through them into their own bodies, they can heat themselves up. In this way, said Roger, each squirrel becomes a sort of low-voltage electric blanket – and will sit up on the wires with a stoned smile for hours.

But the point of Roger's call, it eventually transpired, was to propose an expedition down to Dorset, in order to explore the holloway network of that county.

Holloway: from the Anglo-Saxon *hola weg*, meaning a 'harrowed path', a 'sunken road'. A route that centuries of use has eroded down into the bedrock, so that it is recessed beneath the level of the surrounding landscape. Most will have started out as drove roads, paths to market. Some as Saxon or pre-Saxon boundary ditches. And some, like the holloway near Bury St Edmunds, as pilgrim paths.

The oldest holloways date back to the early Iron Age. None is younger than 300 years old. Over the course of centuries, the passage of cartwheels, hooves and feet wore away at the floor of these roads, grooving ruts into the exposed stone. As the roads deepened, they became natural waterways. Rain drained into and down them, storms turned them into temporary rivers, sluicing away the loose rock debris and cutting the roads still further below the meadows and the fields.

Holloways do not exist on the unyielding rock regions of the archipelago, where the roads and paths stay high, riding the hard surface of the ground. But in the soft-stone counties of southern England – in the chalk of Kent, Wiltshire and East Anglia, in the yellow sandstone of Dorset and Somerset, in the greensand of Surrey and in the malmstone of Hampshire and Sussex – many holloways are to be found, some of them twenty feet deep: more ravine than road. They go by different names in different regions – bostels, grundles, shutes – but they are most usually known as holloways.

These holloways are humbling, for they are landmarks that speak of habit rather than suddenness. Trodden by innumerable feet, cut by innumerable wheels, they are the records of journeys to market, to worship, to sea. Like creases in the hand, or the wear on the stone sill of a doorstep or stair, they are the consequence of tradition, of repeated action. Like old trees – the details of whose spiralling and kinked branches indicate the wind history of a region, and whose growth rings record each year's richness or poverty of sun – they archive the past customs of a place. Their age chastens without crushing.

Gilbert White, in his *Natural History of Selborne* (1788), made a typically attentive study of the holloways in his Hampshire parish. 'Two rocky hollow lanes', he recorded, ran through the parish, 'the one to Alton, and the other to the forest'.

> These roads, running through the malm lands are, by the traffic of ages, and the fretting of water, worn down through the . . . freestone . . . so that they look more like water-courses than roads . . . In many places they are reduced sixteen or eighteen feet beneath the level of the fields; and after floods, and in frost, exhibit very grotesque and wild appearances, from the tangled roots that are twisted among the strata, and from the torrents rushing down their broken sides . . . These rugged gloomy scenes affright the ladies when they peep down into them from the paths above, and make timid horsemen shudder while they ride along them.

To enter these holloways, White said, was to access a world of deep history; an unexpectedly wild world, buried amid the familiar and close-at-hand. He visited his holloways in different weathers, to see how their moods altered with the changing climate. During the fiercely cold January of 1768, when the temperature in Selborne dropped to −34°C, and the leaves of laurel bushes were scorched brown by the cold, and when the snow fell thickly enough to fill the holloways, White observed how it there became sculpted by the wind into shapes 'so striking to the imagination so as not to be seen without wonder and pleasure'. When the sun shone that winter, reflected sunlight from the snow was bright enough to dazzle animals and birds. Poultry sat in their roosts all day long, stupefied into inaction by the land's lustre.

Few holloways are in use now: they are too narrow and too slow to suit modern travel. But they are also too deep to be filled in and farmed over. So it is that, set about by some of the most intensively farmed countryside in the world, the holloways have come to constitute a sunken labyrinth of wildness in the heart of arable England. Most have thrown up their own defences, becoming so overgrown by nettles and briars that they are unwalkable, and have gone unexplored for decades. On their steep damp sides ferns and trailing plants flourish: bright bursts of cranesbill, or hart's tongue, spilling out of and over the exposed network of tree roots that supports the walls.

I think of these holloways as being familial with cliffs and slopes and edges throughout Britain and Ireland – with the Cliffs of Moher in County Clare, or the inland prow of Sron Ulladale on the Isle of Harris, or the sides of Cheddar Gorge or Avon Gorge, where peregrines nest. Conventional plan-view maps are poor at registering and representing land that exists on the vertical plane. Cliffs, riverbanks, holloways: these aspects of the country go unnoticed in most cartographies, for the axis upon which they exist is all but invisible to the conventional mapping eye. Unseen by maps, untenanted by the human, undeveloped because of their steepness, these vertical worlds add thousands of square miles to the area of Britain and Ireland – and many of them are its wildest miles.

Dorset is rich in holloways: they seam the landscape cardinally, leaving the coast and moving northwards, uphill and inland, cutting into the Jurassic lias, the Permian sandstones and mudstones, the oolites and the chalks of the region. Along these routes dray horses, carts and carriages would have moved to and from the harbours and bays, supplying and evacuating the incoming ships. Roger had been tipped off by a friend of a Dorset friend about an especially deep and forgotten holloway, in which he thought we could begin our exploration: it was near the village of North Chideock, which lies in a small lush valley, cupped by a half-moon of low green rabbit-cropped hills, the horns of which rest upon the sea.

So on a hot July day, we set off for Dorset to see if we could find wildness amid the dairy farms.

We drove down in Roger's dark-green Audi, and as we left the outskirts of Cambridge I felt a lift of excitement at having escaped the city and at being on an adventure. The Audi had moss growing in its foot-wells, and in the grykes between the seats. 'Three different sorts,' he said proudly, when I pointed this out. In the glove-box were a variety of knives. The boot held, as it always did, a bivouac bag, a trenching tool of some sort, and a towel and trunks, in case he passed somewhere interesting to sleep, dig or swim.

We got lost several times on the way. When he was unsure of the correct exit to take on a roundabout, which was nearly always, Roger tended to slow almost to a halt, and squint up at the exit signs, while I assumed the crash position in the passenger seat.

We reached Chideock – a one-song drive west of Bridport – in the early afternoon, left the car, and began walking up along the village's main road, keeping where we could to the shade cast by the big green-gold laurel bushes which lapped at the road. The sun roared soundlessly in a blue sky. Hot light glared off every leaf and surface. Dust puffed up from the road wherever we stepped. There was the smell of charred stone.

Where the road ran to its end, we found an emblem for our adventure. Just to the east of the road, set back amid oak trees and laurel bushes, was a small Catholic chapel, built of pale sandstone in a Romanesque style. We pushed open a wooden gate, and walked down a leaf-strewn path to the chapel's porch. Its door was huge, of ridged oak, studded with black square-headed bolts. It opened with an ease that belied its weight, its bottom edge gliding above the flagstones of the porch, which were dipped by the passage of many feet.

The air inside the church was cool, and the sandstone of its walls and pillars was chilly to the touch. There was a faint odour of must, and everywhere the glint of gilt: saints in their niches, a golden altar rail, a gleaming candlestick at either end of the mensa. Striking through the air at angles were needles and poles of sunlight, sieved by the windows, in which dust motes rose and fell slowly, like gold leaf in warm water.

The Chideock Valley has a recusant past. After the Act of Supremacy in 1558, when Catholic priests were banned from Britain, missionaries began to re-infiltrate England in order to keep the faith alive. Chideock had long been a Catholic enclave, and several priests came to the area to offer clandestine ministry. A high-stakes game of hide-and-seek began. The priests went fugitive in the landscape, taking asylum in the woods, caves, copses and holloways of the area. Soldiers combed the countryside for them and their supplicants. Mass was held in secret in a hayloft in one of the Chideock farmhouses. Over the course of fifty years of this recusancy, at least three laymen and two priests were caught, tortured and executed. The chapel had been built in the nineteenth century as a memorial to these 'Chideock Martyrs'.

One of the priests, John Cornelius, had returned in secret to Chideock from Rome in order to act as chaplain to Lady Arundell, the lady of the manor. He was arrested at Chideock Castle on 24 April 1594, being dragged out bareheaded. A relative of the Arundell family, Thomas Bosgrave, was outside the castle that day, and in a spontaneous gesture of solidarity he offered Cornelius his hat. Bosgrave himself was immediately arrested, as were two of the castle servants, John Carey and Patrick Salmon, who were rightly suspected of having assisted Cornelius. Cornelius was taken to London, and tortured, before being transported back to Dorset. And on 4 July he, Bosgrave, Salmon and Carey were hanged in Dorchester. Carey was the first to ascend the scaffold, and before he died he kissed the rope, praising it as a 'precious collar'. Bosgrave delivered a brief and passionate address concerning the rectitude of his faith. Cornelius kissed the gallows, and uttered the words of St Andrew: 'O Cross, long desired', before praying for his executioners and for the queen. After hanging, the body of each man was quartered, and Cornelius's head was nailed to the gibbet.

We left the church's golden cool and set off up into the heat of the hills, to find and follow the holloways. Knowledge of the valley's violent past, of the priests who had gone to ground here for their faith, and the laymen who had died for it, had altered my sense of the landscape and of our adventure.

This was another unexpected change of atmosphere for my journeys: the cold exigent Protestant north had given way, via Ireland, to a sinuous southern Catholicism. In one sense, I thought, all of recusant Britain could be conceived of as a kind of holloway labyrinth: sunk down, almost unnoticeably, into the cultural landscape. In Lancashire, Aberdeenshire, parts of Dorset and Devon, and the other recusant heartlands, existed an alternative culture that was intensely British, but which possessed different strata of custom, language and history. That history was at once real, but also an *utinam*, an 'if only' history, and so it had to keep itself hidden, wild. Even London had its recusant holloways, of which vestiges remained: Tyburn, the shrine of Thomas More off Kingsway, the Bavarian Embassy chapel behind Piccadilly . . . many other recusant routes could still be traced through the city. I thought of a secret map of which I had been told, made by Jesuits around 1590, that showed the Catholic safe-houses in Scotland, and of which one leaf was in an archive in Rome, the second in Salamanca. There were also the Sheldon Tapestries, huge woven hanging maps of Gloucestershire, Oxfordshire, Berkshire, Worcestershire and Warwickshire, into which red threads had been discreetly insinuated to mark many known recusant hide-outs.

The path that Roger and I followed up into the hills was itself the beginnings of a holloway, cut down ten feet or more into the caramel sandstone of the area. Though no traffic other than walkers now passed this way, the road was still being deepened by water. Heavy rain had fallen the previous week, and the holloway floor bore evidence of the water rush that must have flooded it. Leaf and branch jetsam was tangled around tree roots, and here and there patches of smooth surface stone had been rinsed clean and exposed to the air, so that they lay glowing in their first sunlight for nearly 200 million years.

At some point in the history of the road, hedging trees had been planted to either side of it, partly to make way-finding easier in poor weather, and partly to provide shelter from the winds and sea storms that beat in off the English Channel. Over centuries, these hedges had grown, died, reseeded, grown again, and now, unchecked, they had thrust up and out and over the holloway.

One thinks of hedges as nothing more than bristly partitions; field Mohicans. But these hedges had become linear forests, leaning into one another and meshing above the old sunken road to form an interlocking canopy or roof, turning road into tunnel.

Near the summit of the western horn of the half-moon of hills, the road became so overgrown that we had to leave it. We scrambled up its steep eastern side, and into the pollinous air of the flower meadow that bordered it. I looked back over my shoulder, to where the sea lay blue. The heat bred mirages out over the water; false promises of islands and mountain ranges. A few hundred yards further along, in a gap in the hedge by a towering ash tree, we found a way back down into the holloway, and descended into its shadowy depth, abseiling down the sandstone sides using ivy as a rappel-rope. It felt as though we were dropping into a lost world, or a giant version of the gryke in the Burren.

Few people knew as much about hedges as Roger. The twelve acres of his land were separated into four meadows and a small wood by almost a mile of old hedgerow, laid out on a medieval pattern. In certain places – the brink of his woodland, the edge of his moat – Roger had laid his hedges into beautiful lateral structures, which tightened their own meshes as they grew. But mostly he had let the hedges run wild. In places, they had reached twenty feet high and fifteen feet wide. Elder,

maple, hazel and ash trees for the most part formed their central structures; dog rose, blackthorn and bramble billowed spikily outwards; and
bryony, honeysuckle and hop draped and wove themselves around
everything, giving the hedges differing densities and colours through
the year. So thick were some areas of hedge that elms grew there to an
uncommon height, protected from the death-carrying beetles by the
thicket of briars and roses. Elsewhere flourished sloes, crab-apples, hol-
lies, oaks and spindle trees. In autumn, the hedges produced hundreds
of pounds of fruit, which Roger would harvest.

Roger's hedgerows were exceptional, in the sense of rare. For thirty
years he had kept them and let them run to jungle, while on neigh-
bouring farms, mile after mile of hedgerow had been destroyed. Using
a series of old maps, he had researched the changing hedgerow extent in
his parish. In 1970, just after he moved to Walnut Tree Farm, he estimated there to be four miles of hedge within half a mile of his house,
excluding his land, and a total of thirty-seven miles of hedge in the
parish itself. Now only one and a half miles were left in his vicinity, and
no more than eight miles in the entire parish.

All this was a version in miniature of the hedgerow loss that occurred
across England in the decades after the Second World War. The drive to
maximise agricultural productivity, especially in cereals, meant that vast
areas of land – in the Midland and East Anglian shires in particular –
were opened out into increasingly large fields, for the bigger the field,
the more efficiently combine-harvesters and tractors were able to work
it. Farmers were financially encouraged to plough out the woodlands
and grub up hedgerows that divided their land. Nearly a quarter of a
million miles of hedgerow were lost during this conversion; 2,000 miles
are still being lost each year. On the Wessex Downlands and the Essex

marshes, hedgerow systems were destroyed in their entirety. And with the loss of the hedgerows came the loss of the wildlife that thrived in them: tree sparrows, grey partridges and corn buntings, among other species, were brought close to extinction.

Shortly before we left for Dorset, I had driven over to Walnut Tree Farm to plan the trip. That day, by way of rehearsal for our Dorset adventure, we went out exploring Roger's hedgerows. Walking the fields, we reached an unusually deep and thick area of hedge. Roger said he had seen a weasel emerge more than once from there, so we decided to try to crawl inside the hedge, to find what world it held. Pulling our sleeves up over our hands, we pushed under the first row of boughs, trying to avoid the biting blackthorns. A few yards in, we reached a natural hollow, where the trunks of the main trees rose, and we sat there, with our backs against a trunk, looking out into the meadow through the skein of briar and leaves, and listening to the life of the hedge. Paths through the leaf-litter around us testified to the hedge's interior as a high-use animal roadway.

'There is wildness everywhere,' Roger had written once, 'if we only stop in our tracks and look around us.' To him, the present-day and the close-at-hand were as astonishing as the long-gone and the far-afield. He was an explorer of the undiscovered country of the nearby.

Writing in 1938, the painter Paul Nash spoke of the 'unseen landscapes' of England. 'The landscapes I have in mind,' he wrote, 'are not part of the unseen world in a psychic sense, nor are they part of the Unconscious. They belong to the world that lies, visibly, about us.

They are unseen merely because they are not perceived; only in that way can they be regarded as invisible.' Nash found his archetype for these unseen landscapes in the Wittenham Clumps: a hill in Oxfordshire, ring-marked by Bronze and Iron Age earthworks, and topped by an eighteenth-century beech grove. The hill is little more than 300 feet high, and of gently sloping sides; the sort of landform over which your eye might easily slide. But for Nash the Clumps possessed a numinous beauty.

Perhaps it was the effect of my return to England, after the vast wild spaces of Scotland. Perhaps it was reading of Edward Thomas's walking tours, and looking at Palmer's mystical canvases. Perhaps it was living with my daughter Lily, and watching her intense scrutiny of a snail, or a mushroom or a patch of briar. Certainly, it was Roger's influence, and the glimpse into the gryke in the Burren: that miniature wildwood, no more than an arm's-length long and a hand's-span wide. Whatever the combination of causes, I had started to refocus. I was becoming increasingly interested in this understanding of wildness not as something which was hived off from human life, but which existed unexpectedly around and within it: in cities, backyards, roadsides, hedges, field boundaries or spinnies.

Certainly, these islands possessed wild places on massive scales – the Cairngorm massif is greater in area than Luxembourg, and its weather systems can be polar in their severity. But my original idea that a wild place had to be somehow outside history, which had failed to fit the complicated pasts of the Scottish and Irish landscapes, seemed even more improper in an English context. English wildness existed in the main as Nash's 'unseen landscapes': it was there, if carefully looked for, in the bend of a stream valley, in the undercut of a riverbank, in copses and peat hags, hedgerows and quicksand pools. And it was there in the margins, interzones and rough cusps of the country: quarry rim, derelict factory and motorway verge. I had not expected to find this when I had begun, had been all but blind to such places. But now a myopia was setting in, a myopia of a good sort, replacing the long-sight of the early northern and western journeys. Or a thawing of vision – perhaps that was a better way of thinking of it, now that summer had come.

That margins should be a redoubt of wildness, I knew, was proof of the devastation of the land: the extent to which nature had been squeezed to the territory's edges, repressed almost to extinction. But it seemed like proof, as well, of the resilience of the wild – of its instinct for resurgence, its irrepressibility. And a recognition that wildness weaved with the human world, rather than existing only in cleaved-off areas, in National Parks and on distant peninsulas and peaks; maybe such a recognition was what was needed 'to help us end the opposition between culture and nature, the garden and the wilderness, and to come to recognize ourselves at last as at home in both', as an American philosopher, Val Plumwood, had put it.

An artistic tradition has long existed in England concerning the idea of the 'unseen landscape', the small-scale wild place. Artists who have hallowed the detail of landscape and found it hallowing in return, who have found the boundless in the bounded, and seen visions in ditches.

William Blake perceived the world in a grain of sand. John Ruskin was captivated by the growth of lichens and mosses on trunks and rocks. Dorothy Wordsworth kept a series of elegantly attentive journals – the Alfoxden Journal, written when the Wordsworths were living in Somerset in 1797–8, and the Grasmere Journal, kept at Dove

Cottage from 1800–1803, whose precision of observation supports Wordsworth's allusion in 'Tintern Abbey' to his sister's 'wild eyes'. John Clare – from an early age a lane-haunter, a birds'-nester, a night-walker and a field-farer – wrote his artfully simple poems of praise for the landscape around his Northamptonshire home: poems that still carry the suddenness and surprise of the encounters he had during his years of countryside foray.

Over the summer of 1805, the young watercolourist John Sell Cotman spent nearly four months living at Brandsby Hall, north of York, where he was employed as drawing master to the four daughters of Mrs Cholmeley, the Hall's owner. During that time, Cotman began to explore the nearby landscapes: the rivers, fells and woodlands of Durham and North Yorkshire. He took his brush and colours, and went on foot, pushing further and further up the River Greta, and into the fell country near Kirkham. In this period, something remarkable happened to his painting. Cotman's fame had previously come from his grand subjects: Cadair Idris, Newburgh Priory, Durham Cathedral. But that summer, he became fascinated by the local, the small-scale: a drop-gate over a stream arm, a boulder beneath a bridge, a copse of trees, smoke rising discreetly above a river pool. The images he made in those months are subtly close-toned, attentive. He wrote to his patron Dawson Turner to explain that he had spent the summer chiefly 'coloring [*sic*] from nature', making 'close copies of that ficle [*sic*] Dame consequently valuable on that account'. He had been converted to the beauty of the parochial.

The late-Victorian writer Richard Jefferies spent much of his life studying and describing the rural southern counties of Wiltshire, Sussex, Gloucestershire and Somerset: counties that were, to Jefferies, teeming with wildness. Jefferies had no interest in the nineteenth-century North American idea of 'wilderness' on a grand scale – a phenomenon to be experienced only amid the red-rock citadels of the desert or the glacier-ground peaks. For Jefferies, wildness of an equal intensity existed in the spinneys and hills of England, and he wrote about those places with the same wonder that his contemporaries were expressing in their reports on the Amazon, the Pacific, the Rockies and the Rub al-Khali. He found wildness joyful, but also minatory; the vigour of natural wildness was to him a reminder of the fragility of human tenure on the earth. In 1885 he published *After London, or Wild England*, a futuristic fantasia set in the 1980s, by which time, following an unspecified ecological catastrophe, much of Southern England has been flooded, and London has been reclaimed by swamp, scrub and tree:

> Brambles and briars . . . met in the centre of the largest fields. Hawthorn bushes sprang up among them, and, protected by the briars and thorns from grazing animals, the suckers of elm-trees rose and flourished. Sapling ashes, oaks, sycamores, and horse-chestnuts, lifted their heads . . . and these thickets and the young trees had converted most part of the country into an immense forest.

Then there was Stephen Graham. Graham, who died in 1975 at the age of ninety, was one of the most famous walkers of his age. He walked across America once, Russia twice and Britain several times, and his 1923 book *The Gentle Art of Tramping* was a hymn to the wildness of the British Isles. 'One is inclined,' wrote Graham, 'to think of England as a network of motor roads interspersed with public-houses, placarded by petrol advertisements, and broken by smoky industrial towns.' What he tried to prove in *The Gentle Art*, however, was that wildness was still ubiquitous.

Graham devoted his life to escaping what he called 'the curbed ways and the tarred roads', and he did so by walking, exploring, swimming, climbing, sleeping out, trespassing and 'vagabonding' – his verb – round the world. He came at landscapes diagonally, always trying to find new ways to move in or through them. 'Tramping is a straying from the obvious,' he wrote, 'even the crookedest road is sometimes too straight.' In Britain and Ireland, 'straying from the obvious' brought him into contact with landscapes that were, as he put it, 'unnamed – wild, woody, marshy'. In *The Gentle Art* he described how he drew up a 'fairy-tale' map of the glades, fields and forests he reached: its network of little-known wild places.

There was an Edwardian innocence about Graham – an innocence, not a blitheness – which appealed deeply to me. Anyone who could sincerely observe that 'There are thrills unspeakable in Rutland, more perhaps than on the road to Khiva' was, in my opinion, to be cherished. Graham was also one among a line of pedestrians who saw that wandering and wondering had long gone together; that their kinship as activities extended beyond their half-rhyme. And his book was a hymn to the subversive power of pedestrianism: its ability to make a stale world seem fresh, surprising and wondrous again, to discover astonishment on the terrain of the familiar. My 1929 edition of his book was well bound in stiff board and green leather, with gold imprinted lettering. Its corners were bashed and its cover scuffed: it had clearly been in a lot of pockets and knapsacks before I acquired it.

That July day, as Roger and I dropped into the hazy light of our Chideock holloway, one of Graham's remarks came back to me. 'As you sit on the hillside, or lie prone under the trees of the forest, or sprawl wet-legged by a mountain stream, the great door, that does not look like a door, opens.'

Down in the holloway, the bright hot surface world was forgotten. So close was the latticework of leaves and branches, and so tall the sides of the holloway that light penetrated its depths only in thin lances. Roger and I moved slowly up the bed of the roadway, forcing a way through the undergrowth, through clumps of chest-high nettles, past big strongholds of bramble, and over hawthorns that had grown together, enmeshing across the roadbed. Occasionally we came to small clearings in the holloway, where light fell and grass grew. From thorn thickets, there was the scuttle of unseen creatures. Any noise we made thudded into the banks, and was lost. A person might hide out undetected in such a place for weeks or months, I thought.

Lines of spider's silk criss-crossed the air in their scores, and light ran like drops of bright liquid down them when we moved. In the windless warm air, groups of black flies bobbed and weaved, each dancing around a set point, like vibrating atoms held in a matrix. I had the sense of being in the nave of a church: the joined vaulting of the trees above, the stone sides of the cutting which were cold when I laid a hand against them, the spindles of sunlight, the incantations of the flies.

I would like to see a map that represented the country only according

to these old ways, and that was blind to the newer routes, to the roads
which take so little notice of the shape of the land through which they
pass. These old ways, these tradeworn cantons, tended to work round
woodlands, to follow the curve of a valley or the surge of a hill. They
existed in compromise with the land through which they passed. Many
of them had evolved from footpaths that had, both for ease of movement and ease of orientation, attended to the twisting courses of streams
and rivers, or the natural curves of rising and falling land. This relationship of accommodation between way and landform has now been
largely abandoned: bypasses and motorways strike through old woodlands and hillsides.

My own map was filling out, moving towards a state not of completion – it would never achieve that – but of coherence. I did not want it
to be definitive, only to have caught and absorbed something of the
places I had passed through, and something of how they had changed
me, brought me to think differently. Reading the French philosopher of
space and matter Gaston Bachelard, I had come across a paragraph
that summed up my hope for the journeys. 'Each one of us should
make a surveyor's map of his lost fields and meadows,' Bachelard had
written. 'In this way we cover the universe with drawings we have lived.
These drawings need not be exact. But they need to be written according to the shapes of our inner landscapes.'

Later, after our first exploration of the main holloway, Roger and I set
out on a wider reconnaissance of the area. Back at the old ash tree, using
exposed roots for handholds, and the ivy again for a rope, we climbed

up out of the road, and emerged into the lush meadow. After the greeny dusk of the roadbed, the meadow was startlingly bright. The grass blades flashed like steel in the sunshine. We stood blinking, wringing the light from our eyes.

That afternoon, we walked along the curved ridge of the hills that extended east and south of the holloway – Copper Hill, Denhay Hill, Jan's Hill. Sunlight skidded white off every surface. Everywhere we saw evidence of creatures taking refuge in the soil: mason bees, wasps, rabbits – successors to the fugitive priests. Where the sandstone was exposed, it was riddled with burrows of different sizes, with piles of ochreous silt marking the tunnelling work. There were networks of burrows through the gorsy undergrowth, too: miniature green holloways, no bigger in cross-section than a croquet hoop, which had been made by badgers. Following one such tunnel down into a steep copse, we found a badger metropolis. The animals must have been there for many generations, for the earthworks they had thrown up were substantial and long-term: ramparts, tumuli, barrows. I counted ten separate setts. Near the entrance to one of them lay a badger skull. I picked it up, saw the clamp-and-vice of its jaws, and the bulky orbit bones that protected its absent eyes.

As we walked, buzzards turned above us like spotter-planes. Once, a roe deer picked its way nervously into the middle of a field, until something startled it and it escaped in urgent, arched bounds. Hours later, as the air was hazing up, we returned to our holloway hide-out, dropping down by the old ash tree again into the near-darkness. We cleared nettles and briars, moved loose trunks to make seats, and then Roger built a fire to cook supper on – a pyramid of small sticks, with a hot centre of tinder, that produced an intense and almost smokeless fire. We ate a spicy tagine that Roger had made in advance and carried up with him. Firelight flickered off the walls of the holloway and on the hedge canopy above us, and set complicated shadows moving in the leaves. As we sat there in the thickening dark, talking, the day seemed to convene itself around the furnace-point of the flames.

Campfires prompt storytelling, and Roger, never slow to start a story, told me how he had once been shot at by a hunter in the Polish woods, because the hunter had thought he was a bear. The conclusion of the story, it turned out, was not Roger's outrage at having been fired on, but his delight at having been mistaken for an animal. Then we each read out bits from a copy of Geoffrey Household's classic 1939 novel, *Rogue Male*, in which the hero, pursued by Nazi agents, goes to ground in a Dorset holloway almost identical to our own. 'The deep sandstone cutting, its hedges grown together across the top, is still there,' Household had written, 'anyone who wishes can dive under the sentinel thorns at the entrance, and push his way through . . . But who would wish? Where there is light, the nettles grow as high as a man's shoulder; where there is not, the lane is choked by dead wood. The interior of the double hedge is of no conceivable use to the two farmers whose boundary fence it is, and nobody but an adventurous child would want to explore it.'

I chose to sleep not in the holloway itself, but in the deep grass of the upper meadow. I lay in the warm darkness, breathing in the scents of the field, brought out by the gentle dew that had settled after nightfall. I could hear the ongoing business of the meadow – the shifting of grass stalks, the shy movements of animals and insects – and again I felt a sense of wildness as process, something continually at work in the world, something tumultuous, green, joyous. This was a wildness quite

different from the sterile winter asperities of Ben Hope, and perhaps, I
thought for the first time, more powerful too.

I woke at dawn. The air was cool, but the sky was cloudless, and held
the promise of great heat to come. So Roger and I walked back down
the holloway, off the half-moon of hills, and past the chapel hidden in
the laurels. Then we drove to the coast – to Burton Bradstock, where a
pebble beach shelves steeply away from high sandstone cliffs.

The sea was already warm, so we swam straight away, backstroking
out for a hundred yards or so, and then treading the blue water. I
looked back at the ochre sandstone cliffs, and the green hills rising
behind them, and watched my arms and legs moving like phantom
limbs beneath the surface of the sea.

After the swim, we sat on the shingle, talking about Iris Murdoch,
who used to bathe off Chesil Bank, just along the coast, and about
Roger's friend Oliver Bernard, who had inadvertently managed to so
offend the owner of the public house on the nearby cliff-tops that he
had been obliged to run for his life. We gathered piles of flints, and
made Andy Goldsworthyish towers with them. Time passed languidly
in the heat. Roger went for another swim. I lay on the hot shingle,
watching overhead clouds, thinking about Cotman's paintings and
about Stephen Graham's map of his 'unnamed' wild places.

In so many of the landscapes I had reached on my journeys, I had
found testimonies to the affection they inspired. Poems tacked up on
the walls of bothies; benches set on lakesides, cliff-tops or low hill
passes, commemorating the favourite viewpoint of someone now dead;

a graffito cut into the bark of an oak. Once, stooping to drink from a
pool near a Cumbrian waterfall, I had seen a brass plaque set discreetly
beneath a rock: 'In memory of George Walker, who so loved this place.'
I loved that 'so'.

These were the markers, I realised, of a process that was continuously
at work throughout these islands, and presumably throughout the
world: the drawing of happiness from landscapes both large and small.
Happiness, and the emotions that go by the collective noun of 'happiness': hope, joy, wonder, grace, tranquillity and others. Every day, millions
of people found themselves deepened and dignified by their encounters
with particular places.

Most of these places, however, were not marked as special on any
map. But they became special by personal acquaintance. A bend in a
river, the junction of four fields, a climbing tree, a stretch of old
hedgerow or a fragment of woodland glimpsed from a road regularly
driven along – these might be enough. Or fleeting experiences, transi-
tory, but still site-specific: a sparrowhawk sculling low over a garden or
street, or the fall of evening light on a stone, or a pigeon feather caught
on a strand of spider's silk, and twirling in mid-air like a magic trick.
Daily, people were brought to sudden states of awe by encounters such
as these: encounters whose power to move us was beyond expression but
also beyond denial. I remembered what Ishmael had said in *Moby-
Dick* about the island of Kokovoko: 'It is not down in any map; true
places never are.'

Little is said publicly about these encounters. This is partly because
it is hard to put language to such experiences. And partly, I guessed,
because those who experience them feel no strong need to broadcast
their feelings. A word might be exchanged with a friend or partner, a

photograph might be kept, a note made in a journal, a line added to a letter. Many encounters would not even attain this degree of voice. They would stay unarticulated, part of private thought. They would return to people as memories, recalled while standing on a station platform packed tightly as a football crowd, or lying in bed in a city, unable to sleep, while the headlights of passing cars pan round the room.

It seemed to me that these nameless places might in fact be more important than the grander wild lands that for so many years had gripped my imagination. Taken together, the little places would make a map that could never be drawn by anyone, but which nevertheless existed in the experience of countless people. I began to make a list in my head of what would be on my own map of private or small-scale wild places.

There would be the 'Dumble', the steep-sided ditchway in Nottinghamshire, in which I had played with my brother when we were young. There would be the little birch grove near Langdale in Cumbria, whose trees I had climbed and swung between. There would be the narrow strip of broadleaf woodland at the base of the Okement valley in Devon, where I saw a blue-backed falcon slip from an oak and glide off out of sight – a merlin! Such a good guardian for such a magical place.

There would be the patch of moss – soft and intricate as a rug, starred with sea-pinks – on a North Cornish sea cliff, on which I had once spent a night. I had reached the cliff along the coastal path as the day ended, and there, a hundred feet above the breaking sea, I had found my sleeping place. It was just large enough to hold me, and it sloped back inland, so that I did not feel tipped out towards the cliff edge. I lay awake until midnight in my comfortable niche, watching the weather out over the Atlantic. It was a night of odd temperatures: the air cold enough for my breath to show white in it, but warm enough for lightning to gather and strike, bright wires standing again and again far out to sea, their light strobing on the cliffs around me.

There would be the little beach in the intricate terraqueous lands that lie on the southern flank of Suilven, in Sutherland. The beach was two yards wide and three long, made of finely milled yellow gravel, and near it an anonymous waterfall gave into an anonymous loch. The gravel showed deer-hoof prints, in which water welled like ink. It was summer, and at that latitude the northern light was fine and persistent. I washed under the waterfall, and then swam, looking back from the loch's centre at the bactrian form of Suilven. Later, I sat on the beach, when a red-breasted merganser cruised round a corner of the loch. It saw me, and watched me, and then dived, and its dive was almost rippleless, as if it had bored a hole in the water and slid down it beak-first.

And there would be the tree ring I came across by chance in Northumbria, on a summer day so hot that the air shimmered and bare rock was burning to the touch. It was a rough circle of old beeches, unmarked on the map, but within 500 yards of a main road. The earth within it was thick and soft with green moss and golden grass that had been closely cropped by rabbits. In Ireland it would have been called a rath, in Scotland a fairy-mound: Celtic folklore elected these tree circles as the doorways between the human world and the otherworld. Relatively few tree rings remain now; most have been ploughed out. I stepped into the cool shade of the ring, and lay there for half an hour, watching the business of the moor. When I left it, I walked south for two miles over heather, until I found a small black lake, near the edge of a spruce plantation, into whose sun-heated dark water I slipped, and in which my skin showed bronze, like the scales of a carp.

12

Storm-beach

Lying just off the Suffolk coast is a desert. Orford Ness is a shingle spit twelve miles long and up to two miles wide. It is unpopulated, and in its hundreds of grey acres, the only moving things are hares, hawks and the sea wind.

The Ness is the largest and strangest of the series of vast shingle peninsulas that jut from the coastlines of Norfolk, Suffolk, Essex and Kent. To its north are Scolt Head and Blakeney Point, and to its south is Dungeness, the fulcrum on which the North Sea pivots into the English Channel. These spits are created by the action of tides, currents and seasonal storms. Like sand dunes, they are in continual slow migration, forming and reforming their shape as they shift. In their movement, they are as close to organism as anything only mineral can be. Their shingle is made mostly from flint, which lies about in its several forms: big chunks, white and bulbous like knuckle bones, or long translucent bars, shiny and nubbed as the skin on an alligator's back.

There is an exquisite patterning to the structure of these spits. They organise themselves in designs so large that they are best witnessed from the vantage of a falcon or an airman. At Dungeness, the shingle is arranged into giant floreate blooms. Orford forms itself in long parallel ridges, each of which marks a time when a storm cast up thousands of tonnes of gravel along the shore, and fattened the spit. These ridges are the stone equivalents of growth rings in a tree trunk. Aerial images of Blakeney show it to possess the complex beauty of a neuron: the long stem of the spit, and to its leeward a marshland that floods and emerges with every tide – a continually self-revising labyrinth of channel and scarp.

Wave and tidal action will always tend to round things off if they are soft enough. This is as true of a peninsula of several hundred square miles as it is of a stone or piece of sea-glass. Millennia of oceanic massage have given East Anglia its humpish outline, from which the spits strike out. The contrast between the north-western and south-eastern coasts of mainland Britain could not be more marked. On the north-west the long fingers of peninsula and sea lace intricately – a handclasp speaking of pax between rock and water. On the bulge of Norfolk, Suffolk and Essex, however, the land is constantly ceding to the sea, or weaving with it. There is an eeriness to these littorals, born of their perpetual motion, and the dialogue between solid and liquid.

On a hot summer afternoon, I travelled to the East Anglian coast to see these shingle deserts. My aim was to join up some of the spits: to draw a wild ley-line down the coast, from Blakeney through to Orford and perhaps beyond. I was following, too, I realised, a geological logic, or a geo-logic: in my journeys, I had moved down a gradient of mineral resilience – from the igneous coastline of Coruisk and the volcanic north-west, through the soluble limestone of the Burren, down to the sandstone and chalk of the holloway counties, and now to these transient and fraying south-eastern edgelands.

I had begun to think that the history of Britain and Ireland could be well comprehended through the history of its six great rock types – granite, sandstone, slate, chalk, limestone and flint. There were others, of course: basalt, shale, the clays. But these six rocks, it seemed to me, formed the strong mineral skeleton of the archipelago. Whatever we did to the skin of the country, the skeleton would remain.

I reached Blakeney on a warm late-summer afternoon. Big drogue-shaped clouds hung in a blue sky. Above them was a lattice of cirrostratus, hinting at weather trouble to come. A steady wind blew onshore, scouring the face and drying the skin.

I stepped down on to the gravel of the spit, and began the crunching walk out along the spit's four miles. Blakeney is a terrain of extended lines: the gleaming ridges of the gravel ramparts, the water's edge, the wrack, all sweeping away to a distant coincident point. The spit possesses the firm perspectival vision of an Uccello painting, guiding the eye towards its limits.

Only a few hundred yards along, I lay down on the warm dry shingle, and sighted the spit's summit ridge off ahead of me. I looked along it at pebble level, over the gleaming stones, each of which held an ember of the afternoon's abundant light. Scattered here and there were walkers, making dark uprights in this horizontal landscape.

Inland, a big wood fire, burning out of sight, was hazing the air above the marshes, thickening the sky between me and the mainland. Only the simpler shapes of the land were visible: a windmill, a four-square church tower, oak trees, pines. I could hear children's voices and laughter, carrying over the marsh. Ahead of me, two swans were trying to beat out to sea, but the wind was so strong that they were making no advance at all, beating and beating and remaining still. With the loud wooden creaking of their pinions, and their stasis, they seemed like early flying machines being tested in a wind tunnel.

Then a skein of twenty or so wild geese flew inland over my head, the slow Doppler of their honking causing me to look up. As they flew they formed and reformed the pattern of their arrangement, first as an arrowhead, then a horseshoe, and then back to an arrowhead. A single white goose flew just off the nose of the arrow. Thousands of feet above the geese two Tornado jets, out on manoeuvres from RAF Marham, played. Both planes tilted sideways in unison to show their full hawk-ish silhouette – raked back wings, biro-top nose – while their contrails disintegrated behind them.

After an hour of walking, I stopped and hollowed out a seat in the gravel. I sat, watched the sea, drank some water, and picked up flint pebbles. They were beautiful stones to hold. Each was differently pat-terned. Some wore a mesh of chatter lines, like the craquelure of old oil paint. Some had cortical furrowings. Others were patterned with swirls of sediment and colour – cream, blue, beagle-brown – which resembled map-markings, indicating borders, coastlines, islands, seas, and they reminded me of pelts of the Enlli seals.

I got up and walked along, scanning the shingle for the best of these mapstones. Near the water's edge, I found a white flint egg that wore a rough blue map of the spit itself, and a big whelk, bleached chalk-white by salt and sun, hollowed and smashed so that the spiral construction of its interior was visible: a central post about which the shell chamber helixed.

Then, a mile or so further on, as though summoned or anticipated by the barnacle geese's airborne cuneiform, I found an arrowhead. A small one, two inches long, with gently convex outer sides, so that it sat well in the palm of my hand. There must have been something about its form, some indication of its workedness by hand, that caught my eye, lying as it was among those millions of other stones shaped by the sea. At its base it was the blue-black of storm-cloud, a colour that changed to grey towards the head's point. I held it, wondered what other hands had touched it in the thousands of years since it was knapped out. I slipped it into my pocket. I would keep it, I thought, for a year or two, before returning it to the same shore.

Two miles further out along the spit, on the sand plains that stretched away to its seaward side, I reached the hull of a big wooden boat, sunk deep and permanently into the hard sand. The curved lateral timbers of the hull, weed-hung and blackened from unnumbered submersions, stood up like the ribcage of some great beast. Around it, the hard-packed sand was set into ripples, which repeated their own patterns on smaller and smaller scales. I thought of the optical effects of the limestone pavements in the Burren, and also of the sand desert of Forvie, on the coast above Aberdeen: a Saharan zone of the far north, where the dunes were so extensive that you could walk within them for three hours, and their migration so relentless that they had overwhelmed a village.

The old hull was sunk within a hollow of its own making and keeping, eight or nine feet deep, filled with water that had been left behind by the last tide. It lay as a clear brimming pool. I took my clothes off and slipped into it. The water had been simmered all day in the sun, and was warm as a bath. Florid cabbage-like seaweeds grew from the timbers, red and green in colour, and translucent gobies, disturbed by my arrival, darted about: the pool was busy with life. I sank down, until the water ringed my neck, and kept myself buoyant with flutterings of my hands. Looking around, I could see only the gravel ramparts of the spit, and the North Sea, and I watched as wave after wave began its spiralling break on to the shore, and gravel was churned in the base of each wave and then flung from its curling summit.

Natural forces – wild energies – often have the capacity to frustrate representation. Our most precise descriptive language, mathematics, cannot fully account for or predict the flow of water down a stream, or the movements of a glacier or the turbulent rush of wind across uplands. Such actions behave in ways that are chaotic: they operate according to feedback systems of unresolvable delicacy and intricacy.

But nature also specialises in order and in repetition. The fractal habits of certain landscapes, their tendencies to replicate their own forms at different scales and in different contexts: these can lend a near-mystical sense of organisation to a place, as though it has been built out of a single repeating unit.

The Dakotan tribes of North America found evidence of circular forms in nature nearly everywhere, from the shape of birds' nests to the course of the stars. The Pueblo Indians of the American south-west, by contrast, tended to apprehend landscapes in rectangular terms: they found parallelograms and rhomboids to be ubiquitous – a form which they almost certainly derived from the regular dihedral shapes into which the red rock of the south-western deserts erodes. Jonathan Raban has written beautifully about how the recurring unit of the art of the Indians of the British Columbian coast is the lozenge, which he relates to the distinctive shape into which light forms when it falls on gently moving water.

Britain and Ireland have produced their own versions of this natural monadism, this obsessive hunting after singularity in nature. Thomas Browne, in his slender work of 1658, *The Garden of Cyrus*, proposed that the 'quincunx', the disposition of five items with four at the corners of a square and the fifth in its centre, existed with such ubiquity that it ought properly to be considered the figure upon which the universe was constructed. Browne found the quincunx repeating itself throughout natural and artificial forms – in five-leaved flowering plants, and in astral motion – and took it as hermetic proof of a Universal Spirit of Nature. In 1917, the mathematician and biologist D'Arcy Wentworth Thompson published an elegant book, *On Growth and Form*, in which he proposed that the form of the spiral had its play throughout the natural world: in seashells, spiderwebs, the distribution of seeds in the head of a daisy, the curve of a beaver's tooth, the turns of a narwhal's horn and an elephant's tusk, in a pine-cone's configuration of scales, and in the curve of a sea wave as it broke.

As I had travelled, I had become increasingly interested in these monadists, these fearsome concentrators. Roger had told me about his friend John Wolseley, a British-born artist who had become obsessed by the dunes of the Australian deserts, and who in 1991 had spent eight months in the Simpson Desert, trying to map and comprehend the dunes and their shifting sedimentary histories. I had also heard of a contemporary photographer called Kevin Griffin, who for years had been taking images of the Atlantic waves that crash into Dun Loughan Bay in Galway. Griffin's method was to stand in the surf with a camera strapped to his chest, its focal length preset to seventy centimetres, waiting for what he called a 'well-shaped wave' to appear: his images were taken at the instant before the strike of the wave. Immersion, involvement, these were Griffin's fascinations, and they had cost him several broken ribs and near-drownings. Still he continued his project, trying to fathom the behaviour of incoming water along a 200-yard stretch of a single Irish beach.

The oddest and most wonderful monadist of all, though, I came across quite by chance. Finger-walking the shelves of a library one morning, I discovered the books of a man called Vaughan Cornish. In 1895 Cornish had moved into a small house on the Dorset coast near Poole, the precise location of which I was not able to establish. During his years there, Cornish became beguiled by the waves that fell upon the beach beneath his garden. 'Every day,' he recalled in a memoir written near the end of his life:

> the waves of the sea – beautiful, mysterious and insistent – drew me more and more to the path on the cliff whence I could watch them curl and break, and listen to their splash upon the sandy shore. I stood there on the afternoon of a calm day in early autumn at the time of low water of a spring tide. The little waves, gliding slowly in over the flat sands, bent round the ends of a shoal, as waves of light are refracted, and, meeting, passed through each other, each to continue its own course.

Over several years of observation, Cornish convinced himself that the wave was the key to all geographies. So committed was he to the proving of this idea that he sold his home on the south coast, and became instead an itinerant explorer-geographer, moving between wild places, where he could dedicate himself to the pursuit, refinement and proof of his theory. 'I wandered abroad,' he wrote, 'among sandhills, and snow-drifts, explored amphibiously the sandbanks of estuaries, measured waves in storms at sea, timed the throbbing surge of torrents, the heaving of whirlpools, and the drumming thunder of waterfalls.' He sailed out into tempests in the Atlantic Ocean and on Lake Superior in order to observe the formal clash of gale-driven waves. He followed storm surges down the Ure, the Swale and the Tees, tracking the generation of 'roll waves'. He worked often at night and during full moons, in order to catch the right tides to make his measurements, and this research brought him into dangerous situations: out on the sand-flats of estuaries at Morecambe and Southend, for example, where the sea could come in subtly and swiftly. In January 1907, he happened 'by good fortune' to be in Kingston, Jamaica, when an earthquake struck the town. He ran out of the house in which he was staying and 'mapped the seismic waves that traversed the island'.

Over the years, Cornish published widely on the wave form – *Waves of the Sea and Other Water Waves* (1910), *Waves of Sand and Snow* (1914) and *Ocean Waves and Kindred Geophysical Phenomena* (1934) among his books – and he gave a name to the science he had devised: 'kumatology', from the Greek word for 'wave', *kumas*. The study of kumatology, Cornish wrote, had led him 'by an untrodden path to the Land of the Unknown. In this country, there are no sign-posts to direct the traveller, no roads for him to follow, no maps to show him how to shape his course . . . But it is a delightful land, and its call is like the call of the wild.'

I read Cornish's books with increasing wonder at this man, whose eye was so attuned to the wave form that he could see it everywhere, and with increasing fondness for him: his monomania, the way his vision hovered partway between spirituality and hard science. Cornish perceived affinities between phenomena that one would never usually think to connect. He pointed out similarities between the movement of steam quitting a chimney, the arrangement of water-weed tresses in a stream, the way fallen leaves drift before the wind, the composition of quicksand, the rippled cloud effect called 'mackerel' sky, the body-shapes of fish and cetaceans, the wings of birds, and the cahots or undulating tracks that were made by the procession of sledges or carriages over snow or mud. His curiosity was exemplary. Why, he wanted to know, did flowing water create transverse ripples of sand, hard under foot, like the ridges in a cassock? He developed his own esoteric vocabulary for describing his wave forms: he named the 'entrance' and the 'run' of wave-drifts of snow or sand, terms he took from naval architects' language for the swelling fore-part and narrowing after-part of a ship. He was particularly interested by what he called the 'eddy-curve' – the complex form of drift, with a blunt head and a fine tail, that was produced in snow, sand or any other non-liquid particular matter by the effect of a current moving against a fixed obstacle.

Sand became Cornish's preferred substance of study, and he wrote about it with a lyrical intensity that remains moving to read. At Aberdovey, he found dunes that in their 'crescentic form' approximated an 'Aeolian sand-hill, the mound having two arms or horns similar in shape to the cusps of a four-days-old moon'. Such dunes, he noted, had a family resemblance with the *barchan* dunes of the Taklamakan Desert in Central Asia, and with the *medao* dunes of the Peruvian deserts. Back in Dorset, in the 'loose dry sand of the sea-shore between

Branksome Chine and Poole Haven', he studied how sand formed into ridges and ripples around marram grass, and he photographed these shapes obsessively.

Once, Cornish lay down among a range of small dunes, and looked upon them for so long that, with only a depthless blue sky above him, he lost all sense of scale and of era:

> The steep slopes, the sharp arêtes, and the pyramidal peaks of the sand-dunes stood out with an intensity of light and shadow which, combined with uniformity of tint, was more like lunar scenery as viewed with a telescope than any terrestrial landscape which I had hitherto seen. The slopes of the dunes were smooth and unspotted, and in the absence of detail or of objects of known size there was nothing to provide a scale of magnitude. With a low sun, which threw dark, long shadows, the dunes, with their bold, mountainous forms, loomed immense, and an unbiased observer might easily have supposed their height to be thousands of feet.

Anyone who has spent prolonged time in deserts will recognise Cornish's experience: the swift vertiginous loss of scale, the sudden Alice-like shrinking of the self. This can happen elsewhere. Stare for long enough at the surface of a granite boulder in the Mamores, and it will come to seem a mountain range in itself. Several times in the course of my journeys, I found myself affected in this way by the self-similarity of the landscapes through which I was passing, drawn into illusions in which my sense of scale was thrown, and it seemed that I might be able to enter a bird's nest, or the bole of a tree, or pass into the curled lustrous chamber of a whelk, following the whorl of its chamber round, keeping a hand pressed to its shining surface, searching for its top-most spire.

I reached the far tip of Blakeney Point, four long shingle miles out, as dusk was falling. Sea on three sides of me, the air going grainy, and the wind pushing down to my lungs if I turned to face it. Beached in the scrubland of salt marshes inshore from me was the wreck of a small trawler, big rusted anchor-chain holes staring seawards. This far out along the spit, gravel had given way to sand: blond dunes, bound together by mint-green marram grass. In the offshore wind, each long slim blade of grass had leaned over and inscribed a portion of a perfect arc in the sand with its sharp tip, like the pencil arm of a compass.

To the north, across a tidal channel down which the sea was running fast, was a big sand shoal, a hundred feet or so across. Scattered over it were seals, common seals, hundreds of them. Some were lounging in the last sun, their tails and heads bent upwards so that they rocked gently on the braced curve of their own bodies, like weeble toys. Others were hauling themselves towards the channel, slid off the sandbank into the deeper water with a wallop and a splash. The wind carried their pungent marine scent to me; raw fish and wet dog.

The tide was running faster and faster, clapping and chopping aggres-sively in the channel, overwhelming the sand bars. Behind me, in the darkness, I knew it would be snaking coldly through the dunes over which I had walked earlier, infiltrating the channels and miniature bars, and beginning to submerge the old ribs of the hull by which I had bathed.

As the sun dropped beneath the horizon, I found an inclined sand dune, with a flat sloping side, a couple of square yards in area, tufted with marram grass at its summit. There I arranged flint pebbles in the form of the organising patterns of the day: the cross-hatch and the spiral. I found blue stones, the same colour as diesel smoke, and bleached chalk-white stones, and laid them into a double helix, white coiling with blue, which resembled the cloud formation that was at that moment shaping in the sky. Then I returned to a deep hollow between two dunes that I had seen earlier – a gentler southern version of the dune nook on Sandwood Bay – and settled into my sleeping-bag for the night.

As full darkness was falling, a gun boomed along the coast. The birds had begun to move inshore. They came in their dozens, mixed geese and ducks pouring back to their roosts on marshes and flashes. They flew in groups and letter-sets over my dune hollow, moving fast and softly, often passing just a few yards above me, unaware of my presence. These were stealth-fliers, making the transition from predatorless sea to hazardous land, coming in low to avoid danger. Sometimes all I could hear of an incoming group was the tweeting of their wings. Against the dark sky they were visible only as silhouettes. Occasionally the birds sensed me even in the darkness, for they veered off, honking their alarm, and banking from side to side. Some went over so fast that I did not even see them, only heard a squeak and a rush of displaced air, and looked up to see unbroken sky, and a young horned moon.

For an hour or so this fast traffic went on. Then, as the day's last light drained back over the horizon, the flow of birds slowed. Suddenly, it was so dark that I could barely make out the distinction between black sky and black sea to my north. Only the bright lights of distant fishing

trawlers roved slowly back and forth along the horizon, like big com-
bines harvesting the dark, indicated the division between the two.

Putting a hand down to my side, I could feel that a small rim of
wind-blown sand had already built up against me: the beginning of a
dune which would overwhelm me if I were to lie here for long enough.
The rough blades of marram grass skittered quietly against one another.
The honks of the sleeping seals drifted down to me, familial and
soporific. There was the chatter of dinghy lanyards clacking on metal
masts, from the boats moored in the marshes, tittle-tattling to one
another. I fell asleep to these noises, and the drum-talk of the waves.

I slept fitfully, and woke at six, with a pain in my back from the sand,
which under the weight of my body had compressed to the hardness of
concrete. The tide had sluiced up to within thirty feet of my bed, and
the seals' sandbank was submerged. A set of human footprints, which I
was sure had not been there last night, passed just behind my head in
the sand. But the wind had vanished. The sea was placid, sheeny. A thin
band of mist hovered a foot or so above it. It was a mysterious place to
come awake.

In the long silky dawn light, I crunched back over the rinsed shingle,
calling out good morning greetings to the seals, who followed me cheer-
ily in the shallows, bobbing up and down, or disappearing into the
undersea. I passed two dead crabs, lying on their backs, claws locked
behind their heads, pale stomachs presented to the dawn, like a couple
of early sunbathers. Dunlin were out in flocks of twenty or thirty, peck-
ing through the esoteric debris of the wrack-line. Whenever I got within
ten yards or so of them, they would lift off and fly down the beach as a
single whirring flock, their wings making the soft flutter of riffled paper.

Even this early groups of people were on the beach, here and there, staring out to sea, drawn by the sense of being at the salt edge of things. Most were bird-watchers, sitting in fold-out shiny canvas director's chairs, binoculars pressed to their eyes, watching the dawn arrivals pelt in from the sea. An hour later, only a few hundred yards from where the spit joined back to the land, I walked past an elderly man in a deckchair, its legs sunk into the gravel, a tartan rug tucked around him to keep him warm, staring out to sea, as if waiting for an armada to come.

From Blakeney, I drove south along the coast, and inland to Walnut Tree Farm. Roger cooked me breakfast while I told him about my night on the Point, and then he picked fresh mint from the clumps that grew in profusion outside his front door, and we drank cups of mint tea, sitting by the moat in the early light. Then we drove on together to Orford Ness.

In the eleventh and twelfth century, Orford was a thriving port, protected from the North Sea by the comforting arm of the Ness. Then that arm turned murderous. Over the course of several centuries – accurate time-telling is difficult with regard to these shingle formations – it extended down the coast, and strangled the port. Without the flushing action of regular tides, which were deflected by the Ness, the harbour silted up, making it impossible for deep-bellied ships to reach the quays. Orford was turned into a small-boat harbour only, dead to trade.

The weather had been deteriorating since we left Walnut Tree Farm; the yellow dawn of Blakeney curdling into a sour grey day. To reach the Ness you must be ferried across the River Ore. As we stepped from the ferry on to the pontoon on the Ness's shore, it was clear that the Ness was in a wild state. The tide was incoming, and brown currents swirled beneath the pontoon, making it squeak and shift. The easterly wind had strengthened. Looking across the Ness from the pontoon, it was impossible to tell where brown desert gave way to brown sea. The horizon was lost, dissolved into a single rolling beige of shingle, sea and sky. Two Harriers blasted overhead, moving due south, leaving a sandpapery roar in the air. We set off to walk the spit.

For eighty years the Ness was owned by the Ministry of Defence, which prized its natural security cordon as well as its uniformity and expanse. So it was that like many other larger deserts – the Great Victoria in Australia, the Kizil Kum in Kazakhstan, the Mojave Desert in America – the Ness became a site for ordnance testing. Bomb ballistics and weaponry experiments were conducted on the Ness during the First and Second World Wars, and in the 1960s, nuclear detonation devices were trialled in specially built concrete structures now known as the Pagodas. In big concrete halls, the Ness military scientists would stand British fighter planes, and then fire enemy bullets at them from fixed cannon, attempting to locate weak points, and to see how the planes could be better armoured.

All across the Ness, enigmatic military structures still protrude from the shingle – pre-fabricated barracks, listening stations, beacons, watch-towers, bunkers, explosion-chambers. Unexploded ordnance still lies around. It is forbidden to step off certain cleared pathways through the shingle, which have been made safe, and marked out with a rust-red dye and blood-red arrows. By the sides of the pathways we were following lay military debris: twisted sprays of tank tracking, a shattered concrete block, and an exploded boiler, whose inch-thick iron casing had flared into bright rusted thick petals: warnings not to stray.

It is hard to be on the Ness, and not feel its militarising influence upon one's vision. That day, everything I saw seemed bellicose, mechanised. A hare exploded from a shingle divot. Bramble coiled and looped like barbed wire. Geese landed with their undercarriages down. Green and orange lichen camouflaged the concrete of pillboxes.

Roger and I walked out to the mid-north of the Ness, halfway between its inner and outer coasts, and there we climbed up on to the roof of the Bomb Ballistic Building, a black chunky structure which had been used for observing the fall of ordnance from planes. From the summit of the building, we gained a harrier's-eye view of the Ness – or a Harrier's-eye view. To our west, cupped on its landward coast, were salt-meres: Lantern Marshes, Kings Marshes. To the north was the gleaming puffball of Sizewell B, oddly bright on this overcast day. Disappearing into the southern haze was the Ness's distal point, probing ever further down the coast – a thin finger indicating the way to Dungeness. And to the east was the outermost edge of the Ness, where its grey-brown stone shaded into the grey-brown water.

Laid out below and around us, much as it would have appeared to the First World War bomb-watchers, was the main expanse of Ness. Seen from this height, the landscape's own logic became more apparent. There were the longitudinal shingle ridges running and curving its full length – the Ness's storm-born growth rings. Cutting across these were other less regular ridges, made by the vehicles of the bomb-disposal teams. These were the marks of the clean-up operation; of the desert's decontamination. The man-made lines and the storm lines swooped and arced and intersected with one another, to create a single vast fingerprint of shingle, stretching as far as I could see.

Vaughan Cornish died almost unknown, his work on the wave form dismissed as cranky. One person, though, would encounter Cornish's work, and would build on it to become a pioneer in the analysis of the behaviour of particulate matter.

Ralph Bagnold fought as a young man on the Western Front, and then returned to England to train as an engineer. In the 1930s, stationed in Egypt, he led expeditions into the sand seas of Libya, and became fascinated by the abstract beauty of that arid world. Above all, he was interested in the migrations of the Libyan dunes – their slow martial processes of advance and retreat. To Bagnold, the dunes seemed to possess the wilful unpredictability of living beings. He loved, too, the eerie song of the dunes, made when wind played in a certain way on the sand slopes. This song had haunted his Libyan evenings; at times the dunes would emit a low-pitched sound so penetrating that normal speech could be heard only with difficulty. As he travelled more between deserts, he began to catalogue the different songs of the sand: the high keening of the slipfaces of the Libyan sword dunes, and the 'white roaring' of the Kalahari sands.

Bagnold was compelled by the contradictory properties of sand grains. He wanted to know how it was that loose, dry, uncemented grains of sand could settle so firmly against one another that a loaded lorry driven across the surface of the sand would make tracks less than an inch in depth; but that sand grains of the same consistency could form pools of dry quicksand, fluid and deep enough to swallow that same loaded lorry.

His engineer's mind engaged by the behaviour of the sand, Bagnold began to delve into the scientific literature surrounding its properties. What he found was that almost no work had been done, apart from that of Vaughan Cornish, on the physics of dune formation or sand structures. It was true that the dunes had been named and described, making an austere litany of names – *erg, seif, barchan* – and that their forms and habits were known; the star dunes that built and spread out from a still centre, the *seif* dunes that drifted in linked chains miles long, the *barchan* dunes, crescent-shaped and showing their outer curves to the wind. But beyond this, nothing. Empty territory.

So Bagnold began to investigate the topic. The physics involved in the analysis of the dunes was formidably complex. One had to map and anticipate the turbulence patterns of the wind, even before one tried to understand how the sand grains themselves – each of a different weight and shape – behaved within the flows of the wind. Only a brilliant obsessive could have taken on the subject.

Bagnold was such a man. Working by night, he held candles in the slipfaces of the dunes – their 'undercliffs' – in order to determine the 'wind regimes' that controlled the behaviour of sand there. In the heat of the day, he walked for miles through what he called 'the streets' – the corridors of low ground that the dunes preserved between themselves, even as they moved – and he walked along the fine lines of the trailing wing-tips of *barchan* dunes, which reached up to ninety feet high. In an effort to determine the different possible liquidities of quicksand, he took to jumping up and down on the surface of the firmer pools, and recorded that such leaps could make 'a real circular wave radiate outwards for several metres in the undulate sand'. In prose of beautiful precision, Bagnold catalogued the dunes and the physics of their behaviour: their serpentine crests, their rounded windward shoulders, and their steep leeward slipfaces, 'where the slope of the dune surface reaches the limit of steepness imposed by the angle of shear of the deposited material'.

When Bagnold returned to England from North Africa in 1935, he retired from the army, built a wind tunnel for himself, and began a decade's worth of intricate experiments into the physics of blown sand. He found himself occupying a physical universe of exquisite formality, in which dunes travelled before the wind, preserving their individuality by an equality of loss and gain of their component sand-grains.

The massive accumulation of minute particulars: this was Bagnold's method of study, and it could not have been more appropriate to his subject. This was science as devotion. Information, for Bagnold, was not a way to summarise and therefore reduce or close down the desert landscape, but instead a way to make it more astonishing. Science, for him, refined the real into a greater marvellousness.

In 1941, Bagnold published his findings as *The Physics of Blown Sand and Desert Dunes*. William Langewiesche rightly describes the book as 'a small masterpiece of scientific exploration', the consequence of Bagnold's love-affair with sand. 'Instead of finding chaos and disorder,' Bagnold wrote of the desert:

the observer never fails to be amazed at a simplicity of form, an exactitude of repetition and a geometric order unknown in nature on a scale larger than that of crystalline structure. In places vast accumulations of sand weighing millions of tons move inexorably, in regular formation, over the surface of the country, growing, retaining their shape, even breeding, in a manner which, by its grotesque imitation of life, is vaguely disturbing to an imaginative mind.

Late that afternoon, Roger and I reached the furthest seaward point of the Ness, the point at which the coast crooked and the peninsula began its slow sharpening away southwards. The sea had thrown up a ten-foot-high rampart of wet shingle. We scrambled down it, the stones hissing and slithering under our feet, and walked along the tideline for half a mile, picking up pieces of wood, comparing flints, finds. We discussed the driftwood, tried to imagine the story of each stick or shard; where it had floated from, which river had washed it down to which sea. Roger could tell the wood-type of each curled or flattened piece: a waterlogged oak plank; an ash shard that had the brittle texture of cuttlefish bone; even a rare spiralling cherry bough, weathered to a silky silver-grey, like the handle of a well-used implement.

We made a little woodhenge out of the driftwood: a rough circle of poles and spires, pushed down into the gravel – a homage to Derek Jarman's driftwood garden on Dungeness. Our henge would last as long as the next high tide.

Then we sat, watched the sea and talked. I told Roger the story I had been reading of a 'ghost forest' that had been discovered on the eastern coast of Greenland in the 1950s. A young glacier had sheared away volcanic crust to reveal a stratum of 100-million-year-old sandstone, embedded in which were the fossils of long-dead forest: seeds, leaves and bark imprints – the spectres of persimmons, walnuts, sycamores, tulip trees, even eucalypts and breadfruits. A six-man expedition had been mounted to investigate the fossils: the scientists sailed a 'small fine schooner' into the remote bay, across 'a cold grey mirror of water that was sprinkled with icebergs in surrealist shapes', passing through 'eerie arctic twilight'. It was the kind of mission I wanted to be called up for, I said: ghost trees, the tropics haunting the poles, adventure, ice . . . A month or two earlier I had given Roger a book called *The Great American Forest*, by Rutherford Platt, and he had brought it with him to Orford. He got it out from his knapsack, and read a section he liked about chlorophyll and the colours of autumn forests: how the great flaring, which looked like death, was in fact just a sign of the trees hunkering back for winter, ready to go through the sap cycle again.

The shingle rampart behind us locked off the rest of the world. There was only the steep wet gravel to our west, and the sea to our east, brown and frightening. Fast, fat, stone-heavy waves plunged aggressively, and the big wind filled the air with cold spray. I could hear only the detonations of the waves, gravel spattering like bullets, and the wind's steady roar. A single sailing-boat, visible through the haze, marked the edge of the known world.

Perhaps we should not have been surprised by what we found out there, sitting on a concrete housing near the lighthouse. It was a tiny shelter, a little cabin a foot or so high, made of broken bricks and hunks of concrete, with a loop of coat-hanger wire sticking from its ceiling, and a gap for the front door. There was no clue as to who had made it, or why, but the impulse to have done so was no mystery. It was a shelter, however rudimentary and scaled down, for this unprotected front-line space.

At evening, as the sun was low and red in the sky, we crossed back over the River Ore, and into the woods and fields of Suffolk. A single mushroom-cloud of cumulonimbus dominated the eastern sky, and it was soaked in the red fission light of the late sun.

Some time after our day on Orford Ness, Roger became unusually withdrawn. He stopped writing as regularly, and he spent increasing amounts of time alone at the farm. We – his friends and family – thought it was the effect of his book, which he was close to finishing, after so many years' work on it: that he had gone into hibernation for the final stages. I went over with my friend Leo to see him, to find out how he was, and to see if I could help at all with the book. He cooked lunch for us, but did not eat himself: he had lost his appetite, he said – probably the pressure of the work. When Leo and I went for a quick swim in the moat, he stayed on the bank.

Two weeks later, Roger began to slur his speech, and to hallucinate that visitors had come to stay at Walnut Tree Farm, when he was in fact alone. He was taken that night to hospital. A scan revealed an aggressive tumour on the front left lobe of his brain.

The first part of Roger's treatment was at the hospital close to my home. I went to see him there each day that he was in, felt hot-eyed, talked brightly. It seemed impossible at that time, to me as to all of Roger's friends, that the cancer would not ebb away. Roger's unstoppable vitality would simply overpower the disease.

This did not happen. Roger became progressively more ill. There was difficult and exhausting medical treatment. There were long periods of befuddlement, and shorter periods of clarity, and in one of these periods of clarity I saw him. We spoke about some of the journeys I had been on since he had fallen ill, and about *Wildwood*, which he had finished only a few weeks before his diagnosis. He told me about oak trees; how when one of their number was under stress they would share nutrients via their root systems. It was a measure of his generosity and his devotion to nature that, even when so near to death, he could still speak unjealously of the ability of trees to heal themselves. I told him about the birch trees I had been climbing in Langdale, how whippy they were, and how, if you found a young tree slender but strong enough, you could climb to its summit, and allow your weight to bend the tree's tip over and down, so that it deposited you lightly upon the ground from which you had begun, before springing back up to the vertical. Roger asked me to get his copy of Robert Frost down from the shelf, and to read out Frost's poem 'Birches'. It ended:

> *So was I once myself a swinger of birches.*
> *And so I dream of going back to be.*
> *. . . I'd like to go by climbing a birch tree,*
> *And climb black branches up a snow-white trunk*
> *Toward heaven, till the tree could bear no more,*
> *But dipped its top and set me down again.*
> *That would be good both going and coming back.*
> *One could do worse than be a swinger of birches.*

The cancer killed Roger appallingly fast. Five weeks before the equinox, I drove over to Walnut Tree Farm to see him for what I knew would be the last time. He was sitting in the kitchen, and was unable to raise himself from his wicker chair. I bent to give him a clumsy hug, and was shocked to feel how thin he was within his old green jumper. His partner, Alison, his son Rufus, and his friend Terence were there too; they had been taking gentle care of him for weeks. We all sat together in the kitchen, talked, drank tea. When the others moved off to do jobs around the house, I sat alone with Roger for a while, held his hand, spoke a little. I gave him a stone that I had found for him the previous month, on Embleton beach in Northumbria: it was a pyroclast, grey basalt ringed with what I thought was red serpentine, and it had been spewed out by the volcano complex whose eroded roots now formed the Cheviot massif. This was once lava, I said as I passed it to him. Roger held it in his hand, and rubbed his thumb over its rough side, to give himself the answer of a texture. A cricket clicked along the edge of the old biscuit tin that sat on the table. He fell asleep, and I left the room quietly. On the way home, I stopped the car in a lay-by and cried.

Three days afterwards, with Leo and another friend who knew Roger, I travelled by train to the North Norfolk coast: past the ironstone reef that rises near King's Lynn and gives the walls of the older houses a rusty colour, and then out to Holkham Bay. We swam in wild waves at dawn and dusk, saw a marsh harrier hunt over the whin, and in the evening we read out the pages from Roger's book that described his adventures on that stretch of coast. That night, we slept in a clearing in the pine forests which run down almost to the sand at Holkham. I spent half the night in a hammock that Roger had lent me, and half of it down on the thick soft needle carpet, where it smelt of sap and resin.

Roger died six days later, at the age of sixty-three, still in the house that he had built around himself thirty-eight years earlier. He had never worn anything but used clothes, so I turned up for his funeral in shabby brown cords and a jumper with a hole in the shoulder, to find everyone else in suits and black ties. After my initial horror, I realised it didn't matter at all. His oldest and closest friends, several of whom he had

known since childhood or university, spoke movingly about him. There
were readings from his letters and from *Waterlog*. The coffin was cremated with a swatch of full-leaved oak branches upon it. Loudon
Wainwright's 'The Swimmer's Song' was played as the coffin rolled
through the velvet curtains, and the congregation wept.

In the weeks following the funeral, I could not shake off a sadness,
close to depression, at Roger's death. Grief played its tricks: I kept for-
getting he had died, thinking for a second I could ring him up to ask
him something, or call over to see him. I had known him for fewer than
four years, but friendship with Roger did not seem to follow the normal
laws of time. 'I want all my friends to come up like weeds,' he had once
written in a notebook, 'and I want to be a weed myself, spontaneous
and unstoppable. I don't want the kind of friends one has to cultivate.'
That caught it exactly. Spontaneous and unstoppable. Roger had not
just loved the wild, he had been wild. Not in the austere and chastening sense I had once understood the wild to be, but natural, vigorous,
like a tree or a river.

We had shared adventures, and there would have been others to
come, but for the cancer. A night stake-out of a badger in Thornham
Woods, near Walnut Tree Farm. A trip to Cumbria in the coming
autumn, to climb and swim and give a joint lecture. At some point a
journey to Australia, where we had both been invited to speak. When
the invitation had arrived, Roger had wondered if we could earn our
passage out to the Antipodes as oarsmen on a quinquereme. I hadn't
been sure that we could.

I tried not to grieve too much: to do so seemed somehow to deny the
worth of Roger's extraordinary life. But I still could not rid myself of a
sense of waste. I had wanted to know Roger as he aged into his seventies

and his eighties, for he would have grown old, properly old, so superbly. He was an expert in age: in its charisma and its worth. Everything he owned was worn, used, re-used. If anyone would have known how to age well, it would have been Roger.

One night after his death, feeling morose, I read back through our correspondence. His e-mails were sharp, erudite and always inset with beautiful little field-notes, told for the joy of telling. His letters, which he preferred to write by hand, would often be accompanied by a poem, or a leaf or a feather; once a bunch of tiny teasels for Lily. One passage from the correspondence stood out, evoked Roger and his world instantly. It was the spring before his diagnosis, and he was in excitement about new arrivals at Walnut Tree Farm:

> Fox-cubs here, under the shed just beyond the shepherd's hut: the one that's invisible because under an enormous hedgehog of brambles. They are well-grown now and at dusk or dawn, frisking on the flattened grass, somersaulting, vaulting, tumbling as I watch them from my chair in the hedge. What spring means to a fully wound fox-cub!

The next day, someone wrote to me to say that having heard about Walnut Tree Farm, from the obituaries that had been written about Roger, she had added it to her 'list of imagined magical places'. I liked that very much, liked the idea of Roger's home becoming somewhere magical even to people who had never been there: part of the wild maps they held in their minds.

13

Saltmarsh

The autumn equinox was close, and a northerly wind blew down across the east of Britain from Scandinavia, carrying with it cold temperatures and migrating birds. Through the blue skies were arriving fieldfares, mistle thrushes, redwings, starlings, rooks, lapwings, coming in from Siberian river deltas and Finnish forests. They arrived with the Arctic trapped in their feathers, landing in gusts on the newly ploughed fields, or flying overhead in chattering companionable groups. Raptors came too, singly or in pairs: sparrowhawks, peregrines, leaving their boreal roosts, moving south as the Arctic coasts became too cold for them, and the polar sea began to grow its bark of ice. As I walked home one day, a sparrowhawk came past me at a low glide, then rose up to the branch of a glossy laurel tree across the road. It perched there for perhaps half a minute – barred tigerish chest, airman's helmet of grey-blue feathers, burnt-yellow eyes – then pushed off the branch and sculled out of sight, leaving the laurel tree shivering.

As the bird migration got underway, I decided to travel south-east, out to the clays of the Essex coast, where woodland and field frayed away to saltmarshes, and the saltmarshes gave into miles of shining mudflats. Out there I would be able to watch the moving birds, and I hoped the journey might somehow help me shift the sadness of Roger's death, which I was finding impossible to shake off or even lessen. It occurred to me, too, that the mud would complete the mineral dissolve

of my journeys: begun on hard rock, in Essex they would reach the soft-
est and most yielding substance of the archipelago, its tidal muds.

I left home on a bright mid-September morning. Another northerly
was blowing. A pale lemony sun hung low in the sky, throwing a light
that fell unexpectedly hot on the face. There was the vinegary smell
of windfallen apples in my garden. Chestnuts bobbed like little
mines in park ponds. I drove at first through the landscape of Essex –
the poor mocked Essex of jokes and news items – passing chain
pubs with pseudo-Tudor frontages, and business parks in 'Phase II of
Construction': colonies of unfinished corrugated-steel hangars. I
counted ten second-hand car dealerships: showrooms of metal and
glass, blank-plated BMWs and Mercedes parked in obedient ranks on
the outdoor lots, and red and white bunting strung between the arc-
lights overhead. St George's crosses were everywhere, snapping in the
wind on domestic flagpoles, or hanging as air-fresheners from rear-
view mirrors. Somewhere away to my south, I knew, was the industrial
shoreline of Dagenham, and the oil refineries at Coryton, which at
night released sudden air-balloon flares and licks of flame from their
chimneys. Once I passed a roadside shop selling garden ornaments. Its
forecourt was filled with gnomes, and Bambi-like deer, lying at rest with
their legs crooked up beneath them. In pride of place at the front of the
display was a plaster falcon of indeterminate species, perched on a
polka-dotted toadstool twice its size.

But as I got further east, deeper into the county, away from the main
roads and the towns, the marks of this new retail Essex thinned out and
fell back. Farmland began to border the roads. A digger dozed up a pile
of manure twice its own height, which steamed in the morning air.
Tractors gave new naps to thousand-acre fields. Old Man's Beard

climbed profusely through the chain-link fencing on a stretch of road-side. A group of magpies joked in a stand of beech trees. A line of willows leaned out over the road, trailing fingertips over the roofs of passing cars. The density of woodland thickened until it was visible on every horizon.

Near the village of Woodham Walter, I stopped, my eye caught by the sign bolted to a big zinc gate. 'Falconer's Lodge', it read. I got out, and as if by proof of place, a small sparrowhawk slipped from a hedgerow oak a few yards away from me, and made a concave glide to the next tree along. It stood on a low bough, observing me. It seemed to have orange eyes, and from this I guessed it was an old bird. For as sparrowhawks age, the colour of their irises changes. They are born with pale yellow irises, that darken to orange over time, until, in the very oldest birds, the eye blazes red in colour.

Falcons, hawks and other raptors had slipped in and out of all my journeys, and now I had come to Essex to hunt these hunters, and to see if wildness existed in this far south-east of the country. I had come, too, on the path of someone who had himself entered into an obsessive relationship with the birds.

Each autumn and winter, between 1953 and 1963, a man called John Baker tracked the peregrines of coastal Essex. 'Peregrines arrive on the east coast from mid-August to November,' Baker wrote. 'They may come in from the sea in any weather conditions, but are most likely to do so on a clear sunny day with a fresh north-west wind blowing.' Every autumn, once the hawks had arrived, Baker would follow them –

at dusk and dawn, and often for whole cold days – through the mixed landscape of woodland, field, sea wall, mudflat and saltmarsh over which they flew. Baker could not fully explain his fixation with the birds; he knew only that he was committed to a quest whose meaning he did not understand, but whose necessity he could not refute. So absolute was his commitment that, during the months of pursuit each year, he would go almost entirely feral, avoiding human contact as far as possible, keeping to cover wherever he could.

For a decade, while Orion stood bright in the sky, the peregrines hunted and Baker hunted them. Following the falcons for so many miles, he came to know the Essex landscape intimately: its boulder clays and river gravels, its cricket-bat willows and hazel coppices. He moved, once winter arrived, along 'the bone-white coral of frosted hedges', and through 'black hard winter woods'. He watched small waders – knots, plovers, turnstones – form their palping jellyfish-like shoals in the air over the mudflats. He tracked nightingales from the sound of their singing. He collected beautifully marked feathers: partridge, tern, woodpecker, peregrine.

Baker became, during those years of chase, an explorer of what he called the 'beyond-world': the wild world of birds and small creatures that existed in hedgerows, in woodlands, in the air, and out on the coastal borderlands of the mudflats and saltmarshes. This 'beyond-world' was always occurring, mingling with our world of tarmac and cars and pesticides and tractors, rarely more than a turn of the head or a turn in the road away. Most people were entirely blind to this world, but Baker saw it wherever he looked. In his eyes, the Essex landscape – never more than 150 metres above sea-level, only fifty miles from London, heavily farmed – was as inspiring and elemental as the Pamirs or the Arctic.

I had become interested in Baker through *The Peregrine*, the book he wrote about his decade of falcon-hunting, which had been acclaimed as a masterpiece on its publication in 1967. I had read the book again and again, for its wildness and its fierce beauty. It set my imagination aloft, and kept it there.

One reason for Baker's pursuit of the peregrines was that he feared for their survival as a species. By the 1950s, the atrocious impact of pesticides upon bird populations in Britain was becoming clear. In 1939 there had been 700 British peregrine pairs; a 1962 survey showed a decline to half this number, with only sixty-eight pairs appearing to have reared chicks successfully. Sparrowhawks, too, had almost disappeared. It would have seemed likely to Baker that both hawks and falcons would become extinct due to what he called 'the filthy, insidious pollen of farm chemicals'. 'I remember those winter days,' he wrote of the pre-war years, 'those frozen fields ablaze with warring hawks . . . It is sad that it should be so no longer. The ancient eyries are dying.'

The medieval patterns of the Essex countryside, too, were under threat at that time, as the county was drastically reshaped for the purposes of agribusiness. Hedges were grubbed up to make vast open fields. Thousands of spinneys and copses were bulldozed, and many old lanes and shallower holloways were filled in and farmed over. Rivers and streams foamed with surfactants, and became choked with water-weed, that grew in abundance due to nitrogen run-off from fertilisers.

Baker found the decline of the raptors and the damage to the landscape almost unbearable. His only solace came in following the peregrines. Hunting as haunting. Out in the fields, he was brought closer to wildness: he could step through the looking-glass and into the beyond-world. Out there, he was also able to forget the fact that he himself was ill. For Baker was suffering from severe and worsening arthritis, particularly in his arms and legs. It was becoming more and more difficult for him to hold his pen or his binoculars, as his fingers tightened in on themselves, curled over. Hands clenching into talons.

Half a century on, I had come to Baker's hunting ground. I wanted to follow some of the routes he had taken, and to explore this county in his footsteps and through his eyes. To see if, in this month of migration, I could find my way into his beyond-world. My plan was to begin in the county's wooded interior, and from there move out towards the coast, where the migrating birds – redshank, dunlin, gulls of several kinds – would be settling in their thousands on the mudflats.

Before leaving, I had called up copies of the 1950s Ordnance Survey maps of Essex, and read them off against the present-day versions to see what had changed. The woodlands had shrunk, the towns had swollen and the fields had expanded: all this was clear from the comparison. But there were still thousands of acres of native woodland there: ash, maple and hazel woods in the north-west, lime and low elm in the mid-north, and hornbeam in the south. Its distribution dated in the main from the Middle Ages. Scrutinising the new maps, one name in particular had caught my eye: 'The Wilderness' – a long thin skein of broadleaf wood, stretching round to the east of the old village of Woodham Walter. It was an area through which I knew Baker had tracked the peregrines.

I left the car near the entrance to Falconer's Lodge, and began the walk to The Wilderness, following footpaths that led down the edges of freshly ploughed fields, and through small copses. The hedges were still heavy with fruit: plump blackberries, hard orange haws on the turn to red. The smell of ripe fruit and new earth was thick in the air. I ate handfuls of blackberries. A red admiral on a fence post let its wings fall open like a book. The hedgerows were slung with spider's silk, and I recalled the webby corners of Roger's house. Huge females sat in the centres of their webs: big tawny creatures, whose colours reminded me of Rannoch Moor.

The Wilderness was only half a mile from the road. After a few minutes' walk, I turned a corner of a hedge, and followed a faint path into a tunnel of old elders that led into the wood like a secret passage.

There, immediately, at my feet was a kill: a woodpigeon on its back, wings cast out to either side like fans, a pillow-burst of breast feathers. The quills of several of its tail feathers were shorn off halfway through: it had been killed by a fox, not a falcon or hawk. A peregrine or sparrowhawk would have zipped open the chest; the peregrine would have crushed the breastbone, the sparrowhawk would have nipped it out and discarded it.

I stepped over the body, and pushed on into the wood, passing stands of more elders, and ancient coppiced boles of sycamore and hazel. These had run riot, shooting up into groves of vertical poles thirty or forty feet high, which trembled at their summits when I pushed past their bases. The rough path petered out quickly, and the wood thickened around me. I batted away more webs with the back of my hand, and stepped over fallen trunks and outcast branches.

Within a few minutes, I was in wood so deep that it was hard to keep an orientation. Hazy light fell through the branches. The air was thick with the furry hootings of stock-doves. I walked as softly as I could, trying to avoid cracking dry twigs, but woodpigeons still crashed away through the treetops. From further away, I could hear the chatter of crows, probably picking over one of the turned fields that bordered The Wilderness. There were hundreds of burrows in the banks and between the roots of the trees, and in places the clayey soil had been worn to a polish by the passage of animal feet: badgers, rabbits, foxes. Bird corpses were everywhere; I counted a dozen and then gave up.

I came to a dip, a valley or ditch, curving away from me to left and right, perhaps fifteen feet deep and thirty across, with sloping sides. And there, unexpectedly, protruding from the bank, part-buried in the brown soil, I saw a bank of red bricks. I scrambled down one of the steep sides, and up the other, to the exposed masonry. A hundred or so flat thin bricks were visible only, but they were clearly part of some considerable structure. The bricks were now crumbling back into the soil out of which they had originally been fired. I slipped a flat rhomboid-shaped shard of one into my pocket.

There was a mystery to this place I could not quite figure out: the name, the bricks in the heart of the wild wood, the coppiced trees. I thought I would try to get an aerial view. I picked a stand of sturdy coppiced sycamores: six trunks which lacked lateral branches, but whose closeness made it possible to climb one of them while using the others for support. The trunks were leafless except at their tops, where they spread laterally into a quaking green canopy, so that as I climbed them it felt as if I were ascending a whale's spout.

Over the course of two years, Roger and I had carried on an extended discussion of the relative climbing merits of different tree species. Roger had voted for the hornbeam 'as the toughest, least likely to let me down with a rotten branch', and for the oak, 'except for their tendency to stag-headedness these days'. 'Low on my list,' he had said, 'is the crack willow.' I was, of course, an advocate for the beech and the birch, and an unfortunate incident involving a broken branch had turned me against the poplar. Both of us admired the appraisal given to the trees in Calvino's *The Baron in the Trees*, for it was clear that Calvino himself had done some serious practical research on the subject. Cosimo, Calvino wrote, liked best of all to climb holm oaks, olives – 'patient trees with rough, friendly bark on which he could pass or pause' and figs, which 'seemed to absorb him, permeate him with their gummy texture and the buzz of hornets, until he would begin to feel he was becoming a fig himself', and the walnut: 'the endless spread of its branches, like some palace of many floors and innumerable rooms . . . such strength and certainty this tree had in being a tree, its determination to be hard and heavy expressed even in its leaves.' He did not, however, trust elms or poplars, whose 'branches grew upwards, slender and thickly covered, leaving little foothold', or pines, with their 'close-knit branches, brittle and thick with cones, leaving no space or support'. Both Roger and I loved the description of how Cosimo spent nights in the canopy, 'listening to the sap running through its cells, the circles marking the years inside the trunks, the birds sleeping and quivering in their nests, and the caterpillar waking and the chrysalis opening'.

We had several times discussed attempting an aerial traverse of a woodland. Roger had even gone so far as to research and write me a letter on the subject of brachiation. Brachiation, he explained, is the special evolutionary adaptation that enables orang, gibbon and chimpanzee arms to articulate in all directions and support a swinging, hanging body. It is what distinguishes apes from monkeys. By swinging, and moving fast to keep up rhythm and momentum, a heavy gibbon or orang-utan can swing from branches that would never support the ape standing on top of them. Using branches more like ropes than bars, it became possible to utilise the thinner, further reaches of them. The key evolutionary benefit of brachiation was therefore that it allowed the heavy ape to move about among the slender springier branches and reach the fruit at their tips. Brachiation also led naturally to a tendency to uprightness and all that this later entailed in terms of evolution. But it was also dangerous, Roger observed, so animals like the gibbon needed their big brains to remain safe, to make the sophisticated calculations required to stay aloft from branch to branch in the canopy instead of crashing to the ground and killing themselves.

Roger had seemed inexplicably keen that I try the traverse first, with him watching me from the forest floor, on the grounds that I was the climber and he the swimmer. We had never got round to the experiment, but I still aspired one day to fulfil the beautiful description Roger had sent me of the gibbon: 'Gibbons really fly from branch to branch! They fling themselves with great force and glide with a fluency that was surely learned from the birds, the ancient aristocracy of arboreal life. Perhaps they also utilise the energy stored in branches when they are bent, like longbows.'

I had not climbed a coppice-group before, however, and it was with a distinctly ungibbonish inelegance that I reached twenty-five feet up in my sycamores. But from there I was able to look down on to the Wilderness and to get some sense of the land's lie. The ditch was a moat; this much was clear. It ran in a squashed circle around the central area, which looked to be about an acre in size. I could see evidence of earthworks and more exposed ridges of brickwork, suggesting walls and palisades. And beyond the moat in every direction were bands of thistles and waist-high nettles. These were the new fortifications of this area, keeping people out, preserving the land for the creatures that lived in it.

My guess was that the name on the map was a late-eighteenth-century relic: that a big house, perhaps Elizabethan, had once stood here, and had then been taken over by an early Romantic landowner who, following the picturesque taste of the time, had created for his estate a 'Wilderness': an area of rough country, regulated for its irregularity – often with artificial waterfalls and faux rock outcrops – which could be excitingly strayed into by visitors.

But the name had proved a prophecy: two or more centuries later, The Wilderness had become a wild place, properly reclaimed, only a few hundred yards from a road. The building that had once stood here had dilapidated, and had then been steadily and thoroughly reoccupied by nature: by nettle, thistle, elder, hazel, fox, badger and bird.

Swaying up there in the sycamore canopy, I remembered a comment Baker had made to his journal on a late-January day in 1954. 'The view from the gate, beside the wood and past the house seemed wonderful,' he had written. 'The grass was a deep green, whole fields waterlogged and green, . . . grass, which will master us all yet, and cover our shameful rubble in its equality.'

There was something in this long sight, this sense of the human presence as being something temporary, which I recognised. During my journeys, I had seen so many human structures from so many epochs sinking back into the land: the roofless houses of the west of Ireland, the rubble of the Clearance townships mossed over in Scottish glens, and the slate spoil-heaps of Blaenau, where I had spent a day inside a mountain, moving through the abandoned mine-tunnels. I had heard about others: the drowned village of Dunwich on the Suffolk coast, reclaimed by the rising sea, over which Roger had once swum. The thousands of deserted medieval villages of England, painstakingly found and mapped by the historian and archaeologist Maurice Beresford in the 1940s and 1950s, many of them abandoned in the years after the Great Plague. The little Isle of Soay, off Skye, where Gavin Maxwell had established a basking-shark fishery in the 1940s, and where the grass now grew through the eyeholes of shark vertebrae that were scattered in the bone yard, and where rust and damp were slowly breaking down the flensing equipment and the hauling pulleys. South of me here in Essex, I knew, were the so-called 'plotland' woods of Laindon and Thundersley: young woods that had sprung up on land that had been built on in the late nineteenth century, and then again during the great slump in land prices of the inter-war years. Street after street of bungalows, many of them self-built, had rotted back into the ground, and the trees had returned – native oak, ash and hornbeam – and with them had come the creatures.

Abandoned places such as these provide us not only with images of the past but also with visions of the future. As the climate warms, and as human populations begin to fall, increasing numbers of settlements will be abandoned. Inland drought and rising sea-levels on the coasts will force exoduses. And wildness will return to these forsaken places. Vegetable and faunal life will reclaim them: the opportunist pioneer species first – dog-rose, elder, fireweed, crows . . . Just such a reclamation has occurred in the so-called 'zone of alienation': the region of north Ukraine that was placed off-limits after the Chernobyl disaster in 1986. In Pripiat, the town in which the Chernobyl workers were accommodated, silver birch now throng the empty streets and court-yards. Flower meadows of exceptional botanical diversity have grown up

through the paving stones. Forests of pine and willow have populated
the city's outskirts, through which run wolf packs of up to 200 animals.
Moose, deer, lynx and boar pad through the city's suburbs. Black storks
nest in its chimneys, bats in the empty houses, and kestrels in the
unused window boxes. The cooling ponds of the Chernobyl plant itself
are now filled with catfish up to six feet long.

I had spoken once to a climate-change scientist about the subject of
abandonment. The study of her science had changed her perception of
time, she said, and of the relevance of human beings within history.
Though we are now among the dominant species, she said, our age will
pass, and our material legacy – unthinkable though it now is to imagine it vanished – will be absorbed by the land, becoming all but
imperceptible.

Eventually, very much later than this, she said, the sun will swell to
become a red giant, swallowing up all the vast empty space as far as the
earth. Imagine that, she said, an ancient red sun, swollen and massive,
charring the earth.

The band of woods of which The Wilderness was a part extended north
towards the River Chelmer. Baker had spent a lot of time haunting the
overgrown banks of the Chelmer: he would often follow it down to
where it issued into the saltmarsh near Maldon. So after an hour or so
in The Wilderness, I followed the line of the woodland northwards,
keeping to the edge of the tree-line, out of sight. I passed through
regions of ivy-throttled oaks and groves of sweet chestnuts. The vast
field to my west was divided by a row of poplars, whose leaves crackled

in the wind like overhead power-lines. A gang of rooks chakked over the corn stubble. I wondered how many people ever came to this wood, so close to the road, but such a strange place. Hawker dragonflies buzzed around over the grass like quick biplanes. A single green woodpecker passed me, its flight following the line of a stitched thread. Baker had written of watching woodpeckers feed in a nameless wood near his home. 'This quiet ritual took place on the very edge of the world I see,' he had written, 'very near to the world beyond the looking glass, the lost place, the beginning of things.'

I walked for another half a mile. And in the middle of a deep section of oak wood, where it seemed at its deepest, and where a rough little stream cut through it, I came into a glade to find a tyre on a rope, tied to the bough of an oak tree. It was a swing! Suddenly my sense of the wood changed. This was where the children of the village came: to swing on the tyre, to play hide-and-seek, to have adventures. It was a wild place for the kids, and must have been for decades, perhaps centuries. I could see a path worn into the soil by the passage of feet, leading back west through the wood to where the trees thinned, and from there back between two fields towards the church of Woodham Walter.

I left the glade, and walked north-east for two miles to the Chelmer, keeping to the hedgerows and field edges. Just short of the river, passing along the boundary of a newly turned field, I stopped, and picked a curiously shaped flint from a curve of sillion. It was a hand-axe, unmistakably a hand-axe. I couldn't believe my luck. Its interior was blue, a blue which had a depth to it like cloudy water, and its outer side was the colour of old brown bone. It looked to have been abandoned before its flaking had been properly finished. I tested its edge with my thumb, weighed it in my hand, and then set out for the Essex coast and the saltmarshes of the Dengie Peninsula.

The Dengie is a blunt-nosed peninsula in eastern Essex, just under a hundred square miles in area, and bordered on three sides by water – the Blackwater estuary to its north, the North Sea to its east, and the Crouch estuary to its south. Most of it is reclaimed land, below sea-level, saved from the tides by a network of sea walls: grassed-over linear earthworks, fifteen feet high or more. It is provisional land, borrowed land. Stepping onto it, you are stepping into a ghost of water.

At unpredictable moments, the sea reasserts itself in great diluvial acts. The disastrous tide of Martinmas 1099, recorded in the Anglo-Saxon Chronicle: 'This year also, on the festival of St Martin, the sea-flood sprung up to such a height, and did so much harm, as no man remembered that it ever did before. And this was the first day of the new moon.' Or the storm-surging spring tide of 31 January 1953, that killed hundreds, and submerged the Dengie as far inland as Tillingham.

I reached the sea wall near Bradwell late in the afternoon. Crickets and grasshoppers were chirring invisibly from the grass, and the wind was still strong and warm. Streams of birds passed overhead, most too distant or unfamiliar for me to identify. The tide was halfway in, and miles of glossy mud lay open to the air.

Only a few yards short of the beginning of the saltmarsh, next to a little copse of blackthorn, was a barn-like structure, perhaps forty feet at its apex, with a wooden roof, and walls made from mortar and rocks: hunks of ironstone, huge flints, chalky boulders.

I pushed open the front door, which swung silently inwards. The interior was undivided, high and huge. The air was still after the gusting northerly wind. Bluebottles did lazy buzzing laps of the upper space. Light fell at a slant through tall windows.

It was an abbey: St Cedd's, founded in the seventh century. Cedd had been sent south as a missionary by St Finan of Lindesfarne, after much of the region around Essex and London had reverted to paganism. He had been the pioneer of the short-lived East Saxon Celtic Church which, like its western and northern counterparts, was distinguished by mysticism and nature-love.

I walked up to the rough altar. Sunk into its base were three stones. One, dolerite, had come from the Holy Island of Lindisfarne; the second, gneiss, from Iona, where the Celtic mission in Britain began; the third, lias, from Lastingham, in the Yorkshire Moors, the village to which Cedd had travelled from Essex and where he had eventually died of plague. These travelled stones reminded of my own collection, sitting on the shelf above my desk. And the abbey itself, standing out on these edgelands, recalled Ynys Enlli and its *peregrini*: a rare lateral rhyme, binding the country from east to west.

I left the abbey, and walked through the blackthorn copse. There, invisible from outside the trees, nestled a little house: Linnet's Cottage. It was a bird observatory; next to its door a list of recent sightings was displayed, scribbled in marker pen on a whiteboard: peregrine, honey buzzard, marsh harrier, skua, greenshank, little egret, tern . . . The monks had gone long ago, but new watchers on the shore had taken their place.

←

From the wood I turned south, and began walking out along the sea wall. Swallows scudded overhead in twos and threes, moving with fast wing flicks. I saw what I thought was a hare's ear, *Bupleurum tenuissimum*, snug on its short stem. Inland were vast fields, on which three or four black barns sailed like barges. To the seaward of the wall were the marshes, tinged purple.

Saltmarshes form in relatively sheltered coasts, where silt and sand accumulate, becoming colonised by salt-tolerant plants: sea purslane, golden samphire, glasswort, sea aster and others. The plants trap more sediment, and the marsh becomes a kind of filter for the tidal water, meshing off nutrients and foods with each receding tide. The architecture of saltmarshes, and the mudflats into which they dwindle, is formidably complex: a maze of rays, wriggling channels, creeks, fleets, gutways and swatchways, all of which are kept clear by the sluicing action of the tide.

As well as the unusual plants that form them, these saltmarshes are homes to hundreds of rare insects, and provide uniquely safe nesting grounds for waders. They are also among the most effective tidal defences known.

Even the wide saltmarshes of the Essex coastline, however, cannot cope with the rising tides of climate change. Over the past century, sea levels have increased by an average of eight inches worldwide. This creep is primarily due to the thermal expansion of the world's ocean water, warmed by an atmosphere heated by carbon emissions from aviation, industry and energy production. Under pressure from the rising tides, the saltmarshes of the Essex coastline have been in steady decline since the 1970s. At present, around a third of a square mile of saltmarsh is lost each year along the Essex coastline alone: it is anticipated that half the world's saltmarsh area will be lost within seventy-five years. And after the saltmarshes have gone, the sea will be freer to advance inland. The pattern of land-loss occurring in Essex has its parallels across the soft coasts of Britain and Ireland, and across the world.

I walked south along the sea wall for five miles, and in all that time I met no one, and saw only a farmer, turning distantly in his tractor. I stopped to pull fruit from a wild apple tree that was growing on the edge of a dyke and that was heavy with little yellow and pink apples, I ate salty leaves of sea-kale and sea-beet, and chewed on the liquoricey feathery fronds of the abundant fennel. Once, a weasel emerged from long grass at the foot of the sea wall, looked warily around, and then made off in its hooping run for cover in the long grass.

After five miles, I turned back north, and trespassed inland, along a drainage dyke between fields, to a small wood of poplar, hazel and ash. I had seen the wood across the fields, and had thought it might make a good place to sleep. I reached it, and crept into it, pushing low under poplar branches. I remembered exploring the oakwoods of Staverton Thicks in Suffolk with Roger on just such a bright windy day, a year and a half previously, stepping over dozens of fallen oak trunks that were rotting into the ground. Roger had explained to me how essential this decaying matter was to the health of a woodland, that the benign influence of trees continued long after their death. He had stopped by a big prostrate oak limb, and prised off a curved gule of bark; beneath it teemed hundreds of insects: woodlice, ants and others species I could not recognise. Then we had forged on deeper into the wood, to a cleared circle where Roger said he knew local Wiccan enthusiasts came to worship, sometimes naked. I wasn't sure I believed him, but he held to his line. Talismans were hung by wool and string from oak branches;

feathers, rags, fragments of text, spinning and swinging. On the way back through the wood, I had levered a long peat-brown wedge of hard wood from the root of a fallen oak. Later, I sanded it down and gave it to my father as a memento from the Thicks.

The poplars were noisy in the wind. I lay on my back there for a while, in the dense dry leaf-litter and the submarine light of the wood, thinking about Roger. The susurrus of the leaves and the density of the canopy meant that the few sounds I could hear – two gunshots, the honk of a distant ship's horn – seemed to arrive having passed through wood; as though, in Baker's phrase, I were standing at the heart of a tree.

I left the wood just before dusk. I had found it too enclosing: I wanted to spend the night out at the edge, on the sea wall. So I walked out to a remote curving stretch of wall, where only fifty yards of saltmarsh separated me from the high-tide mark. The wind had died away, and there was the smell of grass and salt in the warm air. The sun hung low and yellow over the western fields, diffusing a rich gold light that oiled my hands and face with its colour. I recalled Baker's description of a coastal sunset: 'The yellow orbital ring of the horizon closes over the glaring cornea of the sun.'

A line of dense grass grew on the seaward side of the wall, which hid me from the thousands of migrating birds – dunlins, redshanks, oyster-catchers, curlews, gulls – that were gathering out on the mudflats and bright white cockle-shell beaches, which radiated an intense light. The incoming tide was moving the birds closer to shore, concentrating their numbers. Big waves would send them up in sudden clouds, and then they would rain down again on to the mud a few yards nearer to me. From my hiding place, I could watch without disturbing them.

High tide was reached at about six o'clock. Half an hour later, dusk started to settle on the land, and as it did so the grasshoppers began to stop their chirring, until I could hear only five or six, then two, then one, then none. I watched the light move through its late-day modalities. It became thicker, until just before dark it seemed to consist of single photons, which moved and swarmed with the drugged heaviness of bees.

Suddenly the sky above me was filled with a creaking noise. I looked up and saw a big flock of common gulls – 1,000 birds, perhaps more – flying over me from the west. They reached the water-line, and turned in a single shoaling movement, their white bodies flashing in the dusk as they caught the last light of the low sun, and then they spread and settled on the sea just offshore, turned to face the wind, and formed into a loose bobbing line, one bird every yard or so, that stretched away up and down the coast as far as I could see in both directions.

Full night came; moonless but clear. I lay on my back in my sleeping-bag, watching the silhouettes of the birds as they flew over, and watching the stars pricking into view: first one, then two, then five or six, then too many to count. A scatter of meteors fell – the Piscid showers of September. I started to notice other lit bodies, moving fast: the blipping orbital paths of satellites, but also others, lower than that, visible only as fixed moving lights against darkness. They were passenger planes coming into Stansted airport, 10,000 feet up or more. I realised I was sleeping in the middle of two flight-paths, two migrations: one avian and one human.

Around ten o'clock, I heard a dozen or so big birds move in over me. Geese, I guessed, probably brent geese: pioneers of the major migration of their species that would begin in a few weeks' time. They splash-landed on dyke water only ten yards to my south, and stayed there all night, filling the air with their hound-like barking.

Northern European myth tells of an event called 'The Wild Hunt'. On tempestuous nights, Wodan would lead across the land the troop of warriors who had died in battle, accompanied by their war-hounds. Travellers who found themselves in the path of the Wild Hunt were advised to lie face down. In this way only the cold feet of the black dogs who ran with the hunt would touch them, and they would not be harmed. The purpose of the Hunt was to collect the souls of the recently deceased; its riders were the summoners of the dead. Many different versions of the Hunt exist: in a Christian form of the myth, it was said to occur when Gabriel rallied his angels into battle. The Anglo-Saxon Chronicle detailed how, on 6 February 1127, the Wild Hunt galloped through the deer park of Peterborough and then through the woods up to Stamford: a 'furious host' rushing through the dark forest paths, across the heaths, over the fells, along the coast, and between the places of 'mirk'. Gervase of Tilbury recorded in the thirteenth century that Arthur and his knights still led a Wild Hunt along the holloway that ran between Cadbury and Glastonbury.

The ur-myth of the Wild Hunt was almost certainly an explanation of the autumn migration of wild geese – brent, snow, Canada. Most years, the geese travel in skeins, in groups of fewer than a hundred birds. Some years, however, they fly low and in large numbers, and when they pass overhead in the darkness, the noise of their wings is so loud that it can resemble a plane or – to pre-aviation ears – a war-host of angels. An eerie German soldiers' song, composed in the trenches in 1917, spoke of how 'The Wild Geese rush through the night / With shrill cries to the North. / Beware, beware this dangerous flight / For death is all around us.'

That night on the sea wall, I thought about migration: those strong seasonal compulsions that draw creatures between regions, from one hemisphere to another. More than two million migrating birds used the soft shores of Britain and Ireland as resting points each autumn and winter. Maps could be drawn – had been drawn – showing their flight-paths. They looked not unlike the maps showing the flyways of different airlines. But instead of linking city to city and runway to runway, the bird-migration maps linked wild place to wild place: connected the marshes, mudflats and inland lakes of Britain and Ireland outwards into a wider web of wild places – the boreal forests of Scandinavia, the wide tundra of Siberia. The migrating birds did not shun humans; they were happy to live round them. What they did assess when choosing where to land, though, was wildness: how far the water and the land would allow them to follow their own instincts and fulfil their own needs. Where they could not do this, they did not land.

I woke just after dawn. The sun, over the sea, was round and flat as a coin, orange in colour. Mist hung over the fields, and the wind had died away almost to nothing. I could see no more than 300 yards through the haze. The mist resembled water, as though while I slept a tide had swept in overnight, and flooded the land. The structures of the barns,

footless in the mist, seemed even more ark-like. The copses and spinneys stood out like islands. I walked three miles north, back through the
mist, to St Cedd's. Near the abbey I sat down on a bench that faced out
to sea, to rest and to watch the birds.

After twenty minutes or so, a man and a woman came and sat down
next to me, laying their walking-sticks on the ground, parallel to the
side of the bench. I made to leave. 'Please don't let us drive you away,'
the woman said. We introduced ourselves. They were about seventy, I
guessed. Peter wore big Reactalite glasses, with side shields, and a brown
collared T-shirt. He smiled slowly. Yvonne had a pearl necklace, and did
most of the talking. They came out to St Cedd's every weekend, she
said, unless they were visiting their son in Hong Kong where he worked
teaching English, which they did every two years or so – it was a good
job he had, but it kept him away from England. Yvonne had spent years
living on a yacht moored at Bradwell, when she was a young girl. Her
father had been from the East End, and had moved up to Essex after the
war because he couldn't settle in the city. She explained to me how to
walk on mudflats without sinking in. It's not what you expect, she said,
you have to angle your feet, tilt the insides up, don't keep them flat. And
make sure you keep moving. She got up from the bench, and did a walk
up and down to show me the technique.

Peter told me about a famous photograph of one of the highest
tides he had known, in 1960, when Walter Linnet, who had lived
in Linnet's Cottage, had been floated out of his house. Linnet had
taken his possessions into his duck punt, and had navigated right
up to the eastern wall of St Cedd's, and that was what the photo
showed: him in his loaded duck-punt, floating up against the wall of
the abbey.

I asked Yvonne if she had been here during the 1953 floods. She whistled. She had been on the boat with her mother, she said, when her mother had noticed the water behaving oddly: drawing back to show bare mud, then rushing forwards again shortly afterwards, like, she said, the sea was being shaken somewhere. Yvonne had been sent to get her dad, who had just gone ashore, and bring him back. She found him quickly, and they went back to the boat and cast off, and sailed out up the estuary and into the open water. The weather was terrible, she said, very frightening, and the boat was nearly swamped, and everything fell out of its place in the galley, but it was nothing to what happened onshore.

Peter explained the meteorological physics of the flood to me. When a depression over water is surrounded by highs, he said, the highs begin to rotate around it, and give a spinning motion to the depression. The sea beneath the depression is drawn up into the vacuum created by the low-pressure air. That January, a rotating depression in the North Sea coincided with a northerly wind and a high spring tide. The wind drove the depression south, from the expanses of the North Sea towards the Channel, where the land narrowed the sea down, which caused the tide to surge even higher.

The surge struck the North Norfolk coast first. Blakeney Point was immediately overwhelmed, the Cley marshes flooded, and the Holkham pines stood in water. Warning should have been sent south, but in the chaos it was not, and a short time later, the sea-defences along the Essex coastline were swamped. The sea wall was breached in dozens of places. On Canvey Island alone, about 200 people were drowned. If you had been out at St Cedd's, which remained dry, said Peter, and you had looked back inland across the peninsula, you would have seen only the upper storeys of buildings, and here and there the woodlands.

Later that afternoon, I met my friend Helen. A natural historian, a poet, an artist and a falconer, Helen had a keen sense of the wild, developed from many directions. She had caught a train out to the Dengie, and I met her at the station. After the two days I had spent haunting the woods and the saltmarshes, the shops seemed surprising to me in their brightness and language: a Numark Chemist, a Golden Delight Chinese takeaway, a Pound Store. We drove together back to the village of Dengie itself, where an old friend of Helen's, Ron Digby, lived. Ron was a bird-artist and falconer, renowned within the world of falconry. He had lived in Essex all his life, but had travelled the world painting birds of all kinds. Of all birds, hawks and falcons were the ones he knew best, and painted most often. His manner was gentle, assiduously polite.

We sat in Ron's kitchen, drinking tea. He talked a little about the way in which being a hunter, or being with hunters, changed the way you saw a landscape. He told me that partridges could look almost exactly like clods of earth or big soil-covered flints, and how, when he was hunting regularly, he had come to know some of the field edges so well that he could identify a bird automatically, because he carried a map in his head of where the big stones and clods were. Anything out of the ordinary would likely be a partridge, he said.

He stood up and beckoned us to the kitchen window. There on the back lawn, tethered on wooden stumps, were two peregrines: a plump brown young female, with a cream front, and a beautiful blue-backed male – a tiercel. Their heads bobbed up and down as they watched us: measuring distance, assessing threat.

Ron went out and brought back the tiercel, perched on his gloved hand. The bird's colours recalled the minerals of the coast from which I had come: his beak and back were the silex blue of some of the flints I had found, and there was an orangey ironstone burr to his creamy upper chest. The feathers on his back lay tight and flat as chain-mail, and his sharp wings crossed like sword blades behind him. His eyeballs were the same shiny black as escalator handrails. Around each of his eyes was a rim of pitted yellow skin, like the rind of a lemon. He smelt burnt, of hot stone.

Later, Ron drove us all out through the peninsula and back to the sea wall, just south of where I had slept, his car bouncing over ruts in the road, and Helen sitting in the passenger seat with the hooded tiercel steady on her gloved hand. We discussed the tiercel, and as we did so he tipped his head from side to side, as though embarrassed at being talked about. Once, he creaked open his beak to reveal a tongue as hard and gleaming as plastic.

Right out there on the sea edge, in the depressed land, wading calf-deep through green fields of lucerne, we flew the tiercel. He launched himself from Ron's wrist, flapped his wings clumsily twice, three times, seemed as if he would sink to the grass, and then lifted and flew out on a steep upwards diagonal. We watched him diminish.

He climbed with little hinged flaps, in an effortful but controlled motion, moving in a wide helix, until he reached a high pitch, perhaps 200 feet up, and at that height he levelled off and began to move in big circles, looking down on the land, surveying it.

'The peregrine sees and remembers patterns we do not know exist,' wrote Baker, 'the neat squares of orchard and woodland, the endlessly varying quadrilateral shapes of fields. He finds his way across the land by a succession of remembered symmetries . . . he sees maps of black and white.' The tiercel, up at an altitude greater than any land point in the county of Essex, would have seen out over the sea wall, to where the flocks of waders and gulls were massing on the edge of the incoming tide. He would have seen inland, through the haze, to the rectilinear pattern of the fields and ditches. Beneath him, he would have seen three human figures, moving in a line across the baize of a lucerne field, two figures on one side of a drainage dyke, one on the other. And then he would have seen two partridges startled up from cover, moving trackable objects, one flying south and seaward, the other north-west and inland, out across the crop field, a single feather falling from the northernmost bird as it fled.

The partridges clattered out from our feet, and glancing up I saw the tiercel suddenly tilt into a steep stoop, the lateral bird becoming a near-vertical bird, the ground rising to meet the diving falcon at around 230 feet per second. He missed the partridge, pulled up from his stoop, and began to climb again, regaining his pitch. The partridge had taken cover in the lucerne; when we flushed it out, he stooped again. A longer, more angled dive, perhaps at sixty degrees to the ground, and at the last extension of this stoop he extended a taloned foot and struck the partridge with an impact inaudible to us.

We walked across the field, and when we reached the tiercel we found him mantling: hooding his blue wings over the dead bird, and looking up at us, fearfully.

Later, after the tiercel had fed, we walked up on to the sea wall, where the warm light onshore wind blew the smell of salt and mud on to us. The tiercel perched on Helen's hand, and all four of us sat there, looking out over the saltings, and watching the high migrations pass. Behind us, the late sun blazed in the evening haze, red as an aged sparrow-hawk's eye.

14

Tor

A sequence of clear nights in early November brought the first frosts. Skim-ice formed on standing water. The moon hung low over the city, yellow as it grew, then silver on the wane. After the frost came gales, and the leaves of the horse-chestnut trees, loosened by the frost, ticked down in their hundreds of thousands and drifted up against the kerbs and hedges.

On a day when the wind was buffeting rooks from the trees, I went to the Hope Valley in the Peak District, to see my friends John and Jan Beatty, who had sailed me out to Enlli many months before. I wanted to bring my journeys to some sort of end, and it seemed right to do so in the company of those with whom they had begun. Besides, John had promised to take me to see the snow hares.

John was born and brought up in the Peak, within sight of the Kinder Downfall, and became a park warden while still at school. After working around the world, he settled back in the Peak, in the village of Bamford, near the Ladybower reservoir. Decades spent walking and climbing in the region meant that John rarely used a map, because he carried one in his head. He knew all the Peak's aspects: its bleak upper reaches, its gritstone edges and its wooded cloughs. He knew what time of year each species of migrant bird arrived. Redwings and field-fares in autumn. Golden plover, sandpipers and dunlin in spring. Occasional snow buntings after a midwinter northerly gale. He knew the locations of particular trees: star-leaved field maples, big lone beeches, and the black-barked sweet chestnuts, which flamed a sulphurous yellow in autumn. He knew the locations of the snares and stink-pits set out by gamekeepers on the private swathes of moor, to trap anything which might prey on the grouse. He knew on which south-tilted rocks the adders sunned themselves on hot days. He knew in which larch-tree a pair of goshawks kept their nest, and at the bottom of which heathery down-slope hen harriers had once successfully hatched.

He also knew where the snow hares lived.

The hare had long been my totem animal, and I had been pleased to find hares, like the hawks, appearing throughout my journeys. I had seen them all over the country: hunched discreetly in their forms on Orford Ness, sitting attentively on the turned fields of Suffolk, and scooting over the snow-slopes of Meall nan Tarmachan and the karst shires of the Burren. They had been there too, less expectedly, in the name of Edward Thomas's First World War training camp, and in the hare's ear flower I had seen out on the Dengie Peninsula.

The hawk and the hare: they were the perfect pair of familiars for my map-making. The hawk turning its sentinel circles in the air, looking down on to the land. The hare knowing the land peerlessly at ground level, able to move faster over it than anything else earthbound. My sleepings-out, in cups and dips of rock and earth and snow; this was the habit of the hare. But the pull to the high ground, to the summits and ridges, to look down upon the land; this was in mimicry of the hawk.

Of all hares, it was the snow hare, *Lepus timidus*, that fascinated me most. Smaller and more ancient than their low-altitude cousins, *Lepus europaeus*, the snow hares flourished across Europe during the Pleistocene. When the glaciers retreated, they followed the cold: their winter colouring allowed them to survive in snowbound conditions. Pliny thought that the snow hare went white from eating ice; in fact, it moults into its winter whiteness, shedding the smoky bluish-brown coat that lasts it for most of the year. Its winter moult is instigated by a reduction of the light received through the eyes. Decreased day-length begins the moult in autumn, and winter's low temperature sustains it.

After the recession of the glaciers, the hares were marooned on islands of high ground – Wales, the Pennines, Cumbria, Scotland – before dying out everywhere but the Highlands. Then in the 1840s Scottish snow hares were introduced to the Peak District, in order to diversify the shooting bag on the grouse moors. They survived without flourish-ing: perhaps 200 hares now live across the many miles of high moorland plateaux that spread between the cities of Manchester, Sheffield and Derby. This is the paradox of their presence in the Peak: they have become for many people, including me, a sigil of wildness, but their presence here is entirely a consequence of human management. Even in the Cairngorms, their true fastness, they are under threat from climate change, and severe culls by gamekeepers who believe they are the sec-ondary carriers of a tick-borne grouse-disease.

Snow hares possess, as well as the ghostly beauty of their winter pelage, an exceptionally graceful nonchalance. Poise at rest and ele-gance in motion: this distinguishes the snow hare. Watching one make its curved run over a steep snowfield, you understand why the Egyptian hieroglyph of a hare over a zigzag of water meant the verb 'to be', in the particular gerundive senses of 'being', 'existing', 'persisting'.

For years, John had followed and watched a particular colony of hares which lived in and around a scatter of gritstone tors. The stones are set at 2,000 feet in a remote reach of the moors. There is little cover on the high tundra of the Peak, so it is natural for the hares to be drawn to the tor complexes that extrude here and there, and each of whose stones has its name, its history and its resemblances: to flying saucer, howdah, ostrich egg, quernstone.

It was this colony which John had watched during the great snows of March, when I had gone night-walking in Cumbria, and he had written to tell me of them playing among the ice dunes. In early November, a week before I went to see him, he had called to say that he had been up to the stones, and had found the hares there, on the turn into winter pelage, their brown coats blotched with white. He also said that if I wanted to sleep out, he had found a possible bivouac hole for us: a tunnel, open at both ends, weathered into the north-west face of one of the tors, its floor a blond grit-sand beach. A hare's scrape, really. To sleep *inside* a tor! I couldn't wait.

We began walking late in the afternoon, with a big wind driving rain into our faces, and chopping up the water of the reservoir. We walked north first, through a mile of larch and birch forest. The frost followed by the wind had knocked billions of golden needles from the larches, and they lay in glossy saffron reefs by the side of every road and path, glowing even in that low light, possessing a lustre rather than a colour. John talked as we walked, pointing out birds, trees, plants, describing his love for the moors. There was nothing showy about John's knowledge;

his manner was the emanation of a deep passion. He possessed an integrity and an enthusiasm that reminded me constantly of Roger, and I wished they had been able to meet.

After two miles, he stopped and pointed up to the skyline: the tors, a mile or so from us and 300 feet above, just visible in the dusk. They were formed of gritstone, layers of submarine sand laid down around 300 million years ago, and then compacted over time in a subsiding basin to become rough rock. Ice, wind and water had eventually carved sections of exposed gritstone into the eccentric shapes of the tors. They reminded me of the ventifact sandstone outcrops of the Hoggar Mountains around Tamanrasset in Algeria, which have been abraded by sand-carrying winds into structures impertinent to gravity: boulders the size of houses, balanced on stems of rock.

We began to move steeply uphill, over boggy ground, slipping on bracken and grass. Our clothes, already wet with rain, became slicked with mud. We neared the rocks. Then – Hares! Hares! Two shouts from John, and two hares breaking from cover in the rocks above us, bobbing away uphill. And they were white! They moved so easily, little ghosts slipping between the rocks, over the bilberry and heather. Five seconds and they were gone, leaving my heart thumping.

We walked up into the heart of the tors, alert for more hares. The tors were spread over the rim of the plateau, and they faced twenty clear miles of high moor. At that height the wind was colossal, hurtling out of the black west, and of such strength that it was impossible to stand straight in it. We moved from rock to rock, reaching out to steady ourselves, as though on a ship's deck in a storm. The rain was pelting now in heavy cold monsoon droplets. I took shelter behind a pair of twenty-foot tors that tilted in towards one another to form a wind-gate, and when I stepped from the shelter into the gate itself, the force of the gale was such that it pulled the flesh on my face tight and back. I remembered another gateway to another upper world: the Chalamain Gap, the granite portal that marks the northern entry to the centre of the Cairngorms.

John located the bivouac cave, and I knelt to examine it. It was already flooded out, a pool of water glinting on the mica-sand at its near end. This was a wild night, a wonderful night in its way, and I was glad to have seen the moor in this mood. Certainly, I would have liked to wake among the hares. But it was no night to be out. Sixteen hours of storm-soaked darkness, with almost no cover, would only have been a mortification. The hares could tolerate this, but not us. I found and kept a lozenge of gritstone from the bivouac, and then we retreated behind a tor, blew on our fingers, drank hot coffee from a flask, and shouted at each other above the wind, planning our return in the near-dark over these miles of rough steep ground.

Looking for cover, we walked up and over a shoulder of moor, and there, suddenly, were more hares, dozens of them, white against the dark moor, moving in haphazard darts, zigzagging and following unpredictable deviations, like particles in a cloud chamber. They must, like us, have been driven away from the rocks by the wind, and come here to the peat-troughs for shelter. Their white fur drew the very last of the light, so that they glowed against the dark moor. One, a big male, still dabbed here and there with brown fur, stopped, glanced back at us over his shoulder, and then spun away into the dark.

So few wild creatures, relatively, remain in Britain and Ireland: so few, relatively, in the world. Pursuing our project of civilisation, we have pushed thousands of species towards the brink of disappearance, and many thousands more over that edge. The loss, after it is theirs, is ours. Wild animals, like wild places, are invaluable to us precisely because they are not us. They are uncompromisingly different. The paths they follow, the impulses that guide them, are of other orders. The seal's holding gaze, before it flukes to push another tunnel through the sea, the hare's run, the hawk's high gyres: such things are wild. Seeing them, you are made briefly aware of a world at work around and beside our own, a world operating in patterns and purposes that you do not share. These are creatures, you realise, that live by voices inaudible to you.

By the next morning the storm had blown itself out almost completely, and long slants of sunlight flashed across the moor's edge and down through the village. The sky had a rinsed after-storm sharpness. It was Remembrance Sunday, and at eleven o'clock the Reveille sounded through the cleared air. John and I took part in the service, which was held in the main street of the village. I thought of Gurney, of Thomas, of unnamed and unnumbered others.

After the service finished, we walked up on to Bamford Edge, the broken gritstone rampart that extends along the moor directly above the village. After two or three miles of walking, we found ourselves above a deep wooded valley which dropped steeply away from the moor.

Below us, the valley was ablaze. The great conflagration of autumn was underway. Hundreds of acres of trees on the turn: larch, birch, beech, sweet chestnut, carrying leaves that were orange, carmine, brimstone and gold. The sight ignited in me a sudden series of memory flares, back through my journeys, to the different kinds of phosphorescence I had seen: the glowing seas off the Lleyn Peninsula, the rainbow in Coruisk, the pollen drifting through the pines of

Morlich, the northern lights visible from Ben Hope – and now this autumn wood, a mile from a village.

Autumn leaf colour is an expression of a death which is also a renewal. Through spring and summer, green chlorophyll is the dominant leaf pigment. But as day-length decreases and temperatures fall, chlorophyll production is reduced, eventually to the point of extinction. As the chlorophyll content declines, other pigments begin to shine through: carotenoids – sunlight-capturing chemicals that flame orange, yellow and gold – brown tannins and the rarer redder anthocyanins. The anthocyanins are produced by the action of sustained strong light upon the sugars which get trapped in leaves as the tree's vascular system prepares for leaf-drop. In these ways, deciduous trees burn themselves spectacularly back to their bare branches, in order to survive the winter and prepare for the resurgence of spring.

It was on high ground above the clough that we found the beech tree. A single old tree, no more than twenty feet tall, thriving in a little marshy hollow. This dip was all the beech needed by way of protection from the wind, and it had grown to precisely the level of the surrounding land. It had also created a raft of solid ground in the marsh, binding the bog with its roots so that turf could form. It was a survivor, this tree. Each of its hundreds of branches corkscrewed complicatedly, turned this way and that over the years by the wind. The ground beneath it was golden with shed leaves.

It was a tree that invited ascent. John sat beneath it, looking out over the valley beneath, while I climbed. It was the finest climbing tree I had ever met: the next branch always there, perfectly curved and kinked to take a foot or a hand. It seemed almost to help me up. I perched near its summit for ten minutes or so, thinking south and east, to my own beech tree on top of its little hill. Far beneath, the church clock struck one.

I climbed down, and John and I sat together under the tree for a while. Suddenly we heard a high cheeping, and looked up. A handful of tiny birds had blown in and settled on the upper reaches of the beech. Goldcrests! After a minute or so, swarming the top branches, the birds gusted off, down towards the deeper wood in the clough, to gild some other tree.

15

Beechwood

We shall not cease from exploration,
And the end of all our exploring
Will be to arrive where we started
And know the place for the first time.

The evening I got back from the Hope Valley, I took down my stones from their storm-beach on the shelf, and laid them out on my desk, adding my gritstone lozenge to the pattern. I began to move them around. First I arranged them into a long line of their finding, with the earliest to the left and most recent to the right. Then I moved them into order of their ages, as best I could: Cambrian, Ordovician, Silurian, Devonian, Permian, Jurassic . . . Then I dispersed them into a rough shape of the relative places of their findings, so that they made an approximate mineral map of the archipelago itself, and my journeys within it. Each stone still carried with it some residual memories of the moment of its finding: the smell and temperature of the air, the light's texture.

The blue basalt heart from Ynys Enlli, from the gulch-edge of the pearly sea. The olive-shaped quartz pebble from Coruisk, which I had rolled in my mouth as we left on that hot bright day. The two eyeball-shaped stones, plucked from the peat of Rannoch and the stream-cut near Sandwood, staring back at me. The blue and white oblong taken from the frosted root bole in the Black Wood, which still had winter-wood magic trapped in its layers. The frost-cracked shard from the summit of Ben Hope. The hooped rhombus from the Naver estuary, whose lines recalled wood grain and sand terrace. The mapstone from Blakeney. The dolmen of chalk from the cockle beach at Essex, and the flat red wedge of brick from the Wilderness. And – last of them all – a squashed egg of pale granite flecked with mica, which I had taken from a shelf at Walnut Tree Farm on a visit after Roger's death, to mark the wildness of his home. Other talismans, too: raptor feathers, the dolphin of wood, the broken whelk, the catkins.

My journeys had revealed to me new logics of connection between discrete parts of Britain and Ireland, beyond the systems of motorway and flight-path. There were geological links: tor answering to tor, flint to flint, sandstone to sandstone, granite giving way to mud. There were the migration lines of birds and animals. There were the unpredictable movements of weather and light: the passage of blizzards, mists and darkness, and the wildness they conferred on places. And there were the people, alive and dead, who had dwelled in or passed through the land-scapes. A webbing of story and memory joined up my places, as well as other more material affinities. The connections made by all of these forces – rocks, creatures, weathers, people – had laid new patterns upon the country, as though it had been swilled in a developing fluid, and unexpected images had emerged, ghostly figures showing through the mesh of roads and cities.

I had made more journeys than I have told of here – and there were many more places to which I still wanted to travel. The Orkneys, the Shetland Islands, St Kilda and the Scillies. Skokholm and Skomer, off the Pembrokeshire coast. Secret coves in Devon and Cornwall. Exmoor and Bodmin. The Black Mountains in mid-Wales. The Ardnamurchan Peninsula and the Monadhliaths. Lost little fens in corners of the Norfolk Broads. Parts of Wiltshire and Shropshire. The Borders, where I planned to follow the route taken over the high ground by the fleeing Richard Hannay, in John Buchan's *The Thirty-Nine Steps*. And I wanted to carve a kayak from a big birch and paddle down the Wye. But the making of the map had never seemed like a finite endeavour. There would, anyway, be time to do these journeys, or some of them, in the future, I thought. And in a few years, my children would be old enough to come with me.

The road atlas now seemed even more distorting an account of the islands than when I had begun the journeys. So many aspects of the country go unrepresented by it. It does not observe the pale lines of old drove-ways that seam the soft-stone counties of England, or the tawny outlines of the south-western moors. It fails to record the ceaseless movement of mud within the estuaries of the Wash, and it is inattentive to texture, smell and sound: to the way oak pollen and fireweed seeds drift in wind, to the different shadows cast by mountains, to the angles of repose of boulders at the base of Pennine crags. It ignores the mists of Dartmoor, which are as thick, fluid and quick as milk, and the black peat of Rannoch, so liquid that a human footprint is dissolved within hours. It is blind to the chosen perches of goshawks in the forests of the Dark Peak, or the hunting paths of the sparrowhawks of Cambridgeshire.

Moving the stones around, I thought back over the arc of the journeys: the long cast west and north, and then the retreat south, and eventually down to Essex, unlikely wild Essex. I had a chromatic memory of the change: from the whites, greys and blues of winter

Scotland, through the pewter and cream of the Burren, to the green and gold of the English summer. I had a haptic memory, too, a memory of touch: from the hard rock to the soft mud, from the ice to the grass and the sand. But most powerfully I remembered it as a change of focus: from the long sight-lines from peninsula, moor and mountain summit, to the close-up worlds of hedge and ditch, sea pool and hare scrape.

As I had moved south, my own understanding of wildness had been altered – or its range had been enlarged. My early vision of a wild place as somewhere remote, historyless, unmarked, now seemed improperly partial.

It was not that places such as Hope and Rannoch, the last fastnesses, were worthless. No, in their stripped-back austerity, their fierce ele-mentality, these landscapes remained invaluable in their power to awe. But I had learned to see another type of wildness, to which I had once been blind: the wildness of natural life, the sheer force of ongoing organic existence, vigorous and chaotic. This wildness was not about asperity, but about luxuriance, vitality, fun. The weed thrusting through a crack in a pavement, the tree root impudently cracking a carapace of tarmac: these were wild signs, as much as the storm wave and the snowflake. There was as much to be learned in an acre of woodland on a city's fringe as on the shattered summit of Ben Hope: this was what Roger had taught me – and what Lily did not yet need to be taught. It was something most people forgot as they grew into adults.

One other change had happened, and that was a shift of time-scheme. I had come to feel wildness as a quality that flared into futurity, as well as reverberating out of the past. The contemporary threats to the wild were multiple, and severe. But they were also temporary. The wild prefaced us, and it will outlive us. Human culture will pass, given time, of which there is a sufficiency. The ivy will snake back and unrig our flats and terraces, as it scattered the Roman villas. The sand will drift into our business parks, as it drifted into the brochs of the Iron Age. Our roads will lapse into the land. 'A ghost wilderness hovers around the entire planet,' wrote the poet and forester Gary Snyder, 'the millions of tiny seeds of vegetation . . . hiding in the mud on the foot of an arctic tern, in the dry desert sands, or in the wind . . . each ready to float, freeze or be swallowed, always preserving the germ.'

In between my journeys, I had spent increasing amounts of time exploring the farmland and the copses within a mile or two of my home. The hedgerows, the fields and the little woods that I had once been so avid to leave behind for the far west and north, had come slowly to seem different to me – filled with a wildness I had not previously perceived or understood. Strange things had begun to occur in this landscape. Once, emerging from a high-hedged lane, I put up a flock of white doves from a brown field, and watched as they rose applauding into the sky. On a spring day, I had gone to Nine Wells Wood, and found numberless threads of white gossamer hanging from the leaves and twigs of the spindle trees, and drifting languidly out in the wind like prayer-lines. It was a nursery of thousands of white micro-moths, with each pupa making a single thread of silk. Those trailing silks, some of them five or six feet long, cross-hatched the path at every height, so that it was impossible to move along the wood's narrow tracks without getting snagged and wrapped by the silk, and by the time I reached the far end of the wood I had been part-cocooned.

On a sultry August evening, when the air was still and ripe with humidity, I had run up to the beechwood, passing through hedges thick with bindweed, whose snowy-white trumpets were making their anti-clockwise revolutions. Everything that evening seemed slowed by the heat, and I had the illusion that the air had assumed the consistency of water. I watched from the observatory as a crow took flight from a branch, then moved away with languorous manta-ray wing beats.

In the early days of autumn, with Helen and another friend, and Lily, I walked up to the hedgerows between Nine Wells Wood and the beech-wood. We carried baskets, and picked blackberries, cherry-plums and sloes. Lily poked inquisitively about in the brambles. At an old felled ash trunk, I snapped back a bit of dry bark, and showed her the insects teeming beneath it.

Up near the entrance to the deepest sided of the hedgerow ways, we stopped to see the black walnut tree that Roger and I had found two years previously, when it had been just a self-seeded sapling. Eccentric and independent, it had survived the passage of tractors and the drift of pesticides. It was flourishing, and within a few years it would bear fruit.

One afternoon, a week after the snow hares, the wind was rising, so I went to the beechwood. I walked there, following streets to the city's fringe, and then along field-edge paths. The hedgerows were bright with the ochre of hazels, the doubloon-gold of birch. In the grass of the verges, a few last scabious heads bobbed, and I passed a single cow-parsley inexplicably in flower, lost in its own dream of summer.

Woodpigeons were doing paper-aeroplane swoops, turning in stiff curves, their wings raked up.

From the bottom of the hill, I could hear the noise of the trees with the wind; a marine roar that grew in volume as I approached. Looking up at the swaying wood, I remembered something I had read: when you see a wood or a forest, you must imagine the ground almost as a mirror-line, because a tree's subterranean root system can spread nearly as widely as its aerial crown. For the visible canopy of each tree you have to imagine an inverted hidden one, yearning for water just as its twin yearns for light.

The wood looked drab from the outside that day. But when I stepped into it I found myself inside a light-box. The sunshine streaming through the leaves was throwing gold, copper and silver light into the air. The effect was so unexpected and counter-intuitive that I walked out of the wood and then back into it. The same again. Brown outside – and then a dazzle of colour! I walked on up through the kaleidoscope wood.

The beech will be among the first tree species to die out in southern Britain if the climate continues to warm. Studies of beechwoods show that big old beeches are already beginning to lose their vigour long before their usual time, and trees of fifty years' growth are showing decline more usually associated with trees three times that age. Unlike the elm, however, the beech will not vanish; it will migrate. Beechwoods will follow the isotherms, searching for the cooler land, as the snow hares did after the Pleistocene. The beeches will find fresh habitats and ranges in the newly warmed north. Not the death of a species, then, but its displacement. The loss would still be great, though, and it could happen in my lifetime: the beechwood might die before my eyes.

Up near the long top of the hill, I found my tree. I climbed up past its familiar marks – the crooked branch, the carved 'H', the elephant skin, the missing limb – until I reached the observatory. I settled myself on the forked branch, and looked out over the land.

I have followed a hare's run, I thought: out, round and back to my starting point, turning arc into circle.

Standing there in the observatory, I tried to imagine the effects of the wind across Britain and Ireland. I thought east, to the coasts of Norfolk and Suffolk, where it would be urging the sea to shingled plungings. I thought north, where it would be driving the snow hares of the Peak into shelter, fraying waterfalls into spray in Cumbrian valleys, and moving the sand at the mouth of the Naver. I thought west, where it would be rushing over the summits of Bin Chuanna and Croagh Patrick, scouring the golden island on which I had slept near Rosroe, and probing down into the shearwater burrows on Enlli. And I thought south, where it would be stirring the still air inside the Dorset holloways, and buffeting the birds on the Essex mudflats.

I imagined the wind moving through all these places, and many more like them: places that were separated from one another by roads and housing, fences and shopping-centres, street-lights and cities, but that were joined across space at that time by their wildness in the wind. We are fallen in mostly broken pieces, I thought, but the wild can still return us to ourselves.

Then I looked back out across the landscape before me: the roads, the railway, the incinerator tower and the woodlands – Mag's Hill Wood, Nine Wells Wood, Wormwood. The woods were spread out across the land, and all were seething.

Wildness was here, too, a short mile south of the town in which I lived. It was set about by roads and buildings, much of it was menaced, and some of it was dying. But at that moment the land seemed to ring with a wild light.

SELECTED READINGS

Water

Bachelard, Gaston, *L'eau et les rêves: essai sur l'imagination de la matière* (Paris, 1947)

Carson, Rachel, *The Sea Around Us* (New York, 1950)

Carver, Raymond, *Where Water Comes Together with Other Water* (New York, 1985)

——, *A New Path to the Waterfall* (New York, 1989)

Coleridge, Samuel Taylor, *Collected Letters*, ed. E. L. Griggs (Oxford, 1956–71)

——, *Notebooks: 1794–1808*, ed. K. Coburn (London, 1957–61)

Cornish, Vaughan, *Waves of the Sea and Other Water Waves* (London, 1910)

——, *Waves of Sand and Snow* (London, 1914)

——, *Ocean Waves and Kindred Geophysical Phenomena* (Cambridge, 1934)

Deakin, Roger, *Waterlog* (London, 1999)

Maclean, Norman, *A River Runs Through It and Other Stories* (Chicago, 1976)

Maxwell, Gavin, *The Ring of Bright Water Trilogy* (London, 1960–68)

Raban, Jonathan, *Coasting* (London, 1986)

Simms, Colin, *Otters and Martens* (Exeter, 2004)

Thomson, David, *The People of the Sea* (London, 1954)

Williamson, Henry, *Tarka the Otter* (New York, 1927)

Stone

Ascherson, Neal, *Stone Voices* (London, 2002)

Bagnold, Ralph, *The Physics of Blown Sand and Desert Dunes* (London, 1941)

Bradley, Richard, *An Archaeology of Natural Places* (London, 2000)

Harrison, Robert Pogue, *The Dominion of the Dead* (Chicago, 2003)

Household, Geoffrey, *Rogue Male* (London, 1939)

Langewiesche, William, *Sahara Unveiled* (New York, 1996)

McNeillie, Andrew, *An Aran Keening* (Dublin, 2001)

Meloy, Ellen, *The Anthropology of Turquoise* (New York, 2002)

Murray, W. H., *Mountaineering in Scotland* (London, 1947)

——, *Undiscovered Scotland* (London, 1951)

Perrin, Jim, *On and off the Rocks* (London, 1986)

——, *Yes, to Dance* (Oxford, 1990)

Robinson, Tim, *Stones of Aran: Pilgrimage* (Dublin, 1986)

——, *Mementoes of Mortality* (Roundstone, 1991)

——, *Stones of Aran: Labyrinth* (Dublin, 1995)

Shepherd, Nan, *The Living Mountain* (Aberdeen, 1977)

Thomson, David, and George Ewart Evans, *The Leaping Hare* (London, 1972)

Tilley, Christopher, *A Phenomenology of Landscape: Places, Paths, Monuments* (Oxford, 1994)

Worpole, Ken, *Last Landscapes* (London, 2003)

Wood

Agee, James, *Let Us Now Praise Famous Men* (New York, 1941)

Calvino, Italo, *Il Barone Rampante* [*The Baron in the Trees*], trans. Archibald Colquhoun (London, 1959)

Deakin, Roger, *Wildwood* (London, 2007)

Fowler, John, *The Scottish Forest Through the Ages* (Edinburgh, 2003)

Gurney, Ivor, *Collected Poems*, ed. P. J. Kavanagh (Oxford, 1984)

Harrison, Robert Pogue, *Forests: The Shadow of Civilisation* (Chicago, 1992)

McNeill, Marian, *The Silver Bough* (Glasgow, 1957–68)

Nash, David, *Pyramids Rise, Spheres Turn and Cubes Stand Still* (London, 2005)

Platt, Rutherford H., *The Great American Forest* (New Jersey, 1977)

Preston, Richard, 'Climbing the Redwoods', *The New Yorker*, 14 and 21 February 2005

Rackham, Oliver, *Trees & Woodland in the British Landscape* (London, 1976, rev. 1990)

——, *Hayley Wood: Its History and Ecology* (Cambridge, 1990)

——, *Woodlands* (London, 2006)

Wilkinson, Gerald, *Epitaph for the Elm* (London, 1978)

Air

Bachelard, Gaston, *L'air et les songes* (Paris, 1951)

——, *La poétique de l'espace* [*The Poetics of Space*], trans. Maria Jolas (Paris, 1958)

Baker, J. A., *The Peregrine* (London, 1967)

Drury, Chris, *Silent Spaces* (Thames & Hudson, 1998)

Ehrlich, Gretel, *The Solace of Open Spaces* (New York, 1985)

Heinrich, Bernd, *Ravens in Winter* (London, 1991)

Macdonald, Helen, *Falcon* (London, 2006)

Saint-Exupéry, Antoine de, *Vol de Nuit* (Paris, 1931)

——, *Terre des Hommes* [*Wind, Sand and Stars*], trans. William Rees (Paris, 1939)

——, *Pilote de Guerre* [*Flight to Arras*], trans. Lewis Galantière (Paris, 1942)

Simms, Colin, *Goshawk Lives* (London, 1995)

Wild

Callicott, J. Baird, and Michael Nelson, eds., *The Great New Wilderness Debate* (Atlanta, 1998)

Colegate, Isobel, *A Pelican in the Wilderness* (London, 2002)

Dillard, Annie, *Pilgrim at Tinker Creek* (New York, 1975)

Hinton, David, trans., *Mountain Home: The Wilderness Poetry of Ancient China* (New York, 2002)

Hughes, Ted, *Wodwo* (London, 1967)

Mabey, Richard, *The Unofficial Countryside* (London, 1973)

——, *Nature Cure* (London, 2005)

Muir, John, *The Eight Wilderness Discovery Books* (California, 1894–1916)

Nash, Roderick, *Wilderness and the American Mind* (New York, 1967)

Rolls, Eric, *A Million Wild Acres* (Melbourne, 1981)

Snyder, Gary, *The Practice of the Wild* (San Francisco, 1990)

Stegner, Wallace, *The Sound of Mountain Water* (New York, 1969)

Thoreau, Henry David, *Walden* (New York, 1854)

White, T. H., *The Once and Future King* (London, 1958)

Map

Borodale, Sean, *Notes for an Atlas* (Isinglass, 2005)

Brody, Hugh, *Maps and Dreams* (Toronto, 1981)

Clifford, Sue, and Angela King, *Local Distinctiveness: Place, Particularity and Identity* (London, 1993)

Davidson, Peter, *The Idea of North* (London, 2005)

Dean, Tacita, *Recent Films and Other Works* (London, 2001)

Harmon, Katharine, *You Are Here: Personal Geographies and Other Maps of the Imagination* (New York, 2004)

Least-Heat Moon, William, *PrairyErth: A Deep Map* (Boston, 1991)

Lopez, Barry, *Arctic Dreams* (New York, 1986)

Macleod, Finlay, ed., *Togail Tír* [*Marking Time: The Map of the Western Isles*] (Stornoway, 1989)

Nelson, Richard, *Make Prayers to the Raven* (Chicago, 1983)

Perrin, Jim, and John Beatty, *River Map* (Llandysul, 2001)

Solnit, Rebecca, *A Field Guide to Getting Lost* (New York, 2005)

Turchi, Peter, *Maps of the Imagination* (San Antonio, 2004)

Land

Blythe, Ronald, *Akenfield* (London, 1969)

Craig, David, and David Paterson, *The Glens of Silence: Landscapes of the Highland Clearances* (Edinburgh, 2004)

Fowles, John, *Wormholes* (London, 1998)

Godwin, Fay, *Land* (London, 1985)

——, *Our Forbidden Land* (London, 1990)

——, *The Edge of the Land* (London, 1995)

Goldsworthy, Andy, *Hand to Earth* (London, 1990)

Hunter, James, *A Dance Called America* (Edinburgh, 1994)
——, *The Other Side of Sorrow* (Edinburgh, 1995)
King, Angela, and Sue Clifford, *England in Particular* (London, 2006)
Mabey, Richard, *The Common Ground* (London, 1980)
——, with Sue Clifford and Angela King, *Second Nature* (London, 1984)
Mellor, Leo, *Things Settle* (Norwich, 2003)
Perrin, Jim, *Spirits of Place* (Llandysul, 1997)
Pretty, Jules, *The Earth Only Endures* (London, 2007)
Rowley, Trevor, *The English Landscape in the Twentieth Century* (London, 2006)
Shoard, Marion, *This Land is Our Land* (London, 1987)
Taylor, Kenneth, and David Woodfall, *Natural Heartlands* (Shrewsbury, 1996)

Movement

Ammons, A. R., 'Cascadilla Falls', *The Selected Poems* (New York, 1986)
Coleridge, Samuel Taylor, *Coleridge among the Lakes & Mountains: from his Notebooks, Letters and Poems 1794–1804*, ed. Roger Hudson (London, 1991)
Fulton, Hamish, *Selected Walks: 1969–1989* (London, 1990)
Goldsworthy, Andy, *Passage* (London, 2004)
Graham, Stephen, *The Gentle Art of Tramping* (London, 1926)
Heaney, Seamus, and Rachel Giese, *Sweeney's Flight* (London, 1992)
Holmes, Richard, *Coleridge: Early Visions* (London, 1989)
Lopez, Barry, *Crossing Open Ground* (New York, 1988)
——, *About This Life* (New York, 1998)
McCarthy, Cormac, *Blood Meridian* (New York, 1985)
Sebald, W. G., *Die Ringe des Saturn* [*The Rings of Saturn*], trans. Michael Hulse (Frankfurt, 1995)
Sinclair, Iain, *London Orbital* (London, 2000)
——, *The Edge of the Orison* (London, 2005)
Thomas, Edward, *Wales* (London, 1905)
Thoreau, Henry David, 'Walking' (Boston, 1862)
Twain, Mark, *The Adventures of Huckleberry Finn* (New York, 1884)
Worpole, Ken, and Jason Orton, *350 Miles* (Colchester, 2006)

ACKNOWLEDGEMENTS

I would like to thank above all the following people: my wife Julia, my children Lily and Tom, my parents Rosamund and John, John and Jan Beatty, Peter Davidson, Roger Deakin, Walter Donohue, Michael England, Henry Hitchings, Sara Holloway, Julith Jedamus, Richard Mabey, Helen Macdonald, Garry Martin, Leo Mellor, Jim Perrin, John Stubbs and Jessica Woollard. Each of these people has been vital to the book's shaping. I hope I have already conveyed my deep and specific gratitude to each of you.

I would also like to thank, for various reasons, Stephen Abell, Lisa Allardice, Richard Baggaley, Dick Balharry, Robin Beatty, Martyn Berry, Terence Blacker, Sean Borodale, Aly Bowkett, Sue Brooks, Christopher Burlinson, Ben Butler-Cole, Alan Byford, Jamie Byng, Michael Bywater, David Cobham, Stephanie Cross, Santanu Das, Tom Dawson, Rufus Deakin, Tim Dee, Guy Dennis, Ron Digby, Ed Douglas, Robert Douglas-Fairhurst, Lindsay Duguid, Samantha Ellis, Emmanuel College, Howard Erskine-Hill, Angus Farquhar, William Fiennes, Dan Frank, Edwin Frank, Charlie and Sinéad Garrigan Mattar, Iain Gilchrist, Dinny Gollop, Mark Goodwin, Jay Griffiths, Mike Gross, John Harvey, Alison Hastie, Kitty Hauser, Jonathan Heawood, Caspar Henderson, Jonathan Hird, Mike and Carol Hodges, Andrew Holgate, Jeremy Hooker, Michael Hrebeniak, James Hunter, Michael Hurley, Mary Jacobus, Joanna Kavenna, Peter Kemp, Steve King, Ann Lackie, Bill and Thelma Lovell, Madeleine Lovell, James and Claudia

Macfarlane, John MacLennan, Finlay MacLeod, Annalena McAfee, Christina McLeish, Andrew McNeillie, Rod Mengham, Ann Morgan, Jeremy Noel-Tod, Ralph O'Connor, Redmond O'Hanlon, Jason Orton, Jeremy Over, David Parker, Ian Patterson, Donald and Lucy Peck, Sir Edward and Alison Peck, Jules Pretty, Guy Procter, Simon Prosser, Jeremy Purseglove, David Quentin, Satish Raghavan, Nicholas Rankin, Gary Rowland, Corinna Russell, Susanna Rustin, Ray Ryan, Jan and Chris Schramm, Nick Seddon, Tom Service, Rachel Simhon, Chris Smith, Rebecca Solnit, Barnaby Spurrier, Kenneth Steven, Peter Straus, Kenneth Taylor, Margot Waddell, Marina Warner, Simon Williams, Ross and Lesley Wilson, Mark Wormald and Ken Worpole.

I am very grateful to the following people at Granta for the expertise, care and patience they have shown during the writing and publishing of the book: Sajidah Ahmad, Louise Campbell, David Graham, Ian Jack, Gail Lynch, Brigid Macleod, Pru Rowlandson, Bella Shand, Matt Weiland, Lindsay Paterson and Sarah Wasley.

Certain books, writers and artists have also been influential and inspirational. The most important of these are included in the list of selected readings. The strongest influence, though, has been place itself. I have tried where possible to let the language of the book be thickened, refined or patterned by the forms of the landscapes with which it is concerned.

The map is by Helen Macdonald. The images prefacing 'Island', 'Valley', 'Forest', 'River-mouth', 'Cape', 'Summit', 'Grave', 'Ridge', 'Saltmarsh' and 'Tor', and the image ending 'Tor', are all copyright John Beatty; the images prefacing 'Beechwood', 'Holloway' and 'Storm-beach' are copyright Rosamund Macfarlane; the image prefacing 'Moor' is copyright John Macfarlane. I am grateful to all four of these people for permission to use their fine work here.

INDEX

Keep in touch with
Granta Books:

Visit grantabooks.com to discover more.

GRANTA

Also of interest and available from Granta Books
www.grantabooks.com

MOUNTAINS OF THE MIND
A History of a Fascination

Robert Macfarlane

WINNER OF THE GUARDIAN FIRST BOOK AWARD

To those who love mountains, their wonder is beyond dispute.
To those who do not, their pull is beyond reason. In this groundbreaking
and now-classic work, Robert Macfarlane explores how mountains
have come to hold us spellbound, drawing us up into the
high places – sometimes at the cost of our lives.

'The most exhilarating history of mountaineering ... a riveting read'
Jeremy Paxman

'A marvellous, distinguished book that jolted my heart ...
It simply fizzes with insights into the sublime madness of mountaineering'
Roger Deakin